The Civil War
A History in Documents

Rachel Filene Seidman

OXFORD
UNIVERSITY PRESS

For my father, who taught me to love stories; my
mother, who always wants to hear mine; my daughters,
who fill my life with the best ones; and my husband,
who helps me make sense of them all

OXFORD
UNIVERSITY PRESS

Oxford New York

Athens Auckland Bangkok Bogotá Buenos Aries Calcutta Cape Town
Chennai Dar es Salaam Delhi Florence Hong Kong Istanbul Karachi
Kuala Lumpur Madrid Melbourne Mexico City Mumbai Nairobi
Paris São Paulo Singapore Taipei Tokyo Toronto Warsaw

and associated companies in
Berlin Ibadan

Copyright © 2001 by Rachel Filene Seidman

Design: Sandy Kaufman
Layout: Loraine Machlin
Picture Research: Marty Baldessari

Published by Oxford University Press, Inc.,
198 Madison Avenue, New York, New York 10016
www.oup.com

Library of Congress Cataloging in Publication Data
Seidman, Rachel Filene.
The Civil War: a history in documents / Rachel Filene Seidman.
p. cm. — (Pages from history)
Includes bibliographical references and index.
ISBN 978-0-19-511558-1

1. United States—History—Civil War, 1861–1865—Sources—
Juvenile literature. [1. United States—History—Civil War,
1861–1865—Sources.] I. Title. II. Series.
E464.S48 2000
973.7—dc21   00-037523

9

Printed in the United States of America
on acid-free paper

General Editors

Sarah Deutsch
Associate Professor of History
University of Arizona

Carol Karlsen
Professor of History
University of Michigan

Robert G. Moeller
Professor of History
University of California, Irvine

Jeffrey N. Wasserstrom
Associate Professor of History
Indiana University

Board of Advisors

Steven Goldberg
Social Studies Supervisor
New Rochelle, N.Y., Public Schools

John Pyne
Social Studies Supervisor
West Milford, N.J., Public Schools

Cover: Right panel of artillery man Hunt P.
Wilson's triptych *Battle of Pea Ridge.*

Frontispiece: Gen. Orlando B. Willcox (seated) and his staff pose for a photographer
in their camp.

Title page: An African-American soldier
stands guard over Union cannon headed
for the front lines.

The Civil War
A History in Documents

Contents

What Is a Document?

To the historian, a document is, quite simply, any sort of historical evidence. It is a primary source, the raw material of history. A document may be more than the expected government paperwork, such as a treaty or passport. It is also a letter, diary, will, grocery list, newspaper article, recipe, memoir, oral history, school yearbook, map, chart, architectural plan, poster, musical score, play script, novel, political cartoon, painting, photograph—even an object.

Using primary sources allows us not just to read *about* history, but to read history itself. It allows us to immerse ourselves in the look and feel of an era gone by, to understand its people and their language, whether verbal or visual. And it allows us to take an active, hands-on role in (re)constructing history.

Using primary sources requires us to use our powers of detection to ferret out the relevant facts and to draw conclusions from them; just as Agatha Christie uses the scores in a bridge game to determine the identity of a murderer, the historian uses facts from a variety of sources—some, perhaps, seemingly inconsequential—to build a historical case.

The poet W. H. Auden wrote that history was the study of questions. Primary sources force us to ask questions—and then, by answering them, to construct a narrative or an argument that makes sense to us. Moreover, as we draw on the many sources from "the dust-bin of history," we can endow that narrative with character, personality, and texture—all the elements that make history so endlessly intriguing.

Cartoon
This political cartoon addresses the issue of church and state. It illustrates the Supreme Court's role in balancing the demands of the First Amendment of the Constitution and the desires of the religious population.

Illustration
Illustrations from children's books, such as this alphabet from the New England Primer, tell us how children were educated, and also what the religious and moral values of the time were.

A — In *Adam's* Fall We Sinned all.

B — Thy Life to Mend This *Book* Attend.

C — The *Cat* doth play And after slay.

D — A *Dog* will bite A Thief at night.

E — An *Eagles* flight Is out of sight.

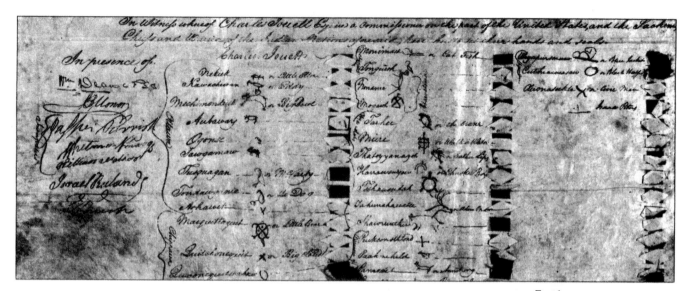

Treaty

A government document such as this 1805 treaty can reveal not only the details of government policy, but information about the people who signed it. Here, the Indians' names were written in English transliteration by U.S. officials, the Indians added pictographs to the right of their names.

Map

A 1788 British map of India shows the region prior to British colonization, an indication of the kingdoms and provinces whose ethnic divisions would resurface later in India's history.

Literature

The first written version of the Old English epic Beowulf, from the late 10th century, is physical evidence of the transition from oral to written history. Charred by fire, it is also a physical record of the wear and tear of history.

How to Read a Document

Primary sources cannot be viewed simply as containing the truth. We need to ask questions about sources as we read them. What message is the author trying to get across? Who was the intended audience? How does that affect the way the author wrote? For instance, a woman writing to her soldier husband at the front might try to mask her difficulties at home so that he would not worry, whereas in a letter to a government official she might exaggerate her problems in order to win his pity. Similarly, a white Southern farmer would probably describe black Union soldiers approaching his neighborhood very differently than a slave would.

Reading documents requires creativity. Historians must read between the lines of primary sources, in order to detect ideas, opinions, and prejudices that are not spelled out directly. For instance, in their descriptions of freedpeople after the war, even some Northern abolitionists reveal paternalistic and racist attitudes toward African Americans. Good historians are also sensitive to their own biases as they interpret this history. Some might have been raised to be suspicious of Northerners as meddling Yankees; others automatically think all Southern whites are racist. Historians try to examine their own conclusions and think about what a devil's advocate might say; what criticisms or questions might someone with the opposite interpretation of these events raise? Historians have to be careful that they do not let their own political or personal goals overshadow their research. Although none of us can escape all our preconceptions, it is important to try to recognize them while reading the following documents.

Caricature

Political cartoonists use exaggerated images and draw on stereotypes to make their characters instantly recognizable and deliver a clear message. Lincoln's followers are portrayed in a distinctly negative light. At the center of the cartoon, the black man is foppishly dressed and the woman behind him is small and surly, showing the artist's disdain for African Americans and women reformers, among many others.

Symbols

In many cases cartoons include symbols that the artist uses to communicate with an audience who knows what those symbols mean. Lincoln rides into an insane asylum on a fence rail, which was a symbol widely used by his political supporters to symbolize Lincoln's modest beginnings as a laborer who split rails for a living.

Text

The text in political cartoons can function in different ways. The text is sometimes meant to convey what the characters are saying, as it is in the balloons in this example. In other places, such as the text below this picture, it is meant to communicate the artist's own opinion. Jokes, puns, and rhymes, such as the play of "right house" on "White House," quickly and humorously convey the cartoonist's message.

Subject

Photographers chose their subjects because they sent a certain message. There was considerable debate about whether it was appropriate for women to enter the field of nursing during the war, and a photograph like this one could be seen as part of that conversation. The woman appears respectable and kind, and, although close to the soldiers, she is not exposed to any part of their bodies other than their heads and arms.

Arrangement

This photograph focuses on the relationship between these three people and does not expose the viewer to much else. Their nearness conveys a sense that the men are well cared for and treated as individuals. A photograph that included the hundreds of beds of other wounded men around them might suggest a different interpretation.

Pose

Because photography during the Civil War could not capture movement, most photographs had to be posed. Both men are looking at the woman, suggesting that she is important to them. The woman holds up a cup, suggesting that her main role is to provide nourishment and strength to the two men.

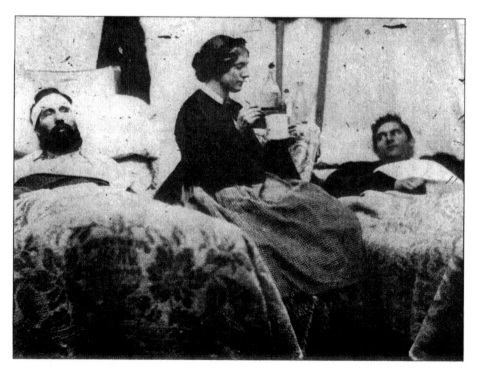

A Defining Moment

For four terrible years, from 1861 to 1865, Americans from the northern and southern halves of the country fought and killed each other in a bloody civil war. Soldiers battled on foot and horseback on land, and on naval ships at sea; they were wounded by cannonballs, rifles, and bayonets; they died by the hundreds of thousands. The country reeled from the destruction. Nearly every adult in the United States either fought in the war or knew someone who did. One out of every five soldiers died, either from a battle wound or disease. Almost as many men died in the Civil War as in all the other wars in which Americans have fought throughout history, combined. Some families lost every male member—sons, fathers, husbands. When it was all over, America was filled with widows and fatherless children. Thousands of veterans faced the rest of their lives with the effects of severe wounds, including the loss of arms or legs shot off in battle or amputated in a surgeon's tent.

Why did it happen? That is a question that people have been asking from the moment the war started right up to the present day, and there have been many different answers. Some historians believe it was inevitable—that by 1860 the North and the South were so different culturally, economically, and politically that there was no other way to settle their conflicts. Others argue that blundering politicians were to blame for widening the gulf between the two sides, and for not figuring out a way to avert the disaster of civil war. Historians still argue passionately over whether slavery caused the war, or was of secondary importance.

The Civil War also fascinates millions of Americans who are not professional historians. Thousands of reenactors research the intricate details of Civil War–era uniforms, weapons, military strategy, and camp life, and then replicate battles and soldiers' lives as closely as possible. *The Civil War*, Ken Burns's 1991 documentary on the war, was one of public television's most successful series ever. New books on the Civil War are published every year, many of them aimed at popular audiences. The war touches a deep nerve in many people that other historical events do not.

What is it about the Civil War, other than the drama of the battlefield, that compels us? Those four years represent one of this country's defining eras. During the crisis of the Civil War, Americans asked themselves many fundamental questions about what their country stood for, and what they wanted it to become. What does it mean to be an American citizen, and who can be one? What does the United States owe its citizens, and what do they owe in return? What role should the federal government play in the daily lives of its people? What price are we willing to pay for our beliefs?

At the very core of the conflict lay what was known as the "peculiar institution," slavery. Most of us today have a hard time imagining what it was like to be a slave, nor do we want to think too deeply about the mind-set of slaveholders. We carry around romanticized notions of plantation life based on movies such as *Gone with the Wind*, but we rarely contemplate the brutality of a system that treated human beings as property. It is the story of the slaves—their lives, their role in the Civil War, their emancipation, and their efforts to defend their freedom during Reconstruction— that forms the most dramatic and important narrative of the war. While most white Northerners went to war to restore the Union, and most white Southerners believed they were fighting to defend their rights and their homes, the Civil War, at its heart, became a war to free the slaves. As such, it was a wrenching, triumphant, and tragically flawed event with more glory and pathos than any novel or movie or miniseries can ever capture.

This book explores the events leading up to the Civil War, the war itself, and Reconstruction, the period after the war, through the eyes of people who lived through them. This collection of primary sources—including letters, diaries, newspaper reports, court testimonies, and military documents—reveals not only what happened, but also how Americans at the time perceived these immensely important events. It opens up questions and provides answers about this turbulent time in our country's past.

Some scholars prefer the term "enslaved people" to "slaves," arguing that it reminds us of the fact of their humanity, and the continuing process by which they were kept under oppression.

Chapter One

One Country, Two Worlds?

Today you can go to almost any part of the United States and find a McDonald's, a Wal-Mart, or other chain store just like one in your area. The different regions of the country have their distinctive features, but they also share a great deal that makes them recognizable and relatively similar to each other. In the middle of the 19th century, however, many people in America saw the northern and southern halves of the country as being so different that they might as well have been two different worlds.

There were significant differences. The North had a much larger population, bigger cities, more industrialization, more advanced transportation and communications systems, and widespread public education. The South had fewer people and was more rural, agricultural, and isolated. Those Southerners who received schooling got it from tutors or private schools. But if you could ask someone from the antebellum period (from 1820 to 1861) what really made the North and the South so different, their reply would probably be simple: "slavery." While the two sides had a great deal in common, including their language, their Constitution, and much of their history, by the 1850s the Southern reliance on slave labor compelled both Northern and Southern Americans to see themselves as not only different, but incompatible as well.

This feeling of difference had not always been so striking. Before the American Revolution, Northern as well as Southern colonists used slave labor. Slavery persisted in some Northern states for decades after the Declaration of Independence pronounced all men created equal. In the early part of the 19th century, there was not much difference in the proportion of Northern and Southern residents engaged in agriculture, nor in their ethnic backgrounds, nor the role education played in their lives.

Even in the South, most people did not own slaves. In 1830, only about one third of white Southerners owned them, and by 1860 an

Twelve years after his dramatic escape from slavery, Frederick Douglass (to the right of the woman in the bonnet) sits on a platform at an abolitionist meeting in 1850. Although his white abolitionist allies originally counseled him to keep his speeches simple, he became one of slavery's most eloquent and sophisticated critics.

even smaller number—only a quarter of them—did. Most whites who did have slaves owned only one or two. "Planters," the very wealthy owners of 20 or more slaves, comprised just 12 percent of all slaveholders. These few men, however, owned 93 percent of the South's agricultural wealth, measured in land and slaves. The image many people today have of plantation life, from the images in Margaret Mitchell's *Gone with the Wind* of grandiose homes and hundreds of slaves, was the reality for only a tiny percentage of Southerners.

But slavery dominated the cultural and economic structure of the South, and both Northerners and Southerners believed that because of this they had different priorities, different customs, and different personalities. In private conversation and in public debates, men and women from both sides were quick to defend their way of life as the better one. Some historians argue that it was this new focus on their differences that allowed Americans to participate in "the brothers' war," as the Civil War was sometimes called. In order to understand the coming of the Civil War, then, we have to examine slavery and how it shaped Northerners' and Southerners' views of themselves and each other. In the following documents, blacks and whites from both sides of the Mason-Dixon Line describe slavery from their own perspective.

North and South Compared

In 1854, George Fitzhugh wrote the following defense of Southern society, in an essay entitled "Slavery Justified." Fitzhugh was one of the country's most influential writers on slavery. His essay reflects the new attitude toward slavery that Southerners adopted after about 1830, when Northern abolitionists became more vocal in their opposition to the peculiar institution. Before then, Southerners had often conceded that slavery was a "necessary evil." But by the time Fitzhugh was writing, most had come to defend the institution as a "positive good," not just for the owners of slaves, but for every white person and even for the slaves themselves.

Fitzhugh's words describe what he thought was wrong with the North as much as what he believed was right about the South. For instance, he reveals his horror of poor white immigrants in Northern cities, and his hatred of labor conflicts in a wage society.

At the slaveholding South all is peace, quiet, plenty, and content-ment. We have no mobs, no trade unions, no strikes for higher wages, no armed resistance to the law, but little jealousy of the rich by the poor. We have but few in our jails, and fewer in our poor houses. . . . We are wholly exempt from the torrent of pau-perism, crime, agrarianism, and infidelity which Europe is pouring from her jails and alms houses on the already crowded North. . . . Actual liberty and equality with our white population has been approached much nearer than in the free States. Few of our whites ever work as day laborers, none as cooks, scullions, ostlers, body servants, or in other menial capacities. One free citizen does not lord it over another; hence that feeling of independence and equality that distinguishes us; hence that pride of character, that self-respect, that give us ascendancy when we come into contact with Northerners. It is a distinction to be a Southerner, as it was once to be a Roman citizen. . . .

In the 1850s, Frederick Law Olmsted, who would later design Central Park in New York City among many other famous projects, traveled extensively in the South and wrote about his impressions. In the following excerpt from his book *The Cotton Kingdom*, he compares how the two regions invested their profits, and reveals the Northern preoccupation with the idea of "progress," both economic and cultural.

Let a man be absent from almost any part of the North twenty years, and he is struck, on his return, by what we call the "improvements" which have been made. Better buildings, church-es, school-houses, mills, railroads, etc. In New York City alone, for instance, at least two hun-dred millions of dollars have been reinvested merely in an improved housing of the people; in labour-saving machinery, waterworks, gasworks, etc., and much more. It is not difficult to see where the profits of our manufacturers and mer-chants are. Again, go into the country, and there is no end of substantial proof of twenty years of agricultural prosperity, not alone in roads, canals, bridges, dwellings, barns and fences, but in books and furniture, and gardens, and pictures, and in the better dress and evidently higher education of

The Civil War has been called the "brothers' war" because Americans fought against their own countrymen, and, in a few instances, brothers actually fought on opposite sides of the conflict.

The Illinois and Michigan Canal con-nected Chicago and the West with the Mississippi River, and allowed for the transportation of goods east and west. The development of the North's transportation system, including its 3,700 miles of canals, strengthened economic ties between the eastern and western parts of the free states. The bonds between them would be of utmost importance during the secession crisis and the Civil War.

the people. But where will the returning traveller see the accumulated cotton profits of twenty years in Mississippi? Ask the cotton-planter for them, and he will point in reply, not to dwellings, libraries, churches, school-houses, mills, railroads, or anything of the kind; he will point to his negroes—to almost nothing else.

Olmsted, like many other Northern whites, was particularly disturbed by the difference that slavery made in the white South's attitude toward work. Because slaves performed most manual labor, Olmsted believed, not only did wealthy whites not have to work hard, but they abhorred work itself. In the following excerpt from one of his many newspaper reports of his travels in the South, Olmsted compares the typical Southern planter's personality to Northern ideals.

The Southerner has no pleasure in labor except with reference to a result. He enjoys life itself. He is content with being. Here is the grand distinction between him and the Northerner; for the Northerner enjoys progress in itself. He finds his happiness in doing. Rest, in itself, is irksome and offensive to him, and however graceful or beatific that rest may be, he values it only with reference to the power of future progress it will bring him. . . .

The Southerner cares for the end only; he is impatient of the means. He is passionate, and labors passionately, fitfully, with the energy and strength of anger, rather than of resolute will. He fights rather than works to carry his purpose. He has the intensity of character which belongs to Americans in general, and therefore enjoys excitement and is fond of novelty. But he has much less curiosity than the Northerner; less originating genius, less inventive talent, less patient and persevering energy. And I think this all comes from his want of aptitude for close observation and his dislike for application to small details. And this, I think, may be reasonably supposed to be mainly the result of habitually leaving all matters not either of grand and exciting importance, or of immediate consequence to his comfort, to his slaves. . . .

Much of the Northern critique of slavery rested on the North's adherence to what has been called the "Protestant work ethic." This ideal holds that work is virtuous in itself and is the only route to self-sufficiency and, therefore, happiness. In the Northern states the members of the Republican Party incorporated these beliefs into their political speeches and writings. Their ideas came to be known as "free labor ideology"

This 1848 advertisement for improved cotton gins appeared in J. D. B. De Bow's Commercial Review *of the South and West. Invented by Eli Whitney in 1793, cotton gins separated seeds and seed hulls from cotton fiber, thereby dramatically increasing cotton plantations' productivity and probably ensuring the survival of the plantation society that De Bow defended.*

COMMERCIAL REVIEW ADVERTISER.

CARVER'S

IMPROVED COTTON GINS.

G. BURKE & CO.,

COTTON FACTORS AND GENERAL COMMISSION MER-
CHANTS, CHIEF AGENTS FOR THE SALE OF

E. CARVER & CO'S

IMPROVED COTTON GINS.

THEY HAVE ON HAND A LARGE ASSORTMENT OF
THE USUAL SIZES,

No. 70 Magazine street,

OPPOSITE THE CANAL BANK,

NEW ORLEANS.

AGENTS:

COBB & MANLOVE,	Vicksburg, Miss.
F. B. ERNEST,	Natchez, do
BROUGHTON & MURDOCK,	Rodney, do
T. McCUNDALL,	Bayou Sara, La.
TITUS & CO.,	Memphis, Tenn.
HORTON & CLARK,	Mobile, Ala.
GILMET & CO.,	Montgomery, do

Slave men load bales of cotton onto ships on the levee at New Orleans. This picture focuses on the men's physical labor, but black men with access to waterways were also important conveyors of information and, at times, fugitive slaves.

and focused on the ideal of a freeman working his way up the economic ladder from a paid laborer to an independent farmer or businessman. In 1859, before he became president, Abraham Lincoln described how the Northern system was supposed to work in this excerpt from a speech to the Wisconsin State Agricultural Society in Milwaukee. His words reveal how free labor ideology justified the fact that many people never did make it beyond the wage labor stage by blaming their failure on flaws in their character.

The prudent, penniless beginner in the world labors for wages awhile, saves a surplus with which to buy tools or land, for himself; then labors on his own account another while, and at length hires another new beginner to help him. This, say its advocates, is *free* labor—the just and generous, and prosperous system, which opens the way for all—gives hope to all, and energy, and progress, and improvement of condition to all. If any continue through life in the condition of hired laborer, it is not the fault of the system, but because of either a dependent nature which prefers it, or improvidence, folly, or singular misfortune.

But by 1859, the world Lincoln described in the previous speech was already changing. More and more people labored in factories rather than in agriculture or small workshops. Many people worked for wages their entire lives, not because they were lazy or because they had "a dependent nature," but because their meager wages did not allow for saving enough money to realize their dreams of a more prosperous life.

Many factory workers considered their own situation unfair and described their lifelong dependence on a factory owner or boss as "wage slavery." In their own critique of the Northern system, they echoed what some Southerners argued were the problems with free labor. Mike Walsh, a newspaper editor and working-class organizer of the Democratic Party, put it to workers this way in 1845:

Demagogues tell you that you are freemen. They lie—you are slaves, and none are better aware of the fact than the heathenish dogs who call you freemen. No man devoid of all other means of support but that which his labor affords him can be a freeman, under the present state of society. He must be a humble slave of capital, created by the labor of the poor men who have toiled, suffered, and died before him.

Abolitionists Speak Out

Most Northerners who opposed slavery did so because they believed it dampened productivity. A few also fervently believed that it constituted a moral wrong for one person to own another as property. People who wanted to abolish or outlaw the slavery system altogether were called abolitionists, and they were a very vocal minority in the North. Ever since the Revolutionary War, some people in both the North and the South had been speaking out against slavery. The early antislavery proponents generally believed that through calm and conciliatory language, they could slowly win the hearts of slaveholders and slavery would gradually die out. In the 1830s, a new breed of abolitionists arose. These men and women took a much more dramatic, forceful approach to the antislavery issue.

One of the first abolitionists to use the new language of immediacy was David Walker, a black man from North Carolina who had settled in Boston. In 1829 he wrote a 76-page pamphlet generally known as *David Walker's Appeal*, in which he called African Americans to militant action on behalf of freedom. Walker's published appeal, along with a violent uprising in 1831 led by a slave preacher named Nat Turner, in which 70 whites were killed, led to a crackdown on all antislavery expression in the South, as well as harsher laws restricting the movements of all blacks, whether freemen or slaves. *Walker's Appeal* read in part as follows:

The Democratic organizer Mike Walsh gives a speech at Tammany Hall in New York in 1843. An enthusiastic orator, Walsh had callused hands that linked him with his working-class audience.

Never make an attempt to gain our freedom or natural right from under our cruel oppressors and murderers until you see our way clear—when that hour arrives and you move, be not afraid or dismayed . . . we are men as well as they. God has pleased to give us two eyes, two hands, two feet, and some sense in our heads as well as they. They have no more right to hold us in slavery than we have to hold them. . . .

. . . Let no man budge us one step, and let slave-holders come to beat us from our country. America is more our country than it is the whites'—we have enriched it with our blood and tears. The greatest riches in all of America have arisen from our blood and tears: and they will drive us from our property and homes, which we have earned with our blood. . . .

Our sufferings will come to an end, in spite of all the Americans this side of eternity. Then we want all the learning and talents among ourselves, and perhaps more to govern ourselves. "Every dog must have its day," the American's is coming to an end. . . .

I speak Americans for your own good. We must and shall be free, I say, in spite of you. You may do your best to keep us in wretchedness and misery, to enrich you and your children, but God will deliver us from under you. And woe, woe, will be to you if we have to obtain our freedom by fighting. Throw away your fears and prejudices then, and enlighten us and treat us like men, and we will like you more than we now hate you. . . . Treat us like men, and there is no danger but that we live in peace and happiness together.

On November 7, 1837, an anti-abolitionist mob in Alton, Illinois, attacked the Godfrey-Gilman warehouse, where the press of abolitionist publisher Elijah Lovejoy had just been delivered and was under guard. The mob threw his press into the Mississippi and killed Lovejoy, making him an early martyr to freedom of the press and helping to solidify opposition to slavery across the country.

In the North, William Lloyd Garrison, a white man, became the best-known abolitionist; he bridged the divide between black and white antislavery activists. He practiced a forceful style of antislavery agitation and took it to new heights. He spread the word through his antislavery newspaper called the *Liberator*, which he began publishing in 1831. Garrison was an outspoken ally of black abolitionists, and argued forcefully that slavery should be immediately abolished. He became famous for his radical ideas and his strident approach, both of which he defends in this excerpt from the first issue of the *Liberator*.

The Female Character

Angelina Grimké and her older sister Sarah paved the way for white women's work in abolition and also in the related movement for woman rights. Angelina focused her energies mostly on abolition, while over the course of her life Sarah began to speak out more and more on the need for equality for women. Although Maria Stewart, a black woman, had addressed public audiences as early as 1831, the Grimké sisters were the first white women to speak out in public in favor of abolition. In doing so, they crossed an important boundary that made many people in the 1830s think about women's roles. Whereas many admired the Grimkés, others denounced their actions. Included among the latter group were the Council of Congregationalist Ministers of Massachusetts, who published a letter that condemned the sisters as unwomanly and un-Christian. Part of their letter reads:

We invite your attention to the dangers which at present seem to threaten the female character with widespread and permanent injury. The appropriate duties and influence of women are clearly stated in the New Testament. . . . We appreciate the unostentatious prayers of women in advancing the cause of religion at home and abroad; in Sabbath-schools; in leading religious inquirers to the pastor for instruction; and in all such associated efforts as become the modesty of her sex. . . . But when she assumes the place and tone of man as a public reformer . . . she yields the power which God has given her for her protection, and her character becomes unnatural.

During my recent tour for the purpose of exciting the minds of the people by a series of discourses on the subject of slavery, every place that I visited gave fresh evidence of the fact, that a greater revolution in public sentiment was to be effected in the free states—*and particularly in New England*—than at the south. I found contempt more bitter, opposition more active, detraction more relentless, prejudice more stubborn, and apathy more frozen, than among slave owners themselves. Of course, there were individual exceptions to the contrary. . . .

Assenting to the "self-evident truth" maintained in the American Declaration of Independence, "that all men are created equal, and endowed by their Creator with certain inalienable rights—among which are life, liberty and the pursuit of happiness," I shall strenuously contend for the immediate enfranchisement of our slave population. In Park-Street church, on the Fourth of July, 1829, in an address on slavery, I unreflectingly assented to the popular but pernicious doctrine of *gradual* abolition. I seize this opportunity to make a full and unequivocal recantation, and thus publicly do ask pardon of my God, my country, and of my brethren the poor slaves, for having uttered a sentiment so full of timidity, injustice and absurdity. . . .

I am aware, that many object to the severity of my language; but is there not cause for severity? I *will be* as harsh as truth, and as uncompromising as justice. On this subject, I do not wish to think, or speak, or write, with moderation. No! No! Tell a man whose house is on fire, to give a moderate alarm; tell him to moderately rescue his wife from the hands of the ravisher; tell the mother to gradually extricate her babe from the fire into which it has fallen;—but urge not me to use moderation in a cause like the present. I am in earnest—I will not equivocate—I will not excuse—I will not retreat a single inch—AND I WILL BE HEARD. The apathy of the people is enough to make every statue leap from its pedestal, and to hasten the resurrection of the dead.

It is pretended, that I am retarding the cause of emancipation by the coarseness of my invective, and the precipitancy of my measures. The charge is not true. On this question my influence,—humble as it is,—is felt at this moment to a considerable extent, and shall be felt in coming years—not perniciously, but as a blessing; and posterity will bear testimony that I was right. I desire to thank God, that he enables me to disregard "the fear of man which bringeth a snare," and to speak his truth in simplicity and power.

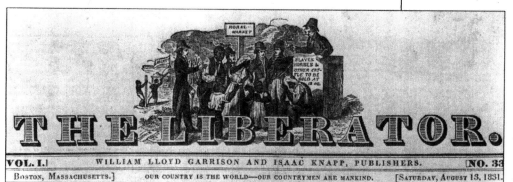

VOL. I.] WILLIAM LLOYD GARRISON AND ISAAC KNAPP, PUBLISHERS. [NO. 33

Boston, Massachusetts.] OUR COUNTRY IS THE WORLD—OUR COUNTRYMEN ARE MANKIND. [Saturday, August 13, 1831.

The masthead of William Lloyd Garrison's radical abolitionist newspaper The Liberator critiques the treatment of human beings as chattel by showing a slave family being sold, along with a horse, while another slave is whipped in the background. The trampled "Indian Treaties" lying on the ground and the capitol building flying the flag of "liberty" in the background illustrate Garrison's concern for wider issues of human justice as well.

Caroline Seabury and her sister traveled from Brooklyn, New York, to Mississippi to teach in the 1850s. They were shocked by the realities of the slave system, having assumed that the stories they heard in the North were exaggerations. The following is an excerpt from Caroline's diary, in which she describes witnessing a "hiring out" of slaves, when one master rented his slaves to other men for the year, separating families without a second thought.

New Year's Day, 1856

By invitation of a friend I went this morning to his plantation twelve miles in the country—my first sight into plantation life. When about half way there we saw quite a large crowd assembled on the "porch" and scattered about the yard of a double log house. My friend at once understood that there was to be a negro hiring & asked if I would like to see it. I assented & we rode up to the door. . . . I sat by an open window & the business soon began. A large block was brought & placed on the highest spot. Around it gathered the crowd of tobacco chewers, now & then I saw a black bottle passed round among them, their voices soon telling of its virtues. [The slaves] stood in the background dressed in their best clothes, of all colors & sizes—in fact this was true of themselves as well as their clothes. There were about 35 in all varying from the real unmistakeable Africans to the pale blue eyed mulatto. My hostess commented on the subject in general, ". . . That yeller one there is the one, you'll hear her called Suey when they put her up. Last year one o' the best men a carpenter wouldn't work, an they made him build a coffin, then made him git into it, and nailed it up to scare him—he was a'most white, a mighty smart feller, could read an write, they said, an so they was afraid to whip him—fear he'd pay back in some way. Well, they kep Jack in a leetle too long, for when they come to knock on the lid, he didn't speak, an

Well-dressed white Southerners look on as a group of barefoot and poorly shod blacks linked by chains passes by under threat of a whip. At the end of the slave coffle a small child holds a woman's hand.

when they opened it, he'd just done breathin—He was Suey's husband. . . . He and Suey was hired to different places 10 miles apart an he would run away every two or three months to see her—when he died she went a'most crazy." For a half hour she had talked on these precise words I answering not one word—I could not doubt the horrid truths she told and never can forget them, or that scene. The auctioneer's loud voice rang out, "genmen, it's a'most time to begin, it's time to bring em on.". . . About a dozen were disposed of, when there came a tall, slender, well-formed light mulatto woman with two children about 7 & 9 years old, and a baby in her arms. "Here's Suey, got no husband to bother her, whall you give—want the children to go along if we can—50—75—85—100—without the children." Here the woman fixed her black eyes on the man bidding. Mrs. H. told me twas "a rich old bachelor, mighty rich from cross the river, but hard on niggers"—Some one kept running against him until it went up to 150—175—& she was "struck off" to the rich man—She said not a word, but her looks told what was in her heart, as she gave up the two older children, she sobbed bitterly— Any other expression of feeling would I suppose have been punished. . . . We spent perhaps two hours there—it seemed to me but a glimpse of the lower world & its foul deeds—and yet it is done at the beginning of every year all over the "Sunny South"—How thankful was I when we rode away from the sight of so much helpless hopeless misery, which I was powerless to relieve.

The Slave System

The great majority of Southern whites did not own slaves and often lived in desperate poverty. Many had little or no schooling, starkly limited diets, ramshackle homes, and tattered clothing. In many ways, then, their physical lives were not all that different from the lives of slaves. Their position in the political and cultural life of the South, however, was very different. Most poor whites did not see themselves as allied with the slaves—and rich whites wanted to make sure

it stayed that way. In a pamphlet published in 1860, James D. B. DeBow of New Orleans, a magazine editor and leading defender of slavery, describes how the slave system benefited even whites who do not own any slaves.

The non-slaveholders, as a class, are not reduced by the necessity of our condition, as is the case in the free States, to find employment in crowded cities and come into competition in close and sickly workshops and factories, and remorseless and untiring machinery. They have but to compare their condition in this particular with the mining and manufacturing operatives of the North and Europe, to be thankful that God has reserved them for a better fate. Tender women, aged men, delicate children, toil and labor there from early dawn until after candle light, from one year to another, for a miserable pittance, scarcely above the starvation point and without hope for amelioration. . . .

The non-slaveholder of the South preserves the status of the white man, and is not regarded as an inferior or a dependent. He is not told that the Declaration of Independence, when it says that all men are born free and equal, refers to the negro equally with himself. It is not proposed to him that the free negro's vote shall weigh equally with his own at the ballot-box, and that the little children of both colors shall be mixed in the classes and benches of the schoolhouse, and embrace each other filially in its outside sports. . . . No white man at the South serves another as a body servant, to clean his boots, wait on his table, and perform the menial services of his household. His blood revolts against this, and his necessities never drive him to it. He is a companion and an equal. When in the employ of the slaveholder, or in intercourse with him, he enters his hall, and has a seat at his table. If a distinction exists, it is only that which education and refinement may give, and this is so

A list of African Americans to be sold at auction in Savannah, Georgia, in 1860. Each slave is rated in the fourth column in terms of his ability to perform the standard day's work of an adult rice-plantation slave (a whole or prime hand as "1," a half hand as "1/2," and so on). The slaves are listed by family, and the prices paid, in the first column, reveal which families were sold together and which were split up.

DESCRIPTIVE LIST
OF
138 NEGROES,
Accustomed to the Culture of Rice.

These Negroes will be sold, deliverable at Savannah, from the 15th to the 20th of January, 1860. For particulars, enquire of

J. BRYAN,
Johnson Square, Savannah, Ga.

No.	NAME.	Age.	FIELD RATE	REMARKS.
1	Adam Adams,	45	1	Prime man, good worker.
2	Molly,	49	1-2	Hearty woman, do.
3	Victoria,	15	3-4	Fine girl.
4	Sarah,	12	1-4	Very good girl.
5	Sophy Adams,	40	1	Very prime and large—mother of fine family.
6	Amy,	19	1	A 1, very likely—daughter of Sophy.
7	Adeline,	15	1-2	A 1, very likely—daughter of Sophy.
8	Lydia,	8		Fine and hearty—daughter of Sophy.
9	Jessica,	7		Fine and hearty—daughter of Sophy.
10	Sannet,	4		Fine and hearty—daughter of Sophy.
11	Adam,	2		Fine and hearty—son of Sophy.
12	Hagar,	60	1-2	Hale woman—excellent midwife.
13	Jimmy,	28	1	Jobbing Carpenter—small, but well built and active.
14	Mina,	26	1	Prime woman—about to be confined.
15	Anthony,	9		Fine boy.
16	Joe,	2		Fine boy.
17	Maria,	30	1	Very prime and fine woman.
18	Juliana,	14	1-2	Very prime and fine girl.
19	Jane Ishmals,	38	1-2	Delicate—slight prolapsis uti.
20	Audley,	9		Fine boy.
21	Adam Bacchus,	32	1	A 1, prime and fine looking.
22	Phœbe (Inis,)	24	1	Right eye injured, but a very prime and likely woman.
23	Ellis,	5		Very fine boy.
24	Sandy,	22	1	Very prime, good ploughman.
25	Old Katey,	aged		Good nurse, hearty old woman.
26	Abraham Bluff,	38	1	A 1, prime and fine looking.
27	Molly,	38		Diseased with wens, capital nurse, intelligent.
28	Henney,	18	1	A 1, very fine girl.
29	Annis,	16	1	A very fine prime girl.
30	Rachael,	12	1-2	A very fine prime girl.
31	Coomba,	9		A very fine prime girl.
32	Bess,	50	1-2	Prolap. uti, good at light work.
33	Belinda,	16	1	A 1, very prime and likely.
34	Chloe,	15	1-2	Very likely.

Slave Drivers

A driver was usually a slave who had been chosen to act as an overseer for the other laborers.

courteously exhibited as scarcely to strike attention. The poor white laborer at the North is at the bottom of the social ladder, whilst his brother here has ascended several steps and can look down upon those who are beneath him, at an infinite remove.

Of course the people who benefited the most from slavery were the wealthy white male slaveholders. They had vast control over their plantations and the lives of both their own families and the families of their slaves. In the following excerpt from his diary, Bennet H. Barrow describes some of the rules he has developed for his Louisiana plantation. From it we can get a sense of his priorities and also the limitations placed on slaves' lives.

1. Rules of Highland Plantation (May 1838)

No negro shall leave the place at any time without my permission, or in my absence that of the Driver the driver in that case being responsible, for the cause of such absence, which ought never to be ommitted to be enquired into—

The Driver should never leave the plantation, unless on business of the plantation—

No negro shall be allowed to marry off the plantation

No negro shall be allowed to sell anything without my express permission[.] I have ever maintained the doctrine that my negroes have no time Whatever, that they are always liable to my call without questioning for a moment the propriety of it, I adhere to this on the grounds of expediency and right. The verry security of the plantation requires that a general and uniform control over the people of it should be exercised. Who are to protect the plantation from the intrusions of ill designed persons When evry body is a broad? Who can tell the moment When a plantation might be threatened with destruction from Fire—could the flames be arrested if the negroes are scattered throughout the neighborhood, seeking their amusement. Are these not duties of great importance, and in which evry negro himself is deeply interested[. T]o render this part of the rule justly applicable, however, it would be necessarty that such a settled arrangement should exist on the plantation to make it unnecessary for a negro to leave it—or to have a good plea for doing so—You must, therefore make him as comfortable at Home as possible, affording him What is essentially necessary for his happiness—you must provide for him Your self and by that means creat in him a habit of perfect dependence on you—Allow it ounce to be understood by a negro that he is to

Men, women, and children all participated in harvesting cotton on large plantations. At the rear are the "big house" where the owner and his family lived, outbuildings, and the plantation's cotton gin, marked by the smokestacks.

provide for himself, and you that moment give him an undeniable claim on you for a portion of his time to make this provision, and should you from necessity, or any other cause, encroach upon his time—disappointment and discontent are seriously felt—if I employ a labourer to perform a certain quantum of work per day and I agree to pay him a certain amount for the performance of said work When he has accomplished it I of course have no further claim on him for his time or services—but how different it is with a slave—Who can calculate the exact profit or expence of a slave one year with another, if I furnish my negro with evry necessary of life, without the least care on his part—if I support him in sickness, however long it may be, and pay all his expenses, though he does nothing—if I maintain him in his old age, when he is incapable of rendering either himself or myself any service, am I not entitled to an exclusive right to his time[?] [G]ood feelings, and a sense of propriety would all ways prevent unnecessary employment on the Sabbath and policy would check any exaction of excessive labor in common.

Whites who owned slaves had a wide spectrum of emotions about their "property," ranging from pure hatred to a kind of paternalistic interest in, and sometimes even fondness for, individuals. In the following entries in her diary, the slave mistress Ella Gertrude Clanton Thomas reveals the complexities of whites' attitudes toward their slaves. Thomas claims to feel some emotional connection to certain individuals, and yet she does not question the practice of splitting up black families, nor does she hesitate to sell her own slaves. Tamah and Isabella were both slaves who worked in Thomas's house.

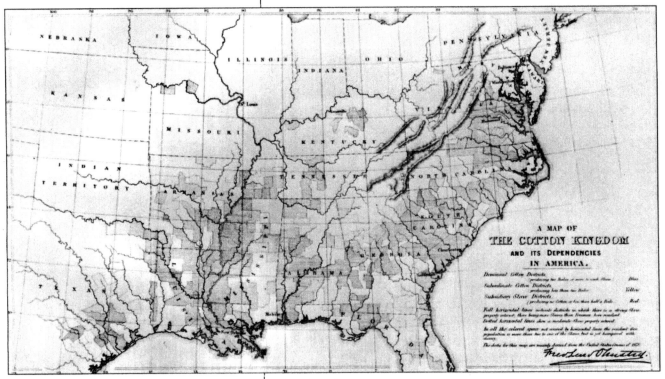

A MAP OF
THE COTTON KINGDOM
AND ITS DEPENDENCIES
IN AMERICA.

This map from Frederick Law Olmsted's Journeys and Explorations in the Cotton Kingdom *shows which districts were more and less dependent on slave labor and cotton production. Olmsted argued that the areas where slave labor was most entrenched saw the slowest economic development.*

Sunday, August 19, 1855

The previous day I had left Isabella at home to finish a shirt for John and to get her things ready to go with me to Aunt Lamkins's—Returning home Sunday night Mr Thomas noticed the disorder among the books in the dining room and soon after found the key to the sideboard. I was certain of having placed it in the sideboard and locking it up with the other key. Upon looking for it, found it missing—Suspicion fully aroused I inquired of Tamah concerning it and she wished to know "why didn't I leave the storeroom keys with Isabella the day before?" Here was another mystery—which when explained proved that she [Isabella] had taken this key and during my absence Saturday unlocked the drawer in which were the storeroom keys and opening that stolen flour and a bar of soap. These Mr Thomas found among her things and she confessed after first denying that she had taken them. Mercy knows what else she took. Oh I have lost all patience with her—It was too late to make any other arrangement so I took her with me the next day but never expect to take her again for I consider her as one not to [be] trusted in the slightest degree. . . .

Wednesday, November —, 1857

[Isabella] is a girl of a good many excellent traits and it [is] very much to be regretted that this incurable habit of stealing should prevent one from placing any confidence in her. . . . I have had so many trials with her that with my consent I don't think I shall ever have her for a house servant. I would like her sold and a good steady woman brought in her place . . . and yet it is strange—that to this girl I have a feeling amounting nearer to attachment than to any servant I ever met with in my life. . . . [Note at bottom of page:] "I wonder what ever became of Isabella. She was afterwards sold and I have never seen her since—she must be living somewhere in the world, and perhaps she may be suffering but I scarcely think so. I hope not. Aug 1879.

Ex-Slaves Remember

No matter what their feelings about their slaves, whites maintained their power over them through violence or the threat of violence. Benjamin Drew, an abolitionist from Boston, traveled to Canada in 1855 to collect the stories of runaway slaves who had made it to freedom. One ex-slave to whom he spoke, Mrs. James Seward, described her experience in slavery and that of her family members.

I am from the eastern shore of Maryland. I never belonged but to one master; he was very bad indeed. I was never sent to school, nor allowed to go to church. They were afraid we would have more sense than they. I have a father there, three sisters, and a brother. My father is quite an old man, and he is used very badly. Many a time he has been kept at work a whole long summer day without sufficient food. A sister of mine has been punished by his [the master's] taking away her clothes and locking them up, because she used to run when master whipped her. He kept her at work with only what she could pick up and tie on for decency. He took away her child which had just begun to walk, and gave it to another woman,—but she went and got it afterward. He had a large farm eight miles from home. Four servants were kept at the house. My master could not manage to whip my sister when she was strong. He waited until she was confined, and the second week after her confinement he said "Now I can handle you, now

In their efforts to catch runaway slaves, slaveholders routinely placed newspaper advertisements like this one that Caroline Seabury pasted into her diary. Despite the fact that at least one of her ancestors—probably her father—must have been white, this blue-eyed, sandy-haired woman was held in bondage.

RAN AWAY

FROM the subscriber, in the month of February last, a woman aged about 30, rather heavy set. short, weighs about 145 pounds, almost white, has long hair, (brown, or sandy,) blue eyes, large mouth, good teeth, and talks freely.

She claims to be free and white, calls herself EMILY RILEY, tells a wonderful tale of her father's being a flat-boatman on the waters of the Tennessee. She is rather clumsy in her walk, has large feet, and had a tetter on one thumb that has injured the nail.

A liberal reward will be paid for her delivery to me or for her confinement in any place so that I may get her.   I. SULLIVAN.

Hayes Creek. Carroll Co., Miss.—4w.

you are weak." She ran from him, however, and had to go through water, and was sick in consequence.

I was beaten at one time over the head by my master, until the blood ran from my mouth and nose; then he tied me up in the garret, with my hands over my head,—then he brought me down and put me in a little cupboard, where I had to sit cramped up, part of the evening, all night and until between four and five o'clock, next day, without any food. The cupboard was near a fire, and I thought I should suffocate.

My brother was whipped on one occasion until his back was as raw as a piece of beef, and before it got well, master whipped him again. His back was an awful sight.

We were all afraid of master: when I saw him coming, my heart would jump into my mouth, as if I had seen a serpent.

I have been wanting to come away for eight years back. I waited for Jim Seward to get ready. Jim had promised to take me away and marry me. Our master would allow no marriages on the farm. When Jim had got ready, he let me know,—he brought two suits of clothes—men's clothes—which he had bought on purpose for me. I put on both suits to keep me warm. We eluded pursuit and reached Canada in safety.

The escaped slave Margaret Garner, realizing that her Kentucky owner was about to recapture her and her children, decided to kill them. She managed to cut her daughter's throat but was stopped before she could cut her sons'. Published after the Civil War, this image reminded Northerners of the terrible price of the Fugitive Slave Law of 1850, which commanded federal marshals (right) to aid slave owners (left.) This tragic episode forms the basis for Toni Morrison's 1987 novel, Beloved.

Frederick Douglass escaped from slavery as a young man. An eloquent author and orator, he became one of the best-known figures of the 19th century. In the following excerpts from his autobiography, Douglass illustrates the vast distance that existed between whites and blacks in the South. In the first, he refutes a popular proslavery argument, that the beautiful songs slaves sang as they worked proved that they were happy. In the second, Douglass explains why slaves often lied when questioned about their experiences. Douglass reminds us that we cannot always take what we hear or read at face value. Sources can lie. Words can mean different things to different people, and depending on what we want to hear, we may mistake their message.

Slaves were expected to sing as well as to work. A silent slave was not liked, either by masters or by overseers. *"Make a noise there! make a noise there!"* and *"bear a hand,"* were words usually addressed to slaves when they were silent. This, and the natural disposition of the negro to make a noise in the world, may account for the almost constant singing among them when at their work. Child as I was, these wild songs greatly depressed my spirits. . . .

I have sometimes thought that the mere hearing of these songs would have done more to impress the good people of the north with the soul-crushing character of slavery than whole volumes exposing the physical cruelties of the slave system; for the heart has no language like song. . . .

The remark in the olden time was not unfrequently made, that slaves were the most contented and happy laborers in the world, and their dancing and singing were referred to in proof of this alleged fact; but it was a great mistake to suppose them happy because they sometimes made those joyful noises. The songs of the slaves represented their sorrows, rather than their joys. Like tears, they were a relief to aching hearts. It is not inconsistent with the constitution of the human mind, that avails itself of one and the same method for expressing opposite emotions. Sorrow and desolation have their songs, as well as joy and peace. . . .

The real feelings and opinions of the slaves were not much known or respected by their masters. The distance between the two was too great to admit of such knowledge; and in this respect Col. Lloyd was no exception to the rule. His slaves were so numerous he did not know them when he saw them. Nor, indeed, did all his slaves know him. It is reported of him, that riding along the road one day he met a colored man, and addressed him in what was the usual way of speaking to colored people on the public highways of the South: "Well, boy, who do you belong to?" "To Col. Lloyd," replied the slave. "Well, does the Colonel treat you well?" "No, sir," was the ready reply. "What, does he work you hard?" "Yes, sir." "Well, don't he give you enough to eat?" "Yes, sir, he gives me enough to eat, such as it is." The Colonel rode on; the slave also went on about his business, not dreaming that he had been conversing with his master. He thought and said nothing of the matter, until two or three weeks afterwards, he was informed by his overseer that for having found fault with his master, he was now to be sold to a Georgia trader. He was immediately chained and handcuffed; and thus without a moment's warning, he was snatched away, and forever sundered from his family and friends by a hand as unrelenting as that of death. This was the penalty of telling the simple truth, in answer to a series of plain questions. It was partly in consequence of such facts, that slaves, when inquired of as to their condition and the character of their masters, would almost invariably say that they were contented and their masters kind.

What, to the American slave, is your 4th of July? I answer; a day that reveals to him, more than all the other days in the year, the gross injustice and cruelty to which he is the constant victim. To him, your celebration is a sham; your boasted liberty, an unholy license; your national greatness, swelling vanity; your sounds of rejoicing are empty and heartless; your denunciation of tyrants, brass fronted impudence; your shouts of liberty and equality, hollow mockery; your prayers and hymns, your sermons and thanksgivings, with all your religious parade and solemnity, are, to Him, mere bombast, fraud, deception, impiety, and hypocrisy—a thin veil to cover up crimes which would disgrace a nation of savages. There is not a nation on the earth guilty of practices more shocking and bloody than are the people of the United States, at this very hour.

—Frederick Douglass, speech to the Rochester, New York, Ladies' Anti-Slavery Society, July 5, 1852

Chapter Two

Expanding Boundaries, Rising Tensions

On September 13, 1856, pro-slavery Missourians met in St. Louis. Two days later the new governor of the Kansas Territory, John W. Geary, used federal troops to break up an army of anti-abolitionist border ruffians nearly 2,500 strong that was about to march on Kansas.

Many 19th-century Americans, both Northern and Southern, felt it was their country's "manifest destiny" to spread from the Atlantic to the Pacific Ocean. They fervently believed that they had the right, and indeed the moral imperative, to carry their traditions and their property—what they considered "civilization"—across the vast reaches of the continent. Westward migration, though, not only destroyed much of the Native American population, it also played a pivotal role in escalating national tensions to the brink of civil war.

Whites uprooted thousands of Native Americans as they pushed West, wiping out much of their culture and causing the deaths of hundreds of thousands of people. While a few white Americans protested this harsh treatment, most believed that westward migration would be good for their own country. But as wagons carried white settlers into the plains and prairies west of the Mississippi, they carried their beliefs and disagreements as well. The issue of slavery, while it had always been controversial, turned dangerously divisive when some Americans sought to introduce the peculiar institution into the enormous new territory. No longer able to ignore the problem, time and again politicians in the North and South fought over what to do about slavery. Time and again, they worked out compromises and policies that might at least hold the problem in check for a while.

One of the earliest decisions over the expansion of slavery dated back to 1787, when the Northwest Ordinance prohibited it from the new territory that encompassed what is now Ohio. But then in 1803 President Thomas Jefferson bought all the land that France had claimed on the continent. This huge new area, called the Louisiana Purchase, stretched all the way from New Orleans in the South to the

In this illustration from Harriet Beecher Stowe's 1852 novel Uncle Tom's Cabin, Little Eva reads the Bible to Uncle Tom, who had risked his life to rescue her when she fell off a steamboat into the river. The book drew on Northerners' emotions to convey to them the horrors of slavery.

"[Americans should not regret] the progress of civilization and improvement, the triumph of industry and art, by which these regions have been reclaimed, and over which freedom, religion, and science are extending their sway. . . . A barbarous people, depending for subsistence upon the scanty and precarious supplies furnished by the chase, cannot live in contact with a civilized community."

—Lewis Cass, governor of the Michigan Territory, from a North American Review article, 1830

Rocky Mountains in the West, and doubled the size of the United States. The Northwest Ordinance did not apply to the new Louisiana Purchase. When settlers started to move into part of the area known as Missouri, the question of slavery had to be reconsidered.

Many Northerners were convinced that Southerners had too much power in the government. In order to prevent the addition of any senators from slaveholding states, they demanded that Missouri be admitted as a free state. Southerners were furious, and the fight over the issue divided the nation. Finally, in 1821 legislators reached what became known as the Missouri Compromise. Missouri was admitted to the Union as a slave state, but a line was established across the rest of the territories at 36° 30', above which slavery could not be introduced. Since most of the land in the Louisiana Purchase lay above the dividing line, Northerners assumed that the majority of the territory would remain free.

The Missouri Compromise managed to calm the nation for the time being, but Thomas Jefferson was right when he called the conflict a "firebell in the night," warning of future troubles over the question of slavery in the West. Eventually the U.S. political system proved unable to contain the conflict. Words gave way to violence, and when fighting broke out in one of the new territories—Kansas—it foreshadowed the coming of the Civil War.

Westward Migration

The most immediate and dramatic impact of westward migration was on the native peoples that it displaced. In some cases, whites pressured Indians into signing treaties giving away their land; in other cases, white settlers simply moved in and fought off the Indians. In still others, the U.S. army attacked Indian villages, or herded Native Americans into wagons, and forced them off their ancestral homes at gunpoint. In addition, thousands of Native Americans died from exposure to diseases brought by the white settlers.

The Sac and Fox Indians of Illinois were forced off their lands after the Black Hawk War, which ended in 1832. Chief Black Hawk made a speech when he surrendered in which he bitterly denounced the actions of whites and the U.S. government.

I fought hard. But your guns were well aimed. The bullets flew like birds in the air, and whizzed by our ears like the wind through the trees in the winter. My warriors fell around me. . . . The sun rose dim on us in the morning, and at night it sunk in a dark cloud, and looked like a ball of fire. That was the last sun that shone on Black Hawk. . . . He is now a prisoner to the white men. . . . He has done nothing for which an Indian ought to be ashamed. He has fought for his countrymen, the squaws and papooses, against white men, who came year after year, to cheat them and take away their lands. You know the cause of our making war. It is known to all white men. They ought to be ashamed of it. Indians are not deceitful. The white men speak bad of the Indian and look at him spitefully. But the Indian does not tell lies. Indians do not steal.

An Indian who is as bad as the white men could not live in our nation; he would be put to death, and eaten up by the wolves. The white men are bad schoolmasters; they carry false books, and deal in false actions; they smile in the face of the poor Indian to cheat him; they shake him by the hand to gain their confidence, to make them drunk, to deceive them, and ruin our wives. We told them to leave us alone, and keep away from us; they followed on, and beset our paths, and they coiled themselves among us, like the snake. They poisoned us by their touch. We were not safe. We lived in danger. We were becoming like them, hypocrites and liars, adulterous lazy drones, all talkers and no workers. . . .

The white men do not scalp the head; but they do worse—they poison the heart. . . . Farewell, my nation! . . . Farewell to Black Hawk.

The Mexican War

In 1844, James K. Polk became President. Polk and his allies wanted even more land for the United States. The 1820s had seen an influx of Americans to Texas, which at that time was a province of Mexico. Mexico abolished slavery, however, and many of the Americans who settled there wanted to keep their slaves. In 1836 Texas won its independence from Mexico, and in 1845 Polk oversaw the annexation of Texas. He wanted even more, though. In 1846 Polk sent U.S. troops to the Rio Grande, the river that ran between Texas and Mexico. Because the border was ill-defined, he could expect that conflict was almost inevitable. Col. Ethan Allen Hitchcock, commander of the 3rd Infantry Regiment, wrote in his diary:

I have said from the first that the United States are the aggressors. . . . We have not one particle of right to be here. . . . It looks as if the government sent a small force on purpose to bring on a war,

The Native American Effort

Once the Civil War began, American Indians fought on both sides of the conflict. Hoping that the new Confederacy would grant them better treatment than the United States had, some chiefs of the five so-called civilized tribes (Cherokees, Chickasaws, Choctaws, Creeks, and Seminoles) signed treaties of alliance with the Confederacy, sent delegates to the Confederate Congress, and supplied soldiers to the Southern army. Stand Watie, a Cherokee leader, became a brigadier general in the Confederate army. He is famous for being the last Confederate general to surrender his troops to the Union, a month after the rest of the army had done so. About one-half of the members of the five tribes, however, remained loyal to the Union.

so as to have a pretext for taking California and as much of this country as it chooses, for, whatever becomes of this army, there is no doubt of a war between the United States and Mexico. . . . My heart is not in this business . . . but, as a military man, I am bound to execute orders.

When Mexicans killed first a quartermaster, and then, the next day, a patrol of soldiers, Gen. Zachary Taylor wrote to Polk that "hostilities may now be considered as commenced." In his message to Congress on May 11, 1846, President Polk placed the blame for starting a war directly on Mexico.

Mexico has passed the boundary of the United States, has invaded our territory and shed American blood upon the American soil. She has proclaimed that hostilities have commenced, and that the two nations are now at war. . . . I invoke the prompt action of Congress to recognize the existence of the war, and to place at the disposition of the Executive the means of prosecuting the war with vigor, and thus hastening the restoration of peace. . . .

When the Mexican War began, neither the U.S. nor the Mexican army was well organized, but the Americans had better supplies and a large force of volunteers, and they won the

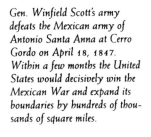

Gen. Winfield Scott's army defeats the Mexican army of Antonio Santa Anna at Cerro Gordo on April 18, 1847. Within a few months the United States would decisively win the Mexican War and expand its boundaries by hundreds of thousands of square miles.

war relatively easily. For many Mexican civilians who lived through the war, however, there was nothing easy about it. Some residents of a village called Burrita, which was located near a U.S. encampment, sent the following complaint of outrages to American officials.

Bernando Garza, a respectable citizen of Burrita making complaint against the 6th Regiment, under the command of Col. Featherston: That on the night of the 25th, and morning of the 26th, his house, occupied as a bakery in Burrita, was pulled down and consumed for fire wood by the soldiers of the 6th Regiment. That from the 22nd inst. To the present time the fence around his corn field has been used by the soldiers for fire wood, his corn cut & taken from the field near and below Burrita, watermellons [sic] used & destroyed. And his frequent complaints to the officers in the fort were unavailing.

Antonio Treneria, also a respectable citizen of Burrita, complains that his corn field, immediately opposite to Burrita has been entered and destroyed by the soldiers. . . .

They further state to their own personal knowledge that there have been seven houses belonging to the citizens of Burrita torn down and destroyed.

The Fugitive Slave Law

The acquisition of lands from Mexico brought renewed conflict to the United States as politicians fought over whether to allow slavery into the new territories. Trouble had been brewing over California's entry into the Union as a free state. Many Southerners started to talk about seceding from the Union, and violent rhetoric became the norm. The conflict reached crisis proportions in 1850. On April 17, a senator from Mississippi pulled out a revolver and pointed it at another senator. Clearly, something had to be done—and done quickly—to ease the tensions.

Henry Clay, Kentucky's prominent senator, secured peace by introducing the Compromise of 1850, a collection of resolutions that was supposed to offer each side something that it wanted. This agreement averted disaster for the time being. But while many Americans welcomed the relative calm it achieved, others was outraged by its specifics. By far the most controversial piece of the Compromise of 1850 was the last resolution, which came to be known as the Fugitive Slave

The Wilmot Proviso

David Wilmot, a Democratic congressman from Pennsylvania, suggested even before the Mexican War was over that slavery be forbidden from any land won in the contest. His proposal never became law, but the Wilmot Proviso had an enormous impact on the U.S. political scene. Almost all Northern congressmen, whether Democratic or Whig, voted for the proviso, and almost all Southerners voted against it, regardless of party. This was the first time that the geographical roots of Congressmen affected their vote more than their party affiliation. Because it suggested that the party system was breaking down, this was an ominous sign for the times ahead.

The Compromise of 1850

According to the Compromise of 1850, California would be admitted as a free state, but the rest of the territory acquired from Mexico would not forbid slavery. The slave trade in Washington, D.C., would be abolished, but slavery itself would be guaranteed. Two more resolutions declared that Congress would have no authority to interfere with the interstate slave trade, and also instituted a stronger federal law to make it easier for slave catchers to recapture fugitive slaves.

Law. The Fugitive Slave Law created a new category of federal officials, called commissioners, who had the power to issue warrants for the arrest of fugitive slaves. It declared that a Southerner's statement that a certain person belonged to him was sufficient proof of ownership, and it prohibited fugitives from testifying on their own behalf. Commissioners received a fee of $10 if they decided the case for the slaveholder, but only $5 if they released the slave, which many Northerners viewed as bribery, pure and simple. Finally, a commissioner had the power to force any citizen to serve as his deputy and help capture slaves, and could fine or imprison him if he refused. For many Northerners, black and white, this law crossed a boundary they could not accept.

Northerners preached resistance to the Fugitive Slave Law. In Philadelphia, a group of outraged African Americans met on October 31, 1850, to discuss their reaction to the new law. The resolutions they passed reveal their anger, their disappointment, and their determination to resist.

1. Resolved, That while we have heretofore yielded obedience to the laws of our country, however hard some of them have borne upon us, we deem this law so wicked, so atrocious, so utterly at variance with the principles of the Constitution; so subversive of the objects of all law, the protection of the lives, liberty, and property of the governed; so repugnant to the highest attributes of God, justice, and mercy; and so horribly cruel in its clearly expressed mode of operation, that we deem it our sacred duty, a duty that we owe to ourselves, our wives, our children, and to our common nature, as well as to the panting fugitive from oppression, to resist this law at any cost and at all hazards; and we hereby pledge our lives, our fortunes, and our sacred honor to do so.

2. Resolved, That we deem the laws of God at all times paramount to any human laws; and that, in obedience to the command, to 'hide the outcast and betray not him that wandereth,' we shall never refuse aid and shelter and succor to any brother or sister who has escaped from the prison-house of Southern bondage, but shall do all we can to prevent their being dragged back to a slavery inconceivably worse than death.

3. Resolved, That whenever a Government "frameth mischief by law," or "decrees unrighteous decrees," or concentrates all its power to strengthen the arm of the oppressor to crush the weak, that Government puts itself in an attitude hostile to every principle

Effects of the Fugitive-Slave-Law.

Four fugitive slaves, two of whom have been shot, seek shelter in a cornfield, while six gun-toting whites threaten in the distance. The quotes beneath the image are from the Old Testament and the Declaration of Independence, the abolitionists' two main sources.

of justice—hostile to the liberal spirit of the law, hostile to that God who executeth righteousness and judgement for all that are oppressed.

4. Resolved, That in our resistance to this most cruel law, we appeal to our own boasted Declaration of Independence, to the inherent righteousness of our cause, to the moral sense of enlightened nations all over the world, and to the character of that God, who by a series of the most astounding miracles on record, declared his sympathy for the oppressed and his hatred of the oppressor.

5. Resolved, That feeling the need in this trying hour of the Wisdom that erreth not, and the arm that is invincible to defend and guide us, we therefore call uppon all the colored pastors of our churches in the Free States (so called) to set apart the first Monday night in each month for public prayer and supplication, that the hearts of this people may be so turned to the weak and the oppressed, that the operation of this cruel law may be powerless, and that the time may soon come when "liberty shall be proclaimed throughout ALL the land unto ALL the inhabitants thereof."

6. Resolved, That we will hold up to the scorn of the civilized world that hypocrisy which welcomes to our shores the refugees from Austrian tyranny, and at the same time would send the refugees from American Slavery back to a doom, compared with which, Austrian tyranny is a mercy.

7. Resolved, That we endorse, to the full, the sentiment of the Revolutionary patriot of Virginia, and should the awful alternative be presented to us, will act fully upon it—"Give me Liberty or give me Death."

8. Resolved, That a Committee be appointed to draft an appeal to the citizens of the Commonwealth of Pennsylvania, setting forth the Anti-Republican, Anti-Christian, Anti-human nature of the Fugitive Slave Bill, and asking of them their sympathy and succor.

9. Resolved, That having already witnessed to some extent the cruel operations of this law; having felt such anguish as no language can describe in seeing the wife flying from her home and the embraces of her husband, and the husband compelled to fly from his wife and helpless children, to gain that security in the land of a Monarchy which they could not enjoy in this Republic; we ask, calmly and solemnly ask, the American people, "What have we done to suffer such treatment at your hands?" And may we not, in the sight of that God with whom there is no respect of persons, appeal to your sense of justice and mercy to have this most cruel law repealed as soon as Congress shall reassemble, and in the meantime may we not ask you to create, by all lawful means, such a public sentiment as shall render its operation upon us powerless?

10. Resolved, That, not in the spirit of bravado, neither or affected unconsciousness of the cruelties of public sentiment and law, in regard to our unfortunate and abused race, but seeing clearly, and knowing fully, the unjust prejudice existing against us, and using only those moral means of truth, sufficient as we deem them by a certain process, to the "pulling down of the stronghold" of the injustice and wrong that now afflict us; yet in view of the unheard of atrociousness of the provisions of this infernal FUGITIVE SLAVE BILL, we solemnly declare before the Most High God, and the world, to resist to death any attempt to enforce it upon our persons.

Four years after its passage, the Fugitive Slave Law was put to a terrible test. On May 24, 1854, Anthony Burns, an escaped slave from Virginia, was suddenly seized in Boston. The city was soon in a furor over his capture, and black and white abolitionists assaulted the federal courthouse where he was being held. The attackers killed one of the deputy marshals guarding Burns, but did not succeed in freeing the captive. Although the city offered to purchase Burns's freedom, the

"We went to bed one night old-fashioned, conservative, Compromise Union Whigs, & waked up stark mad Abolitionists."

—Amos A. Lawrence, former leader of the more conservative wing of the Whig Party

THE
BOSTON SLAVE RIOT,
AND
TRIAL
OF
Anthony Burns,

CONTAINING THE
REPORT OF THE FANEUIL HALL MEETING; THE MURDER OF
BACHELDER; THEODORE PARKER'S LESSON FOR THE DAY;
SPEECHES OF COUNSEL ON BOTH SIDES, CORRECTED
BY THEMSELVES; VERBATIM REPORT OF JUDGE
LORING'S DECISION; AND, A DETAILED AC-
COUNT OF THE EMBARKATION.

Fugitive slave Anthony Burns appears in an 1854 pamphlet containing speeches from the Faneuil Hall meeting where Boston abolitionists decried the Fugitive Slave Law that allowed Burns to be returned to his owner. Boston's resistance to Burns's capture—eventually abolitionists in the city purchased his freedom—set the stage for personal liberty laws that made the enforcement of the Fugitive Slave Law in Massachusetts extremely difficult.

federal government refused and sent in the U.S. Army. As thousands of bitter New Englanders watched, the troops marched Burns through the streets of Boston to a ship waiting in the harbor to take him back to slavery in Virginia.

The Anthony Burns affair had a profound and lasting impact on the United States. Both whites and blacks were shocked and deeply moved by the spectacle of a man being marched through the streets back to slavery. In an editorial written a few days after the Burns fiasco, the assistant editor of *Frederick Douglass's Newspaper*, William J. Watkins, wrote about the event.

"A good revolver, a steady hand, and a determination to shoot down any man attempting to kidnap. Let every colored man make up his mind to this, and live by it, and if needs be, die by it. This will put an end to kidnapping and to slaveholding, too."
—Frederick Douglass, "True Remedy for the Fugitive Slave Bill," 1854

Slavery is murder in the highest degree. Every slaveholder is a murderer, a wholesale murderer. Those who apologise for them are worse than murderers. If one of these midnight and noonday assassins were to rush into the house of a white man, and strive to bind him hand and foot, and tear God's image from his brow, and be shot in the attempt, no one would characterize the act as murder. Not at all. It would be considered an act of righteous retribution. . . . Now take the following case. A colored man is living quietly in Boston, one mile from Bunker Hill Monument. He is a free man, for God created him. He stamped His image upon him. Slavery has well nigh murdered him. He has contrived to break loose from its iron grasp. He is pursued by his murderers. The hall of justice has become a den of thieves. A man leaves the honorable occupation of driving horses, and consents, for a "consideration," to be appointed Deputy Marshal, consents to be invested with power to rob him of his God-given rights. The miserable thing is shot in the attempt. Is that man a murderer who sent the well-directed bullet through his stony heart? He would not be so considered if the parties were white.

Popular Sovereignty

In the year following the Anthony Burns affair, a new controversy arose over settlement in the region west of Missouri. Sen. Stephen A. Douglas of Illinois presented a bill to introduce two new territories into the Union: Kansas, just west of Missouri, and Nebraska, north of Kansas. His bill left it up to the people who settled the area to decide whether or not to allow slavery. This tactic for dealing with the slavery issue became known as popular sovereignty.

Douglas's bill caused an incredible furor because it repealed the part of the Missouri Compromise that had drawn a line across the country at 36°30', above which was not supposed to be any slavery. The bill passed, and set the country up for renewed conflict and deadly battles.

Douglas had several motives for sponsoring the Kansas-Nebraska Act. He probably believed that popular sovereignty would lead to two more free states. But in a letter he wrote in 1853, he suggested that part of his motivation had little to do with the question of slavery, but instead with the "problem" of Native Americans living on the land.

It seemed to have been the settled policy of the government for many years, to collect the various tribes in the different States and organized Territories, and to plant them permanently on the western borders of Arkansas, Missouri and Iowa under treaties guaranteeing to them perpetual occupancy, *with an express condition that they should never be incorporated within the limits of territory or state[s] of the Union.* This policy evidently contemplated the creation of a perpetual and savage barrier to the further progress of emigration, settlement and civilization in that direction. . . . It was under these circumstances, and with a direct view of arresting the further progress of this savage barrier to the extension of our institutions, and to authorize and encourage a continuous line of settlements to the Pacific Ocean, that I introduced the first Bill to create the Territory of Nebraska. . . . The Indian barrier must be removed. The tide of emigration and civilization must be permitted to roll onward until it rushes through the passes of the mountains, spreads over the plains, and mingles with the waters of the Pacific.

Because whoever settled Kansas and Nebraska would decide whether or not to admit slavery, Northern abolitionists formed organizations to encourage antislavery settlers to inhabit the region. In order to convince Northerners to move west, emigration societies published pamphlets and books describing all the benefits of the new territories. The following is an excerpt from such a book, published in Boston in 1854:

It is to be remembered that all accounts agree that the region of Kanzas [sic] is the most desirable part of America now open to the emigrant. It is accessible in five days continuous travel from Boston. Its crops are very bountiful, its soil being well adapted to the staples of Virginia and Kentucky, and especially to the growth of hemp. In its eastern section the woodland and prairie-land intermix, in proportions very well adapted for the purposes of the settler. Its mineral resources, especially its coal, in the central and western parts, are inexhaustible. A steamboat is already plying on the Kanzas [sic] river, and the territory has uninterrupted steamboat communication with New Orleans, and all the tributaries of the Mississippi river. All the overland emigration to California and Oregon, by any of the easier routes, passes of necessity through its limits. Whatever roads are built westward must begin in this territory. For it is here that the emigrant leaves the Missouri river. Of late years the demand for provisions and breadstuffs, made by

Personal Liberty Laws

As the result of the Anthony Burns affair and other similar incidents involving fugitive slaves, many Northern states passed "personal liberty laws," which in effect nullified the Fugitive Slave Law. In Massachusetts, a personal liberty law stated that if an attorney worked for a slave catcher, he gave up his right to appear before the courts of the state. Arresting anyone as a fugitive brought a fine, and it became illegal to use the state's jails to detain fugitive slaves.

"Call to Kansas"

This song by Lucy Larcom calls on both men and women to plant not only crops but "freedom" and "truth" in the new land.

Yeomen strong, hither throng—
Nature's honest men—
We will make the wilderness
Bud and bloom again.
Bring the sickle, speed the plough,
Turn the ready soil;
Freedom is the noblest pay
For the true man's toil.
Ho, brothers! come brothers!
Hasten all with me,
We'll sing, upon the Kansas plains,
The song of liberty. . . .

Father haste! O'er the waste
Lies a pleasant land;
There your fire-side altar-stones
fixed in truth shall stand;
there your sons, brave and good,
Shall to freemen grow,
clad in triple mail of right,
Wrong to overthrow.
Ho, brothers! come brothers!
Hasten all with me,
We'll sing, upon the Kansas plains,
A song of liberty! . . .

Brothers brave, stem the wave,
Firm the prairie tread;
Up the dark Missouri flood
Be you canvas spread.
Sister true, join us too,
Where the Kansas flows;
Let the Northern lily bloom
With the Southern rose.
Brave brother, true sister,
List we call to thee:
We'll sing, upon the Kansas plains,
A song of liberty.

One and all, hear our call
Echo through the land—
Aid us with a willing heart
And a strong right hand—
Feed the spark the pilgrims struck
On old Plymouth rock;
To the watch-fires of the free
Millions glad shall flock.
Ho brothers! come brothers!
Hasten all with me,
We'll sing upon the Kansas plains
A song of liberty.

emigrants proceeding to California, has given the inhabitants of the neighboring parts of Missouri a market at as good rates as they could have found in the Union.

In this pamphlet, the Massachusetts Emigrant Aid Company argued that migration west was the perfect opportunity for ordinary people to take part in the antislavery crusade.

It must be that the settlement of the new territories by the best population which can be given them shall command the active effort of all true lovers of their country. This effort ought not to be spoken of as a little affair, or as incidental or subsidiary to other enterprises, but as the greatest duty now before American patriots and Christians. It is a way of work more hopeful than any which has been opened for years. . . . In the long, painful, irritating, and perplexing discussion which has sought to check and hem in the institution of slavery, the great difficulty has been the want of a field of action, where working men should not feel that they were wasting life in mere talk or wordy protest of prophecy. That field is found in Kanzas [sic]. To send men to Kanzas [sic], or to go to Kanzas [sic], resolved that free labor shall be honored in Kanzas [sic], and shall make itself honorable, is an effort which can enlist the energies of every man. It is an effort which the whole providence of God demands, and which is made easy by the wonderful arrangements of his wisdom. . . . Two free states planted west of the Missouri are two new securities for American freedom. . . . So far as their long frontier stretches, the wave of southern slavery will break on a rock which will not let it pass. No caravans of unwilling servants shall be led over their deserts or through their valleys. And if any one of the western regions should ever seek to introduce slave labor, it must not look to the mountain passes for its supply.

Not everyone who went to Kansas found life to be as easy as they had been led to expect. In 1856, Mrs. Miriam Davis Colt and her husband set out for Kansas from New York State. They had read about a new settlement for vegetarians, and wanted to move there. They sent money to the company in charge, and were told that by the time they got there, houses would be built, as well as mills and other necessary buildings. The following are excerpts from Mrs. Colt's diary of her trip to her new home.

May 12th—Full of hope, as we leave the smoking embers of our camp-fire this morning. Expect tonight to arrive at our new home.

It begins to rain, rain, rain, like a shower; we move slowly on, from high prairie, around the deep ravine—are in sight of the timber that skirts the Neosho river. . . . We move slowly and drippingly into town just at nightfall. . . . We leave our wagons and make our way to the large camp-fire. It is surrounded by men and women cooking their suppers—while others are busy close by, grinding their hominy in hand mills.

Look about, and see the grounds all around the camp-fire are covered with tents, in which the families are staying. Not a house is to be seen. . . .

The ladies tell us they are sorry to see us come to this place; which plainly shows that all is not right. Are too weary to question, but with hope depressed go to our lodgings, which we find around in the tents, and in our wagons.

May 13th—Can any one imagine our disappointment this morning, on learning from this and that member, that no mills have been built; that the directors, after receiving our money to build mills, have not fulfilled the trust reposed in them, and that in consequence, some families have already left the settlement. . . .

Expected a saw-mill would be in operation, a grist-mill building, and a temporary boarding-house erected to receive families as they should come into the settlement, until their own houses could be built. . . . As it is, we find the families, some living in tents of cloth, some of cloth and green bark just peeled from the trees, and some wholly of green bark, stuck up on the damp ground, without floors or fires.

Because slavery was legal in Missouri, people who lived there did not want their new neighbors to forbid it. They feared that, surrounded by free-soilers on all sides, they would be unable to keep their slaves from running away. So when it came time for elections in the new territory, proslavery Missourians crossed the border into Kansas to cast their votes illegally. These "border ruffians" came in such numbers that they managed to win the election, and set up a proslavery government in the city of Lecompton. Northern settlers were furious, and, declaring the election a fraud, set up their own government in Topeka. Soon border ruffians came in droves, this time with weapons, to support the Lecompton legislation. The emigrant aid societies that

Free-Soilers

were men and women from Northern states who settled in Kansas and believed in free labor as opposed to slavery.

The Battle of Hickory Point on September 13, 1856, was only one in a series of skirmishes between proslavery border ruffians from Missouri and antislavery settlers in Kansas that gave rise to the name Bleeding Kansas.

had originally been set up to help Northerners settle in Kansas now turned their efforts to transporting rifles to the Northerners.

With both sides heavily armed and tensions mounting, conflict was almost inevitable. In May 1856, 700 proslavery men descended on the city of Lawrence, attacked the two newspaper offices, looted the stores, and burned down the hotel and other buildings.

Even before this "sack of Lawrence," not only Northerners in Kansas but those back East as well were becoming enraged over the border ruffians' tactics and the increasing violence. One of those who expressed his anger was an antislavery senator from Massachusetts, Charles Sumner. His sharp-tongued speech on the Senate floor, called "The Crime Against Kansas," occurred over two days and used the metaphor of rape to describe what was happening in the West. He also made several derogatory remarks against Sen. Andrew Butler of South Carolina in his speech of May 19 and 20, 1856.

Let us tell the North. . . . Your sympathy for Sumner has shaken our confidence in your capacity for self-government more than all your past history, full of evil portents as that has been. . . . In the main, the press of the South applaud the conduct of Mr. Brooks, without condition or limit. . . . [Abolitionists] must be lashed into submission. Sumner, in particular, ought to have nine-and-thirty [lashes of the whip] early every morning.

—*Richmond Enquirer,* June 9, 1856

The Senator from South Carolina has read many books of chivalry, and believes himself to be a chivalrous knight, with sentiments of honor and courage. Of course he has chosen a mistress to whom he has made vows, and who, though ugly to others, is always lovely to him,—though polluted in the sight of the world, is chaste in his sight: I mean the harlot Slavery. . . . If the Slave States cannot enjoy what, in mockery of the great fathers of the Republic, he misnames Equality under the Constitution,—in other words, the full power of the National Territories to compel fellow-men to unpaid toil, to separate husband and wife, and to sell little children at the auction-block,—then, Sir, the chivalric Senator will conduct the State of South Carolina out of the Union! Heroic knight! Exalted Senator! A second Moses come for a second exodus!

Drawing on the Southern "code of honor," which he compelled him to restore his family member's honor, Butler's cousin, Rep. Preston Brooks, also of South Carolina, walked over to Sumner's desk two days after his speech and began beating him over the head with a cane. Sumner's injuries and shock were so bad that he did not return to the Senate for three years. While witnesses described the attack on the elderly and unarmed Sumner as vicious, Brooks defended his actions.

As soon as I had read the speech I felt it to be my duty to inflict some return for the insult to my State and my relative. . . . I waited until the last lady left [the Senate Hall] and then approached Mr. Sumner in front and said—Mr Sumner I have read your last speech with care and as much impartiality as is possible under the circumstances, and I feel it my duty to say that you have libeled my State and slandered my kinsman who is aged and absent and I have come to punish you for it. As I uttered the word 'punish' Mr. Sumner offered to rise and when about half erect I struck him a slight blow with the smaller end of my cane. He then rose fully erect and endeavored to make a battle. I was then compelled to strike him harder than I had intended. . . . When Mr. Crittenden [Kentucky senator] took hold of me and said something like "don't kill him," I replied that I had no wish to injure him seriously, but only to flogg him.

Under the domed ceiling of the Capitol building on May 22, 1856, Rep. Preston Brooks attacks Massachusetts senator Charles Sumner for a speech in which the elderly statesman had lambasted the South and insulted Brooks's cousin, Sen. Andrew Butler. "Bleeding Sumner," along with the events of "Bleeding Kansas" that same spring, outraged Northerners and spurred the dramatic rise of the Republican Party.

The Dred Scott Decision

Both the Compromise of 1850 and the Kansas-Nebraska Act were meant to settle the question of slavery in the Western territories, but both actually divided the nation further. In 1856–57, the U.S. Supreme Court tried to settle the question again with its decision in the case of *Dred Scott* v. *Sanford*, but it, too, managed to inflame rather than quiet sectional passions.

Dred Scott was a slave from Missouri whose owner took him along when he went to live in the free state of Illinois and in Wisconsin Territory, which also was free. After his owner died, Scott sued for his freedom, arguing that because he had lived for years in a free state and territory, he was legally free. After a lengthy series of court battles and appeals, the case reached the Supreme Court.

The Court announced its decision in the spring of 1857. Rather than limiting himself to the question of whether or not Scott was a free man, Chief Justice Roger Taney's majority opinion addressed two other issues: As a slave and a black man, was Scott a citizen with the right to sue in federal courts; and was the Missouri Compromise, which had made Wisconsin Territory free in the first place, constitutional? Dominated by Southerners, including Taney, the Court ruled "no" on all three questions. Scott was not free, neither he nor any other black man, free or slave, was a citizen, and the Missouri Compromise was unconstitutional because Congress had no power to exclude slavery from a territory.

The question is simply this: Can a negro, whose ancestors were imported into this country, and sold as slaves, become a member of the political community formed and brought into existence by the Constitution of the United States, and as such become entitled to all the rights, and privileges, and immunities, guaranteed by that instrument to the citizen? One of the rights is the privilege of suing in a court of the United States in the cases specified in the Constitution. . . .

The words "people of the United States" and "citizens" are synonymous terms, and mean the same thing. They both describe the political body who, according to our republican institutions, form the sovereignty, and who hold the power and conduct the government through their representatives. . . . The question before us is, whether [persons who are the descendants of Africans who were imported into this country and sold as slaves] compose a portion of this people, and are constituent members of this sovereignty? We think they are not, and they are not included, and were not intended to be included, under the word "citizens" in the Constitution. . . .

They had for more than a century before been regarded as being of an inferior order; and altogether unfit to associate with the white race, either in social or political relations; and so far inferior that they had no rights which the white man was bound to respect; and that the negro might justly and lawfully be reduced to slavery for his benefit.

While white Southerners rejoiced over Taney's ruling, Northerners were bitter. Abolitionists were particularly upset over Taney's discussion of blacks' status at the time of the framing of the Constitution.

Robert Purvis, a black Philadelphia businessman and community leader, responded angrily to Taney's judgment at the American Anti-Slavery Society's 1857 annual meeting in New York City. In his speech, Purvis attacked some abolitionists' arguments that the Constitution's framers had intended slavery to die out, asserting that Taney's decision made a mockery of them.

Sir, this talk about the Constitution being anti-slavery seems to me so utterly at variance with common sense and what we know to be facts that, as I have already intimated, I have no patience with it. I have no particular objection, Mr. Chairman, to white men, who have little to feel on this subject, to amuse themselves with such theories; but I must say that when I see them imitated by coloured men, I am disgusted! Sir, have we no self respect? Are we to clank the chains that have been made for us, and praise the men who did the deed? Are we to be kicked and scouted, trampled upon and judicially declared to *"have no rights which white men are bound to respect"* and then turn around and glorify and magnify the laws under which all this is done? Are we such base, soulless, spiritless sycophants as all this? Sir, let others do as they may, I never will stultify or disgrace myself by eulogizing a government that tramples me and all that are dear to me in the dust. (Applause.)

1. That the original policy of the Government was that of slavery restriction.

2. That under the Constitution Congress cannot establish or maintain slavery in the territories.

3. That the original policy of the Government has been subverted and the Constitution violated for the extension of slavery, and the establishment of the political supremacy of the Slave Power.

—Sen. Salmon P. Chase (Ohio) in a letter to Charles Sumner, 1850

Chapter Three

The Rail Splitter and the Splitting Country

Maj. Robert Anderson kneels in prayer beneath the American flag that has just been raised at Fort Sumter in the Charleston, South Carolina, harbor. Anderson's stealthy occupation of the fort after dusk on December 26, 1861, outraged South Carolinians who, having recently seceded from the Union, viewed the fort as their property. Less than four months later, Fort Sumter would be the target of the first shots fired in the Civil War.

I t is sometimes hard for us to imagine the passion with which 19th-century Americans followed politics. They avidly read newspapers for information about candidates. They excitedly attended rallies, speeches, and other political events as a means of entertainment as well as political participation. In the years before the Civil War, as tensions between the free and slave states mounted, politics became more important and more heated than ever before.

Emotions ran high after the passage of the Kansas-Nebraska Act, and a new political entity arose on the American landscape. In Ripon, Wisconsin, a group of men met on February 28, 1854, to discuss their anger over popular sovereignty and what was known as the "Nebraska outrage." They founded a new political organization that they called the Republican Party. Across the North that spring and summer, other groups met for the same purpose and took other names, but eventually "Republican" caught on. Those people who joined this new party mostly came out of the old Whig Party or the more recently formed Free-Soil Party, but there were also some Democrats and some people who had been affiliated with the Know-Nothing Party, which had focused on limiting the rights of immigrants and had reached the height of its power in 1854. In addition to opposing the Kansas-Nebraska Act, most Republicans were Protestant and antislavery, and they believed in using the federal government to help modernize the country through education, transportation, and technology.

The Republicans faced their first Presidential election in 1856. The campaign reflected the fractured political situation in the country. In fact it was really more like two elections, one in the North and one in the South. In the North voters chose between the Republican John C. Frémont, a colorful young explorer and Mexican War hero, and the Democratic James Buchanan. In the South Buchanan ran against Millard Fillmore, nominated by the vestiges of the crippled American and Whig Parties. The campaign was a passionately fought race. Republicans in the North marched in parades chanting "Free Soil, Free Labor, Free Men, Frémont," while Southerners threatened a revolution if Frémont won. In the end, enough conservative Northerners voted for Buchanan to secure the office of the Presidency for the Democratic nominee.

Within the next year, a poor man's son, who had reportedly earned his living splitting rails as a youth and was at that time practicing law in Illinois, would become a lightning rod for some of the most intense political debate in the country's history. He would also become the symbol of the Republican Party. That man, Abraham Lincoln, first made a name for himself in a campaign that he lost, against Stephen Douglas, the senator responsible for the Kansas-Nebraska Act, in the race to represent Illinois. The meteoric rise of Lincoln "the rail splitter" would bring the Republican Party to prominence, but it would also finally split the Union in two.

The Lincoln-Douglas Debates

In one of the most famous events of American political history, Abraham Lincoln and Stephen Douglas participated in a series of debates in their campaign to win a seat representing Illinois in the U.S. Senate. They traveled across the state and met in seven towns to debate each other before thousands of spectators. Farmers, merchants, mechanics, and their families came into town to watch and listen for hours as the candidates argued over the most important issues facing the country.

In these intense Lincoln-Douglas Debates, the two men repeatedly addressed the issue of how to decide whether or not to allow slavery into new territories—a topic of deep interest to many who had watched with horror as Kansas erupted in violence over this very problem. In their seventh debate, in Alton, Illinois, on October 15, 1858, Douglas reiterated his support for popular sovereignty, and Lincoln replied. Lincoln referred to earlier debates, when Douglas had asserted that he did not care whether Kansas voted to be

free or slave. Lincoln asserted this as the real difference between their positions—he viewed slavery as wrong, while Douglas does not. Lincoln's concern in this 1858 exchange was not particularly about black Americans, but rather the impact of slavery on whites.

Douglas: The whole South are rallying to the support of the doctrine that if the people of a Territory want slavery, they have a right to have it, and if they do not want it, that no power on earth can force it upon them. I hold that there is no principle on earth more sacred to all the friends of freedom than that which says that no institution, no law, no constitution, should be forced on an unwilling people contrary to their wishes; and I assert that the Kansas and Nebraska Bill contains that principle. . . . I will never violate or abandon that doctrine, if I have to stand alone. . . . I have defended it against the North and the South, and I will defend it against whoever assails it, and I will follow it wherever its logical conclusions lead me. I say to you that there is but one hope, one safety for this country, and that is to stand immovably by that principle which declares the right of each State and each Territory to decide these questions for themselves. This government was founded on that principle, and must be administered in the same sense in which it was founded. . . .

Lincoln: . . . Now, irrespective of the moral aspect of this question as to whether there is a right or wrong in enslaving a negro, I am still in favor of our new Territories being in such a condition that white men may find a home,—may find some spot where they can better their condition; where they can settle upon new soil and better their condition in life. I am in favor of this, not merely (I must say it here as I have elsewhere) for our own people who are born amongst us, but as an outlet for *free white people everywhere*—the world over—in which Hans, and Baptiste, and Patrick, and all other men from all the world, may find new homes and better their conditions in life.

I have stated upon former occasions, and I may as well state again, what I understand to be the real issue in this controversy

The dramatic contrast in height between Abraham Lincoln, at six feet four inches tall, and Stephen A. Douglas, almost a foot shorter, was only one of their extreme differences. The debates between Lincoln and Douglas during their campaign for the U.S. Senate constitute one of American political history's most famous events.

THE REPUBLICAN PARTY GOING TO THE RIGHT HOUSE.

Lincoln is carried on a rail (his modest roots were often encapsulated in his nickname of "the rail-splitter," a job he held as a young man) into a lunatic asylum. Caricatures of free-love advocates, African Americans, women's rights advocates, alcoholics, thieves, and other supposed adherents followed him. Democratic critics often portrayed the Republican Party as a motley collection of radical fanatics.

between Judge Douglas and myself. . . . The real issue in this controversy—the one pressing upon every mind—is the sentiment on the part of one class that looks upon the institution of slavery *as a wrong*, and of another class that *does not* look upon it as a wrong. The sentiment that contemplates the institution of slavery in this country as a wrong is the sentiment of the Republican party. It is the sentiment around which all their actions, all their arguments, circle, from which all their propositions radiate. They look upon it as being a moral, social, and political wrong; and while they contemplate it as such, they nevertheless have due regard for its actual existence among us, and the difficulties in getting rid of it in any satisfactory way, and to all the constitutional obligations thrown about it. Yet, having a due regard for these, they desire a policy in regard to it that looks to its not creating any more danger. They insist that it should, as far as may be, *be treated* as a wrong; and one of the methods of treating it as a wrong is to *make provisions that it shall grow no larger.* They also desire a policy that looks to a peaceful end of slavery at some time. . . . The Democratic policy in regard to that institution will not tolerate the merest breath, the slightest hint, of the least degree of wrong about it. Try it by some of Judge Douglas's arguments. He says he "don't care whether it is voted up or voted down" in the Territories. I do not care myself, in dealing with that expression, whether it is intended to be expressive of his individual sentiments on the subject, or only of the national policy he desires to have established. It is alike valuable for my purpose. Any man can say that who does not see anything wrong in slavery; but no man can logically say it who does see a wrong in it, because no man can logically say he don't care whether a wrong is voted up or voted down. . . . He contends that whatever community wants slaves has a right to have them. So they have, if it is not a wrong. But if it is a wrong, he cannot say people have a right to do wrong.

Harpers Ferry

The political climate grew even more heated after a radical white abolitionist, John Brown, made a dramatic attempt to start a slave uprising in the South. Brown had already engaged in violence in Kansas, where in 1856 he and his sons had massacred five proslavery settlers, sparking the worst bloodshed in the area. On October 16, 1859, the extremely religious Brown, who believed himself God's tool for uprooting slavery, carried out a plan he had hatched with the support of northeastern abolitionists. He recruited seventeen white and five black men to go with him to Virginia and capture the federal arsenal at Harpers Ferry. His assumption was that the slaves in the area would quickly join forces with him, and, using weapons from the arsenal, would overturn slavery in a swift revolution.

Brown and his men did capture the arsenal, but they had no plan for the next stage. They simply waited inside the arsenal for the slaves in the area to join them. Instead of word of their raid reaching local slaves, though, it got out to local whites who, along with militia companies, seized the area outside the building. They were later joined by the U.S. Marines, led by Col. Robert E. Lee and Lt. J. E. B. Stuart. In the ensuing fight, ten of Brown's men, including two of his sons, died, and Brown himself was wounded.

While his plan to start a slave insurrection failed miserably, Brown did in fact have a major impact on the country. Southerners were enraged by his actions and especially by the support he received from Northern abolitionists. They felt newly justified in their belief that antislavery activists were not content simply to contain slavery, but planned to destroy it completely. Meanwhile, although Northerners

A House Divided

Lincoln gave his famous "House Divided" speech when he accepted the Republican nomination for the Senate at the Illinois State convention on June 17, 1858. He argued that the country could not survive half slave and half free, and suggested that under Stephen Douglas, the country might become all slave. In their ensuing debates, Douglas tried to turn the tables by linking Lincoln to abolitionists and the ideal of black people's equality with whites. Following is an excerpt from Lincoln's speech.

In my opinion [agitation over slavery] will not cease until a crisis shall have been reached and passed. "A house divided against itself cannot stand." I believe this government cannot endure permanently half slave and half free. I do not expect the Union to be dissolved; I do not expect the house to fall; but I do expect it will cease to be divided. It will become all one thing, or all the other. Either the opponents of slavery will arrest the further spread of it, and place it where the public mind shall rest in the belief that it is in the course of ultimate extinction, or its advocates will push it forward till it shall become alike lawful in all the States, old as well as new, North as well as South.

U.S. Marines storm the engine house where John Brown and the last four men of his original band of eighteen are holed up, bringing Brown's raid on Harpers Ferry to a deadly end on October 18, 1859. Brown apparently had not planned an escape route in case of attack, and his raid cost the lives of 17 men, including 2 of his sons.

A Holy Cause

John Copeland, a fugitive slave who joined Brown in his raid, wrote to his parents and siblings from jail a few weeks before he was hanged.

Dear Parents, my fate so far as man can seal it, is sealed, but let not this fact occasion you any misery; for remember the *cause* in which I was engaged; *remember it was a holy cause,* one in which men in every way better than I am, have suffered & died. Remember that if I must die, I die in trying to liberate a few of my poor & oppressed people from a condition of servitude against which God in his word has hurled his most bitter denunciations, a cause in which men, who though removed from its direct injurious effects by the color of their faces, have already lost their lives, & more yet must meet the fate which man has decided I must meet. If die I must, I shall try to meet my fate as a man who can suffer in the glorious cause in which I have been engaged, without a groan, & meet my Maker in heaven as a Christian man who through the saving grace of God has made his peace with Him.

Good-bye Mother & Father, Goodbye brothers & sisters, & by the assistance of God, meet me in heaven. I remain your most affectionate son,

—John A. Copeland

initially denounced Brown's violent tactics, his dignity during his trial changed many opinions. When they heard about his refusal to escape hanging with an insanity plea, read copies of his articulate and selfless speech at his trial, and marveled over his composure at his death at the gallows, quite a few people began to think of him as a saintly martyr. His religiosity was apparent in his speech at his trial for murder, treason, and insurrection, during which he drew on biblical justifications for his actions.

I have, may it please the Court, a few words to say.

In the first place, I deny everything but what I have all along admitted—the design on my part to free the slaves. I intended certainly to have made a clean thing of that matter, as I did last winter, when I went into Missouri and there took slaves without the snapping of a gun on either side, moved them through the country, and finally left them in Canada. I designed to have done the same thing again, on a larger scale. That was all I intended. I never did intend murder, or treason, or the destruction of property, or to excite or incite slaves to rebellion, or to make insurrection.

I have another objection; and that is, it is unjust that I should suffer such a penalty. Had I interfered in the manner which I admit, and which I admit has been fairly proved (for I admire the truthfulness and candor of the greater portion of the witnesses who have testified in this case),—had I so interfered in behalf of the rich, the powerful, the intelligent, the so-called great, or in behalf of any of their friends,—either father, mother, brother, sister, wife, or children, or any of that class,—and suffered and sacrificed what I have in this interference, it would have been all right; and every man in this court would have deemed it an act worthy of reward rather than punishment.

This court acknowledges, as I suppose, the validity of the law of God. I see a book kissed here which I suppose to be the Bible, or at least the New Testament. That teaches me that all things whatsoever I would that men should do to me, I should do even so to them. It teaches me, further, to "remember them that are in bonds, as bound with them." I endeavored to act up to that instruction. . . . I believe to have interfered as I have done—as I have always freely admitted I have done—in behalf of His despised poor, was not wrong, but right. Now, if it is deemed necessary that I should forfeit my life for the furtherence of the ends of justice, and mingle my blood further with the blood of my children and with the blood of millions in this slave country whose rights are disregarded by wicked, cruel, and unjust enactments,— I submit; so let it be done!

Election 1860

The more the North supported John Brown, the more furious and panicked the South grew. It was in this highly charged atmosphere that the Republicans nominated Lincoln for the Presidency of the United States in 1860.

The Democratic Party was in shambles. At its national convention in Charleston, South Carolina, the Northern and Southern halves of the party reached such an impasse over a platform supporting a federal slave code that the Southerners walked out. They called a second convention in Baltimore six weeks later, but the pattern repeated itself. Southerners walked out, held their own convention, and nominated John C. Breckinridge, Buchanan's vice president, while the Northern Democrats nominated Douglas. In addition, the old Whig Party formed its own party, the Constitutional Union Party, and nominated John Bell for President and Edward Everett for Vice President. As in 1856, the Presidential campaign in reality consisted of two separate elections: Lincoln vs. Douglas in the North, and Breckinridge vs. Bell in the South.

During the campaign, Americans of all sorts took an active interest in politics. The following letter from a young girl shows that even the littlest citizens were encouraged to think politically. Grace Bedell's fascination with the campaign

"I John Brown am now quite certain that the crimes of this guilty land will never be purged away but with Blood." —John Brown, note handed to his jailers as he walked to the gallows, December 2, 1859

John Brown, wounded during his raid on Harpers Ferry, lies in bed during his trial. Although his plan to liberate the slaves failed miserably, Brown's reputation as a madman was transformed into that of a saint by his stately demeanor and simple eloquence during his trial and hanging.

Presidential candidate John Bell is encircled by the 33 stars of the American flag in this 1860 campaign banner for the Constitutional Union Party. Bell and his running mate, Edward Everett, had no hope of winning the election, but their base of support in the Upper South hoped to prevent a Republican victory.

is especially interesting since adult women did not even have the vote at this time in history.

Although our most familiar images of Abraham Lincoln show him with a full beard, early in his career he was clean-shaven. Grace Bedell's is the most famous, but not the only, suggestion Lincoln got to grow some facial hair.

NY
Westfield, Chatauque Co
Oct 15, 1860
Hon A B Lincoln

Dear Sir

My father has just [come] home from the fair and brought home your picture and Mr. [Hannibal] Hamlin's [Lincoln's running mate]. I am a little girl only eleven years old, but want you should be President of the United States very much so I hope you won't think me very bold to write to such a great man as you are. Have you any little girls about as large as I am if so give them my love and tell her to write to me if you cannot answer this letter. I have got 4 brother's and part of them will vote for you any way and if you will let your whiskers grow I will try and get the rest of them to vote for you[.] [Y]ou would look a great deal better for your face is so thin. All the ladies like whiskers and they would tease their husband's to vote for you and if I was a man I would vote for you to but I will try and get every one to vote for you that I can I think that rail fence around your picture makes it look very pretty. I have got a little baby sister she is nine weeks old and is just as cunning as can be. When you direct your letter dir[e]ct to Grace Bedell Westfield Chatauqe County New York

I must not write any more answer this letter right off Good bye.
Grace Bedell

Lincoln wrote the following reply to Grace's advice.

Springfield, Ills
Oct. 19, 1860
Miss Grace Bedell
My dear little Miss.

Your very agreeable letter of the 15th is received.

I regret the necessity of saying I have no daughters. I have three sons—one seventeen, one nine, and one seven, years of age. They, with their mother, constitute my whole family.

As to the whiskers, never having worn any, do you not think people would call it a piece of silly affect[at]ion if I were to begin it now? Your very sincere well-wisher, Lincoln

As the election drew near, political tempers continued to flare. Southerners associated Lincoln and the Republican Party with abolitionism and a hatred for slavery, and were convinced that with him as President, their peculiar institution was in immediate danger. "Fire-eaters," the most radical Southerners, threatened to secede from the Union if Lincoln were elected.

Secession

Once the news of Lincoln's election reached the press, reaction was swift and varied. In the lower South many viewed it as the final straw, and the movement for secession began in earnest. South Carolina was the first state to secede, on December 20, 1860. In this speech to the Talladega Methodist Church in Alabama, on November 26, 1860, U.S. Congressman Jabez L. M. Curry urged his fellow Alabamians to support secession. Alabama seceded on January 11, 1861, and within a few weeks a total of seven states in the lower South had formed a new Confederacy.

The Presidential election, with its hopes, its excitements, its banners, its candidates, its alienations, its divisions, is past. What is unprecedented in party warfare there is no rejoicing over local victories; we are overwhelmed with the intelligence of the Abolition success. The appalling danger looms up in terrible distinctness before us. The black flag will soon wave over the Federal Capitol. The crimson dagger of fanaticism has been deliberately plunged into the very vitals of the Constitution. . . . "Darkness visible" wraps the future, and the imperiled South calls upon every son and daughter to do their duty. . . . My advice to Alabama is to act for herself, and seek the simultaneous co-operation of neighboring States, who will join her, not to propose terms to our enemy, but to secure permanent security

A Kind and Fatherly Man

In December 1860, Lincoln traveled by train to Washington, D.C., for his inauguration as President. His train stopped in the town of Westfield, New York, and he came out to talk to the throngs gathered there. He said: "Some three months ago I received a letter from a young lady here; it was a very pretty letter, and she advised me to let my whiskers grow, as it would improve my personal appearance; acting partly upon her suggestion, I have done so; and now, if she is here, I would like to see her." A little boy shouted "There she is!" and Lincoln walked over to her, "amid yells of delight from the excited crowd" and gave her cheek "several hearty kisses." During the Civil War, Lincoln became widely reputed to be a kind and fatherly man, who would pay special attention to the needs of women and children. This impression was strengthened when he lost his beloved 11-year-old son Willie to illness in 1862. Americans whose own sons were in danger related to him even more as a grieving father.

Abraham Lincoln, Republican candidate for President in 1860, is flanked in this campaign poster by the symbols of Justice, carrying scales and a sword, and Liberty, carrying the Constitution. The national symbol, the eagle, spreads its wings over all.

ABRAHAM LINCOLN,
REPUBLICAN CANDIDATE FOR PRESIDENT OF THE UNITED STATES.

in a Southern Confederacy. . . . I rely with strong confidence the State of my allegiance and affections, and can say of her:

My heart, my hopes, are all with thee;
My heart, my hopes, my prayers, my tears,
My faith triumphant o'er my fears,
Are all with thee—are all with thee.

Men and women throughout the deep South debated whether or not their state should join South Carolina in the new Confederacy. For many women, the events of this tumultuous time overrode the common belief that women ought not express opinions on politics because doing so was unladylike. Even without a formal political voice or vote, women nevertheless found ways to make their ideas heard. The *Mercury,* a newspaper in Charleston, South Carolina, printed the following resolution by a group of women from Georgia. Georgia joined South Carolina in the Confederacy on January 19.

Waynesboro, Burke Col, Ga.,
January 1, 1861

The following patriotic resolutions were adopted . . . by the ladies of this town and county at an enthusiastic meeting held by them on Saturday last.

And if the incoming Administration shall attempt to carry out the line of policy that has been foreshadowed, we announce that, when the hand of Black Republicanism turns to blood-red . . . we will reverse the order of the French Revolution, and save the blood of the people by making those who would inaugurate a reign of terror the first victims of a national guillotine. . . .

—James S. Thayer, addressing the New York Democrats' State Convention, January 1861

The following was presented by Mrs. Co. I. Carter and received with a joyous outburst of applause:

Resolved, That the ladies of Burke county do tender their warmest sympathies and pledge their love and devotion to the proud, gallant, chivalrous and "free people" of South Carolina for the fearless and heroic act of December 20th, 1860, which has opened a page in the history of human greatness that the pride of man shall herald through all time, and woman's holiest and noblest affection embalm for all eternity.

A committee of young ladies presented the following, which was adopted:

Resolved, That we, the young ladies of Burke county, do henceforth reject with haughty scorn and proud disdain all civilities from any gentleman who refuses . . . to join the ranks of any Southern state that shall in her sovereign capacity withdraw her allegiance from [the Union] holding it to be self-evident that a dastard's glove can never win a woman's love or defend her honor.

In the North, of course, many rejoiced at Lincoln's election. The following letter from a Wisconsin man to the new President shows the very personal interest people took in the election.

La Crosse, Wis. Novbr. 27th, 1860
Abraham Lincoln, Esqr.
Springfield

I hope you excuse me if I take the liberty and ask you one question.

My wife got on the Election day a little Girl, and I made the proposition that if it is a girl to give your wifes name, and if it is a boy your name Abraham. Will you have the kindness and give me a line what your wifes name is? I am very much oblige to you for any truble.

Very Respectfully Yours, etc.
G. C. Neumeister

Increasing Tensions

Even those Northerners who welcomed Lincoln's election were not sure exactly how to respond to secession. Lincoln would not take office until March 4, and meanwhile President Buchanan suggested contradictorily that while the

The American eagle triumphantly carries off a dead snake in this drawing from Ye Book of Copperheads, *published in Philadelphia in 1863. Republicans considered northern Democrats who wanted to end the fighting and compromise with the South treasonous snakes that threatened the country and so referred to them as "Copperheads."*

Jefferson Davis is sworn in as provisional President on February 18, having been elected by the Confederate Constitutional Convention on February 9, 1861. The convention chose Davis in part because he was known as a moderate who would not alienate the more cautious Upper South states, which the convention hoped would soon join the Confederacy.

government must enforce the laws in all the states, it could not coerce a seceding state back into the Union. Some abolitionists argued that the North should happily just let the sin-filled South go, and good riddance. Others wanted to work out a compromise.

Sen. John J. Crittenden of Kentucky introduced the following peace resolutions as an effort to avoid war between the United States and the Confederacy, but they were rejected by Lincoln.

Whereas, serious and alarming dissensions have arisen between the Northern and Southern States, concerning the rights and security of the rights of the slave-holding States, and especially their rights in the common territory of the United States; and whereas it is eminently desirable and proper that these dissensions which now threaten the very existence of this Union, should be permanently quieted and settled, by constitutional provision, which shall do equal justice to all sections, and thereby restore to the people that peace and good will which ought to prevail between all the citizens of the United States:

Therefore . . . the following articles . . . are hereby, proposed and submitted as amendments to the Constitution of the United States. . . .

Article 1. In all the territory of the United States now held, or hereafter acquired, situation North of Latitude 36° 30', slavery or involuntary servitude, except as a punishment for crime, is prohibited while such territory shall remain under territorial government. In all the territory south of said line of latitude, slavery of the African race is hereby recognized as existing, and shall not be interfered with by Congress, but shall be protected as property by all the departments of the territorial government during its continuance. And when any Territory, north or south of said line . . . shall contain the population requisite for a member of Congress . . . it shall, if its form of government be republican, be admitted into the Union, on an equal footing with the original States, with or without slavery, as the constitution of such new State may provide.

Article 2. Congress shall have no power to abolish slavery in places under its exclusive jurisdiction. . . .

Article 3. Congress shall have no power to abolish slavery within the district of Columbia so long as it exists in the adjoining States of Virginia and Maryland. . . .

Article 4. Congress shall have no power to prohibit or hinder the transportation of slaves from one State to another. . . .

And whereas, also, besides these causes of dissension embraced in the foregoing amendments proposed . . ., there are others which come within the jurisdiction of Congress. . . . Therefore

1. Resolved . . . That the laws now in force for the recovery of fugitive slaves are in strict pursuance of the plain and mandatory provisions of the Constitution . . . they ought not to be repealed. . . .

2. That all State laws which conflict with the fugitive slave acts of Congress . . . are null and void.

When Lincoln gave his inaugural address on March 4, 1861, he knew that the fate of the country rested in how he chose to deal with the secession crisis. He tried to reassure the South that he would not attack slavery where it existed. But he also maintained that he would make sure that the laws of the U.S. Constitution were upheld in every state. In his famous words, he declared that the South would be responsible if a civil war started. He urged Americans to be thoughtful, and to remember that their history and the "mystic chords of memory" bound them all together.

President James Buchanan seems unsure how to handle "that spunky little colt Miss South Carolina." Contemporaries and historians have both criticized Buchanan's annual message of December 3, 1861, in which he stated that secession was illegal and that the federal government would "enforce the laws" in all the states, but that the government could not "coerce" a state back into the Union.

"The difficulties in the way of the seceders are so great, that I fear we shall not get rid of them long enough. My desire is that four or five should go out long enough to be completely humbled and chastened and to leave us in control of the Government."
—Sen. Charles Sumner, letter to Samuel Gridley Howe, December 1860

Lincoln purposely left much of his message ambivalent in his effort to reach as many people and alarm as few as possible. Predictably, Southern secessionists reacted with fury to the speech, while Northern Republicans praised it and Northern Democrats criticized it.

Fellow-Citizens of the United States:

—In compliance with a custom as old as the Government itself, I appear before you to address you briefly, and to take in your presence the oath prescribed by the Constitution of the United States to be taken by the President 'before he enters on the execution of his office.'. . .

Apprehension seems to exist among the people of the Southern States that by the accession of a Republican administration their property and their peace and personal security are to be endangered. There has never been any reasonable cause for such apprehension. Indeed, the most ample evidence to the contrary has all the while existed and been open to their inspection. It is found in nearly all the published speeches of him who now addresses you. I do but quote from one of those speeches when I declare that "I have no purpose, directly or indirectly, to interfere with the institution of slavery in the States where it exists. I believe I have no lawful right to do so, and I have no inclination to do so. . . ."

I now reiterate these sentiments; and, in doing so, I only press upon the public attention the most conclusive evidence of which the case is susceptible, that the property, peace and security of no section are to be in any wise endangered by the now incoming administration. I add, too, that all the protection which, consistently with the Constitution and the laws, can be given, will be cheerfully given to all the States when lawfully demanded, for whatever cause—as cheerfully to one section as to another. . . .

I take the official oath to-day with no mental reservations, and with no purpose to construe the Constitution or laws by any hypercritical rules. And, while I do not choose now to specify particular acts of Congress as proper to be enforced, I do suggest that it will be much safer for all, both in official and private stations, to conform to and abide by all those acts which stand unrepealed, than to violate any of them, trusting to find impunity in having them held to be unconstitutional. . . .

A disruption of the Federal Union, heretofore only menaced, is now formidably attempted.

I hold that, in contemplation of universal law and of the Constitution, the Union of these States is perpetual. Perpetuity is implied, if not expressed, in the fundamental law of all national governments. It is safe to assert that no government proper ever had a provision in its organic law for its own termination. Continue to execute all the external provisions of our national Constitution, and the Union will endure forever—it being impossible to destroy it except by some action not provided for in the instrument itself.

Again, if the United States be not a government proper, but an association of States in the nature of contract merely, can it as a contract be peaceably unmade by less than all the parties who

Lincoln's inauguration on March 3, 1864, took place in front of the uncompleted Capitol dome. Lincoln insisted that work on the building continue throughout the war as a symbol of the inextinguishable life of the Union.

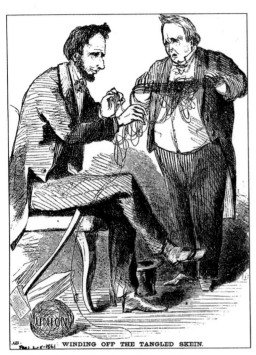

WINDING OFF THE TANGLED SKEIN.

President-elect Lincoln inherits the "tangled skein" of the Union from outgoing President James Buchanan. Buchanan's lack of political skills, lame duck position, and, perhaps, unwillingness, combined with the influence of Southern advisors, meant that he did not deal decisively with the Southern states during the secession crisis, leaving Lincoln with a difficult situation to unravel.

made it? One party to contract may violate it—break it, so to speak; but does it not require all to lawfully rescind it? . . .

I therefore consider that, in view of the Constitution and the laws, the Union is unbroken; and to the extent of my ability I shall take care, as the Constitution itself expressly enjoins upon me, that the laws of the Union be faithfully executed in all the States. Doing this I deem to be only a simple duty on my part; and I shall perform it so far as practicable, unless my rightful masters, the American people, shall withhold the requisite means, or in some authoritative manner direct the contrary. I trust this will not be regarded as a menace, but only as the declared purpose of the Union that it will constitutionally defend and maintain itself.

In doing this there needs to be no bloodshed or violence; and there shall be none, unless it be forced upon the national authority. The power confided to me will be used to hold, occupy, and possess the property and places belonging to the Government, and to collect the duties and imposts; but beyond what may be necessary for these objects, there will be no invasion, no using of force against or among the people anywhere. . . .

That there are persons in one section or another who seek to destroy the Union at all events, and are glad of any pretext to do it, I will neither affirm nor deny; but if there be such, I need address no word to them. To those, however, who really love the Union may I not speak?

Before entering upon so grave a matter as the destruction of our national fabric, with all its benefits, its memories, and its hopes, would it not be wise to ascertain precisely why we do it? Will you hazard so desperate a step while there is any possibility that any portion of the ills you fly from have no real existence? Will you, while the certain ills you fly to are greater than all the real ones you fly from—will you risk the commission of so fearful a mistake? . . .

My countrymen, one and all, think calmly and well upon this whole subject. Nothing valuable can be lost by taking time. . . .

In your hands, my dissatisfied fellow-countrymen, and not in mine, is the momentous issue of civil war. The government will not assail you. You can have no conflict without being yourselves the aggressors. You have no oath registered in heaven to destroy the government, while I shall have the most solemn one to 'preserve, protect and defend' it.

I am loathe to close. We are not enemies, but friends. We must not be enemies. Though passion may have strained, it must not break, our bonds of affection. The mystic chords of memory, stretching from every battle-field and patriot grave to every living heart and hearthstone all over this broad land, will yet swell the chorus of the Union when again touched, as surely they will be, by the better angels of our nature.

War

Eloquent as Lincoln was, he could not stem the tide of war. When he took office, the President hoped that the secession fury would die down if only he and the country could stay calm. He wanted to maintain the visible symbols of federal authority in the South, such as Fort Sumter in the harbor of Charleston, South Carolina, but not to provoke too much Southern anger in doing so. Just two days after he moved into the White House, though, the commander of Fort Sumter, Robert Anderson, informed Lincoln that his troops would have to abandon their station unless they received more food and supplies.

Lincoln knew that to send warships to resupply the soldiers would be seen by the Confederacy as unacceptable, and that he would be seen as the aggressor. So he came up with a plan in which he would send in supplies on an unarmed ship, and tell the Confederates ahead of time what he was doing. Therefore, if they fired, the burden of starting the war would be their own. When they received Lincoln's message, the Confederates responded by demanding the surrender of the fort. When Anderson refused, they bombarded his men. Despite thousands of rounds of cannons, and the destruction of the fort building, not a single man died on either side. It was not an accurate predictor of the war that was to follow.

Mary Chesnut was the wife of Sen. James Chesnut of South Carolina. Her social circle consisted of the most important politicians and social figures in Charleston, and throughout the war she kept a detailed journal, which she later published. In these dramatic entries in her diary, Chesnut describes her experiences leading up to the night the Civil War began.

April 7, 1861

. . . The air is too full of war news. And we are all so restless [after visiting during the day] . . . We came home, and soon Mr. Robert Gourdin and Mr. Miles called.

Governor Manning walked in, bowed gravely, and seated himself by me.

Again he bowed low, in mock heroic style and, with a grand wave of his hand, said, "Madame, your country is invaded."

When I had breath to speak, I asked, "What does he mean?"

"He means this. There are six men-of-war outside the bar. Talbot and Chew have come to say that hostilities are to begin. Governor Pickens and Beauregard are holding a council of war."

Mr. Chesnut then came in. He confirmed the story. . . .

In any stir or confusion, my heart is apt to beat so painfully. Now the agony was so stifling—I could barely see or hear. The men went off almost immediately. And I crept silently to my room, where I sat down to a good cry.

Mrs. Wigfall came in, and we had it out on the subject of civil war. We solaced ourselves with dwelling on all its known horrors, and then we added what we had a right to expect, with Yankees in front and negroes in the rear.

"The slave-owners must expect a servile insurrection, of course," said Mrs. Wigfall, to make sure that we were unhappy enough.

At 4:30 A.M., April 12, 1861, Confederates fired on Fort Sumter in Charleston harbor, South Carolina, beginning the Civil War. Despite 33 hours of bombardment and heavy damage to the fort, not a single man died on either side.

Suddenly loud shouting was heard. We ran out. Cannon after cannon roared. We met Mrs. Allen Green in the passageway, with blanched cheeks and streaming eyes.

Governor Means rushed out of his room in his dressing gown and begged us to be calm.

"Governor Pickens has ordered, in the plenitude of his wisdom, seven cannon to be fired as a signal to the Seventh Regiment. Anderson will hear as well as the Seventh Regiment. Now you go back and be quiet: fighting in the streets has not begun yet." . . .

No sleep for anybody last night. The streets were alive with soldiers, men shouting, marching, singing. . . .

Today [probably April 11th] at dinner . . . [the] men all talked so delightfully. For once in my life I listened.

That over, business began. In earnest, Governor Means rummaged a sword and red sash from somewhere and brought it for Colonel Chesnut, who has gone to demand the surrender of Fort Sumter.

April 12, 1861.

Anderson will not capitulate.

Yesterday was the merriest, maddest dinner we have had yet. Men were more audaciously wise and witty. We had an unspoken forboding it was to be our last pleasant meeting. . . .

I do not pretend to go to sleep. How can I? If Anderson does not acept terms—at four—the orders are—he shall be fired upon.

I count four—St. Michael chimes. I begin to hope. At half-past four, the heaving booming of a cannon.

I sprang out of bed. And on my knees—prostrate—I prayed as I never prayed before.

There was a sound of stir all over the house—pattering of feet in the corridor—all seemed hurrying one way. I put on my double gown and a shawl and went, too. It was to the housetop.

The shells were bursting. . . .

I knew my husband was rowing about in a boat somewhere in that dark bay. And that the shells were roofing it over—bursting toward the fort. If Anderson was obstinate—he was to order the forts on our side to open fire. Certainly fire had begun. The regular roar of the cannon—there it was. And who could tell what each volley accomplished of death and destruction.

The women were wild, there on the housetop. Prayers from the women and imprecations from the men, and then a shell would light up the scene.

"Our new government is founded upon exactly the opposite idea; its foundations are laid, its cornerstone rests, upon the great truth that the negro is not equal to the white man; that slavery—subordination to the superior race—is his natural and normal condition. This, our new government, is the first in the history of the world based upon this great physical, philosophical, and moral truth."

—Confederate Vice President Alexander Stephens on the Declaration of Independence's statement about the equality of man, as quoted in the *Augusta Daily Constitutionalist* on March 21, 1861

Chapter Four

Filling the Ranks

"I feel so interested in Major Anderson," wrote 20-year-old Susan Trautwine, on the morning of April 13. "I hope this mrng's news is not true. 'Lord, have mercy upon us!'" Two days later she reported feverishly on Philadelphia's reaction to the bombardment of Fort Sumter: "News of Major Anderson's surrender! People much excited! Quite a mob collected today. Flags of Union flying every where. Lincoln orders the raising of 70,000 men— 'Lord have mercy upon us!'"

After years of tension that had been slowly gathering like heavy storm clouds, the news from Fort Sumter had the force of a lightning bolt breaking open the sky. People throughout the North and South responded to the start of civil war with a mixture of excitement, fear, outrage, and enthusiasm. In the North, there was a sudden political transformation as many Democrats swiftly rallied behind Lincoln's administration in response to the attack by the Confederacy. In the Upper South, states that had resisted secession after Lincoln's election now hurriedly joined the Confederacy. The few that did not were known as Border States—slave states that stayed with the Union but were home to many Confederate sympathizers—including Maryland, Delaware, Kentucky, and Missouri.

The transformation in the country was profoundly visible not just on the political maps but in people's own lives as well. Thousands of men on both sides eagerly enlisted in their armies. Everyone believed it would be a short and relatively easy war—and everyone believed their side was bound to win. Young men did not want to miss the excitement of being in the army or the honor of helping their cause. Spectators filled the streets, waving and cheering wildly, when the soldiers marched off in their brand-new regiments. While families harbored fears of losing their sons, fathers, husbands, and brothers to the war, at least in public they tried to hide those feelings.

In the early months of the war, the Twenty-Second Indiana Volunteers arrive in St. Louis, Missouri. Men who eagerly joined the armies on both sides expected the war to be short and glorious, and many of them looked forward to traveling to parts of the country they had never seen.

The reality of the Civil War was a rude shock to many who had thought only in terms of glory and victory. Military camp life meant fatigue, boredom, heavy labor, poor food, and the constant risk of disease. Long hours of drilling, marching, and waiting turned out to be physically draining and mentally exhausting. Many youths who had never left their homes before struggled between trying to maintain their sense of morality and being tempted by the gambling, drinking, swearing, and prostitution that by some accounts filled the camps.

While camp life was often boring, it was punctuated by the awesome reality of battle. No one was prepared for the horror of war as it developed in this conflict. Men carried with them images of valor and courage that were severely tested in battles unlike any that had come before. No one witnessed the carnage of the Civil War without being shocked and profoundly moved.

Death was pervasive, due as much to disease as to wounds. While doctors did what they could to treat army casualties, their knowledge was severely limited by today's standards, and infections and other complications could turn even minor wounds into death sentences. Epidemics of measles, dysentery, and yellow fever swept through camps, killing more men than did bullets and cannonballs. Poor diet, lack of clothing, long marches, and exposure to extremes of weather all contributed to a shocking death rate in both armies.

The men who joined the army, especially those who volunteered in the heady early months, underwent dramatic changes. They often signed on as naïve, enthusiastic young soldiers and soon found themselves transformed into weary, hardened fighters. They witnessed more death than they could possibly have imagined, and, no matter how deeply they cared about the cause for which they fought, soon their most fervent wish was simply to get home alive.

A Glorious Adventure

People in both the North and the South reacted to the start of the war with a kind of feverish excitement. The following report from the *Daily Richmond Examiner* describes the raucous scene in that city after the capture of Fort Sumter, when war seemed like a glorious adventure about to begin. Men, women, and children all joined in the demonstrations. Virginia would join the Confederacy soon afterward.

The news of the capture of Fort Sumter was greeted with unbounded enthusiasm in this city. Everybody we met seemed to be perfectly happy. Indeed, until this occasion we did not know how happy men could be. Everybody abuses war, and yet it has ever been the favourite and most honored pursuit of men; and the women and children admire and love war ten times as much as the men. The boys pulled down the stars and stripes from the top of the Capitol, (some of the boys were sixty years old) and very properly run up the flag of the Southern Confederacy in its place. What the women did we don't precisely know, but learned from rumour that they praised South Carolina to the skies, abused Virginia, put it to the Submissionists hot and heavy with their two-edged swords, and wound up the evening's ceremonies by playing and singing secession songs until fifteen minutes after twelve on Saturday night.—The boys exploded an infinite number of crackers . . . and sky-rockets and Roman candles can be had for no price, the whole stock in trade having been used up Saturday night. We had great firing of cannon, all sorts of processions, an infinite number of grandiloquent, hifaluting speeches, and some drinking of healths, which has not improved healths; for one half the people we have met since are hoarse from long and loud talking, and the other half have a slight headache, it may be, from long and patriotic libations.

In this letter to his older brother Henry, New Englander Fred Spooner describes the atmosphere in Providence, Rhode Island, two weeks after the attack on Fort Sumter. Spooner's belief that Confederates were traitors who had started the war, and his confidence that the Union would easily win it, were widespread in the North. Like many others, he believed the North's superior resources would ensure its victory.

Cattle are used to drag the heavy, old-fashioned Confederate cannons along a Southern road, less than two weeks before the Battle of Bull Run. The Confederacy had far fewer guns and other weapons than the Union, and almost no foundries in which to make them.

Uncle Sam lights a cannon that explodes the Confederate demon, sending the monstrous secessionist states flying. Before the first Battle of Bull Run, each side was confident that it would easily destroy the other in one decisive battle. This cartoon, published in June 1861, represents the Northern version of that fantasy.

Providence, Rhode Island
April 30, 1861

Dear Henry,

Your letter was received, and I now sit down in my shirt sleeves (as it is warm) to write in return.

For the last few weeks there has been great excitement here, and nothing has been thought of scarcely except that one subject which now receives the undivided attention of the whole North,—war.

And well may war, so hideous and disgusting in itself receive such attention when carried on for such noble and just principles as in the present case.

Traitors have begun the conflict, let us continue and end it. Let us settle it now, once and for all.

Let us settle it, even if the whole South has to be made one common graveyard, and their cotton soaked in blood. Let us do it *now* while the whole North is aroused from the inactivity and apparent laziness in which it has been so long.

There are plenty of men, an abundance of money, and a military enthusiasm never before known in the annals of history, all of which combined will do the work nice and clean, and if need be will wipe out that palmetto, pelican, rattlesnake region entirely. The holy cause in which our volunteers are enlisted will urge them on to almost superhuman exertions. The South *may* be courageous but I doubt it, they can *gas* and *bag* first rate; they can lie and steal to perfection, but I really do believe that they cannot fight— "Barking dogs never bite." Southern Senators can bluster, bully and blackguard, but I believe them to be cowards at heart. . . .

But granting them to be brave (wh[ich] I dont believe can be proven) they have no chance to overturn this government. They havent the resources, the "almighty dollar," that powerful ally, or formidable enemy,—is against them. They have no money—their property has legs and will be continually disappearing.

They have prospered dealing in human flesh,—let them now take the results of it.

They have had what *they* call the *blessings* of slavery,—let them now receive the *curses* of it. . . .

The volunteering still goes on, although the first regiment have left us for the scene of battle. . . .

I'm much surprised at some who have enlisted, persons whom you would have supposed would have shrunk from the fatigue and dangers of war.

Only think of Mose Jenkins set to work throwing up a breastwork! Or that big bull-headed Goddard getting his muscle up on salt junk and crackers! I'm afraid "Mose" will want to know what the last style of coat is before the three months are up, and that Goddard will miss his accustomed drinks; but never mind, it shows patriotism in the right place, and I say "Bully for them.". . .

The departure of the first detatchment was very imposing. The deck was all covered with the soldiers dressed in their neat and easy uniforms, while the wharves were literally jammed with human beings, and the vessels swarmed with persons all eager to bid them good bye. Cheers after cheers rent the air, while the band played all the national airs. Greene played on his bugle beautifully, he surpassed himself, and I dont believe he could be beat.

And as the steamer slowly moved from the wharve the strains of "Auld Lang Syne" were wafted back to the friends whom they had left behind,—friends mournful that they had left them, yet rejoicing that they went to "fight the good fight."

African-American Soldiers

Among the most eager to enlist in the Union army were free blacks in both the North and the South. Perhaps more than anyone else, they were spurred on by deeply held convictions: they believed the war could crush slavery, and so they wanted to fight for the freedom of their family and their people. They also understood that serving in the military was a cornerstone of American citizenship, and they hoped that by proving themselves worthy soldiers, they might be rewarded with the full rights of citizens. Finally, they hoped that by fighting courageously, they could destroy the image many whites held of black Americans as childlike, cowardly, and untrustworthy.

The United States resisted enrolling black men for a variety of reasons. Lincoln feared it would anger the Border States, who might then decide to join the Confederacy. Many white politicians recognized the same implications of military service that blacks did; it would reinforce African Americans' claims to full citizenship and legal rights, which they were routinely denied in the North. Eventually, the loss of white men on the battlefield, coupled with the Emancipation

Crowds of ladies and gentlemen repair every afternoon to the "Camp of Instruction" of the Virginia Volunteers, at the Hermitage Fair Grounds; to the encampment of the South Carolina Regiments, near the Reservoir, and to the other places of military interest, near the city, to view the battalion drills and dress parades. The proficiency of the Lexington Cadets, who are quartered in the first mentioned place, is something wonderful to behold, and worth going a long distance to see.

—*Richmond Daily Whig*, May 1861

Black men hoist the cannon at Morris Island, South Carolina, for the attack on Fort Sumter in April 1861. The Confederate army used slaves for such labor extensively, allowing it to save white men for the actual fighting. Eventually the Union army recognized that sending fugitive slaves who made their way to Union camps back to their masters only provided the enemy with more manpower, and the North changed its policy requiring officers to do so.

Proclamation in 1863, convinced Northerners of the need to enlist black soldiers. This letter to Secretary of War Simon Cameron comes from two black men in Cleveland, and represents many others that were similarly ignored by the Lincoln administration in the early part of the war.

15th November, 1861

Hon. Simon Cameron,
Secretary of War

Sir: . . . [W]e would humbly and respectfully state that we are colored men (legal voters); all voted for the present administration.

The question now is will you allow us the poor privilege of fighting, and, if need be, dying, to support those in office who are our own choice? We believe that a regiment of colored men can be raised in this State, who, we are sure would make as patriotic and good soldiers as any other.

What we ask of you is that you give us the proper authority to raise such a regiment, and it can and shall be done.

We could give you a thousand names, as either signers or references, if you required. . . .

W. T. Boyd
J. T. Alston
P.S. We await your reply.

The Battle of Bull Run

The Battle of Bull Run, fought in the dreadful heat of July 21, 1861, marked the first decisive battle of the Civil War, and a turning point in popular attitudes toward the conflict. Bull Run was a small river that ran through Virginia, less than 30 miles outside Washington, D.C. The *New York Tribune* had been calling repeatedly for an attack on the Confederacy—it blared "Forward to Richmond" on its masthead day after day—and the Union finally decided to try to capture a critical railroad junction in Manassas. U.S. Congressmen and other Northerners rode out in carriages to watch the battle, carrying with them naïve images of war along with their picnic lunches. Raw troops, heat, confusion, and strategic mistakes led to delays and problems at the front. The end result was that the Union soldiers, after nearly beating the "rebels," were forced back and eventually gave up, running for safety, toppling some of the spectators who got in their way.

Caught off guard, civilians watched in horror as men were shot and fell in what seemed like immense numbers. A total of about 600 men on each side died from wounds received in this battle. Although in a short time that would seem like a mercifully small number, it was more than had ever died in a battle on U.S. soil until that time. Bull Run made it clear that the war would not be bloodless, easy, or short.

In the following letter to his brother, George H. Sargent of Manchester, New Hampshire, describes his role in the Battle of Bull Run. Sargent advises his brother not to join the army, but after the Union loss, thousands of men determined that they were needed to help their country. Like Sargent, though, many others soon lost their initial enthusiasm for the war. Sargent was wounded on July 2, 1863, at the Battle of Gettysburg, along with 23,049 other Union soldiers and approximately 26,000 Confederates, and was mustered out of service on June 21, 1864.

Washington, D.C.
July 28, 1861

Dear Brother:

Yours of the 18th is at hand. I was verry glad to here from you. In my last I told you we were to go farther south. We have been and got back one week ago today. Today is Sunday. We had the

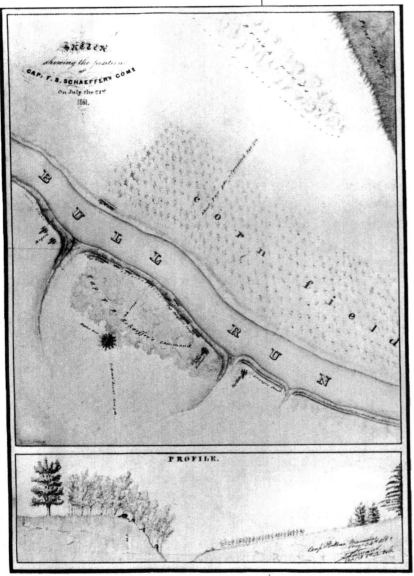

The cross section (below) shows the geological features at the Battle of Bull Run, named after the creek. The depth of the water and the slope of the hills, as well as the height of the corn, made fighting difficult for the outnumbered Union soldiers, who were defeated by the Confederates.

hardest Battle ever fought in this Country. We started for the south. We went to Fairfax Court House as soon as we got there. It was evacuated and our Brigade was encamped the nearest the Court House. We were encamped in the yard.

The rebels left in such hast that they left there blankts and a few other small things which we boys soon found use for. Took all we could cary with ease but we had to throw them away when to the field of Battle. When we got there we had a tough time of it. Went to fighting at 11 o'clock in the forenoon and fought till 4 in the afternoon when we had to retrete. I will tell you how it was.

We were the first to go onto the field and the last to leave it. We had to fight hard. We were drawn up in line of Battle when a masked Battery began to play on us with great loss on our side. In a short time the Riflemen opened on us and we fell like hail. Soon other masked Batteries began to play on us, then our cannon began and we had tough and tight, but after 4 or 5 hours we gained an advantage and we kept it. We drove them from one of their Batteries at the point of the Bayonet. When they were reinforced by about 30 thousand fresh men and we had to retrete in hast. Our orderly of our Company and five others with about 30 of other Regmts. went through or part way through some woods, we went through when we were on the way to Battle. We had got part through on our way back when we surrounded by 200 hundred Rebels when we broke away and ran for life. I got home the first one of our camp and on the whole I went over sixty miles and fought over six hours in 30 hours. I call that a good days work, don't you. I guess that [you] would have given out if you had been me. Some of the men were taken prisoners. Thurl Emerson is one, so I guess he will not write you very soon.

If you have not enlisted, dont you do it. If you do, you will wish you had not. Now don't you do it and if you have enlisted,

Death and mutilation are prominent in this sketch of the Battle of Bull Run that appeared in Frank Leslie's Illustrated Newspaper *on August 3, 1861. Because photographic technology could not yet capture movement, citizens on both sides relied on the sketches of newspaper correspondents to convey to them the chaos of battle.*

get out of it as soon as you can. I shall come at the first opitunity. It is not the Cannon Ball or the Bomb Shells of which I come for, although we had plenty of them. It [sic] not them but don't you enlist in a company. We had one Ball took the legs off three boys at one time. They marched right behind me.

As for Mother, I must see here [sic]. I think she is sick. Write me all about her. I want to see you all, that wood of the old house.

Conscription

As men like Sargent wrote home about the devastation of battle, and newspapers were filled with the names of the dead and wounded, enlistment slowed to a trickle. Eventually the North and the South both instituted conscription. In the spring of 1863, the North passed the Enrollment Act, which made every male citizen between the ages of 20 and 45 eligible for the draft. The only men who were exempt were those whom a doctor deemed unfit for soldiering, or those who were the sole source of financial support for a widow, elderly parents, or children.

The primary purpose of the Enrollment Act was to persuade men to enlist voluntarily before they were drafted. Many Northern localities implemented bounties—cash rewards—in order to persuade men to join the army. In some cases, men joined the army in one town, collected the bounty, deserted, and reenlisted in another town to get more

"You are green, it is true, but they are green also; you are all green alike."

—Abraham Lincoln, in response to a request by Gen. Irvin McDowell for more time to train his troops before the march on Bull Run

A Poor Man's Fight

One of the war's ironies is that the Confederacy, founded to protect individual states' rights, resorted to the draft before the North did. With fewer men than the North, the South faced a shortage of soldiers by the spring of 1862. In April of that year, the Confederacy passed a law making all white men between the ages of 18 and 35 eligible to be drafted for three years' service, unless they were employed in war production or served as militia officers, civil servants, clergymen, or teachers. That fall, the law was amended to excuse one white man for every 20 slaves on a plantation, and to allow men to pay substitutes $300 to join the army for them.

These loopholes in the law angered poor Southern whites who owned no slaves and could not afford the cost of a substitute. In both the North and the South, many complained that it was a "rich man's war and a poor man's fight." Historians have argued over whether that was true. Recent research has suggested that in fact working-class men did not participate more than wealthier men; although more of them may have died in the fighting because they tended to serve in the infantry rather than in the cavalry or as officers. Working-class soldiers also tended to be less healthy and therefore less resistant to the waves of disease that swept through the camps.

cash. Men who had enlisted early in the war before the institution of bounties particularly disdained bounty jumpers.

Some working-class men felt they were unfairly forced into joining the army when their families could least afford to lose a breadwinner. People voiced their opposition in a variety of ways, from letters to newspaper editors to stoning draft officials and chasing them out of town, as the wives of miners did in Pennsylvania coal-mining towns in 1862.

The worst case of draft resistance was the New York City Draft Riots of 1863. Workers in New York were angered by the draft law's stipulation that a man could hire someone to go into the army in his place or pay the government $300—about a full year's wages for a laborer—to find a substitute for him. Egged on by the leaders of the city's large Democratic Party, protesters took to the streets on July 13, 1863. After a rally in Central Park, they marched to the draft lottery offices and burned them down. Soon their anger against the draft metamorphosed into rage against those they saw as responsible for the start of the war—African Americans. Rioters chased the children out of the African-American orphan asylum and looted and burned the building to the ground. The rioters lynched a dozen African Americans from lampposts. All in all, 100 people, white and black, died in the riots.

In the following entries in his diary, George Templeton Strong, a wealthy Unionist, describes the New York City Draft Riots and his impression of the rioters. He expresses sympathy for African Americans, although his statements are laced with paternalistic and racist comments, and his descriptions of the rioters are filled with anti-Irish prejudice, common among the upper class in that city as elsewhere. While many Irish workers were involved in the riots, the Irish also provided the Union army with some of its most courageous soldiers, among them the New York City Irish Brigade, who returned to their hometown from the battlefield to help suppress the riots.

[I heard] of rioting in the upper part of the city. . . . Reached the seat of war at last, forty-sixth Street and Third Avenue. Three houses on the Avenue and two or three on the street were burned down. . . . The crowd seemed just what one commonly sees at any fire, but its nucleus of riot was concealed by an outside layer of ordinary peaceable lookers-on. Was told they had beat off a squad of police. . . . At last, it opened and out streamed a posse of

perhaps five hundred, certainly less than one thousand, of the lowest Irish day laborers. The rabble was perfectly homogeneous. Every brute in the drove was pure Celtic—hod-carrier or loafer. They were unarmed. A few carried pieces of fence-paling and the like. . . . The fury of the low Irish women in that region was noteworthy. Stalwart young vixens and withered old hags were swarming everywhere, all cursing the "bloody draft" and egging on their men to mischief.

July 14 . . . Many details come in of yesterday's brutal, cowardly ruffianism and plunder. Shops were cleaned out and a black man hanged in Carmine Street, for no offence but that of Nigritude. . . .

July 19 . . . Not half the history of this memorable week has been written. I could put down pages of incidents that the newspapers have omitted, any one of which would in ordinary times be the town's talk. Men and ladies attacked and plundered by daylight in the streets; private houses suddenly invaded by gangs of a dozen ruffians and sacked, while the women and children run off for their lives. Then there is the unspeakable infamy of the nigger persecution. They are the most peaceable, sober, and inoffensive of our poor, and the outrages they have suffered during this last week are less excusable—are founded on worse pretext and less provocation—than that of St. Bartholomew's or the Jew-hunting of the Middle Ages. This is a nice town to call itself a centre of civilization! . . . How this infernal slavery system has corrupted our blood, North as well as South! . . . But how is one to deal with women who assemble around the lamp-post to which a Negro has been hanged and cut off certain parts of his body to keep as souvenirs? Have they any womanly privilege, immunity, or sanctity?

You will no doubt be hard on us rioters, tomorrow morning, but that 300-dollar law has made us nobodies, vagabonds and cast-outs of society, for whom nobody cries when we must go to war and be shot down. We are the poor rabble, and the rich rabble is our enemy by this law. Therefore we will give our enemy battle right here, and ask no quarter. Although we got hard fists, and are dirty without [on the outside], we have soft hearts and have clean consciences within, and that's the reason we love our wives and children more than the rich, because we got not much besides them, and we will not go and leave them at home for to starve. . . . Why don't they let the nigger kill the slave-driving race and take possession of the South, as it belongs to them.

—Letter to the *New York Times*, signed "A POOR MAN, BUT A MAN FOR ALL THAT," July 13, 1863

Immigrant Troops

Southerners often derided the Northern army as composed mainly of "foreigners," whom they described as "riffraff." In reality, the Union army's immigrant soldiers represented an estimated 26 percent of the white forces. Because 31 percent of white males of military age living in the Union were foreign-born, immigrants were actually underrepresented in the army. Different groups, however, were represented differently. British and German Protestants joined up in numbers equal to their population percentage, while Irish and German Catholics did not. One reason for this difference is that many Irish and German Catholics were committed to the Democratic Party, and saw the war as a Republican crusade.

When immigrants and the sons of immigrants did join the army, they often did so in groups. Sometimes entire regiments were made up of men of a particular ethnicity. In the Union army, the 11th Corps, under Gen. Oliver O. Howard, contained many regiments of German-Americans. They fought at Chancellorsville, Virginia, and were defeated by Stonewall Jackson's men; when they fought the same corps at Gettysburg, they were routed again.

One of the most famous regiments in the Union army was the Irish Brigade of the Army of the Potomac. The Irish Brigade was specifically created to help Irish Catholic men retain their identities and to show Northerners, who were often prejudiced against Irish immigrants, the contributions that they were making to the war. Known for colorful and dashing officers, many of whom were veterans of European armies, the Irish Brigade saw some of the worst fighting of the war. They earned themselves a distinguished reputation by their courage and hard fighting against desperate odds at Marye's Heights at Fredericksburg, Virginia, the Bloody Lane at Antietam, and in the battlefields of Gettysburg and Spotsylvania, Virginia. The brigade was known not only for its courage on the battlefield, but also for its high spirits and camaraderie, and its sense of Irish and Catholic identity. They held legendary celebrations of Saint Patrick's Day, which included horse racing, athletic contests, dances, theatricals, and recitations, as well as a good amount of hard drinking.

July 20 . . . For myself, personally, I would like to see war made on Irish scum as in 1688.

Abuse of Black Troops

Just two days after the murdering of free blacks on the streets of New York City had finally been stopped, African-American soldiers courageously led a doomed assault on Fort Wagner at the entrance to Charleston Harbor in South Carolina. Their valiant efforts and bravery in battle despite horrendous losses won them fame and new respect from many who had doubted the ability of black soldiers.

When African Americans were finally enlisted in the army, after Lincoln issued the Emancipation Proclamation in January 1863, they were segregated into separate regiments and forbidden to serve as commissioned officers. While white soldiers were paid $13 per month and extra money to buy a uniform, until 1864 black soldiers were paid only $10 and from that had to buy their own uniforms. The following letter from a black soldier who served with the 54th Massachusetts Regiment describes to his brother-in-law some of the insults African Americans faced in the service of their country, even after the attack at Fort Wagner.

Jacksonville, Florida
March 26, 1864

Dear William

I will devote some spare moments I have in writing you a few lines which I hope may find you and all your family the same, also all of my many Friends in Worcester Since the Regiment Departure from Morris Island I have enjoyed the best of health. the weather here is Beautiful it is warm here as it is home in July. the Regiment in general are in Good Health but in Low Spirits and no reason why for they have all to a man done there duty as a soldier it is 1 Year the 1st Day of April since I enlisted and there is men here in the regiment that have been in Enlisted 13 Months and have never received one cent But there bounty and they more or less have family, and 2 thirds have never received anny State Aid, and how do you think men can feel to do there duty as Soldiers, but let me say we are not Soldiers but Labourers working for Uncle Sam for nothing but our board and clothes . . . we never can be Elevated in this country while such rascality is

Performed Slavery with all its horrors can not Equalise this for it is nothing but work from morning till night Building Batteries Hauling Guns Cleaning Bricks clearing up land for other Regiments to settle on and if a Man Says he is sick it is the Doctors Priveledge to say yes or no if you cannot work then you are sent to the Guard House Bucked Gagged and stay so till they see fit to relief You and if you don't like that some white man will Give you a crack over the Head with his sword. now do you call this Equality if so God help such Equality there is many things I could relate on this matter but I will say no more I want You to consult some counsel in Relation to the Matter and see if a man could not sue for his Discharge and get his views on the Subject and let me know immiedeitely for I am tired of such treatment Please answer soon as you can and Oblidge Your

    T.D. Freeman

Camp Life

African-American soldiers faced particularly galling injustices in the army, but all soldiers, Northern and Southern, dealt with terrible conditions. In the North, a national organization, the United States Sanitary Commission (USSC), was set up to help alleviate some of the suffering due to disease, poor nutrition, and sanitation, as well as to help surgeons deal with the massive requirements of wartime medicine. The USSC oversaw the work of more than 7,000 local aid societies and provided food, medicine, clothing, and bandages to the soldiers, as well as nurses, doctors, and ambulances for the army hospitals. Drawing on the work of Florence Nightingale, who had organized hospitals and trained nurses to help the British army in the Crimean War, the USSC's main goal was to make sure that the soldiers did not suffer more than was necessary from unsanitary conditions in the army and hospitals.

    The following is a set of instructions for inspecting army camps, sent out by the USSC in 1862. The advice the inspectors were supposed to give the soldiers reveals the sorts of conditions prevalent in army camps.

V.—INSPECTION OF COMPANY QUARTERS

Proceed thoroughly to scrutinize the camps, visiting the tents of one company after another, having, if possible, the captains of each

[W]hen provision and clothing were cheap we might have got a long But every thing now is thribble and over what it was some three year back. . . . i think it a piece of injustice to have those soldiers there 15 months with out a cent of money for my part i Cannot see why they have not the same rite to thirteen dollars per month as the Whites.

—Rachel Ann Wickford, the wife of a black soldier, in a letter to the federal government, 1864

A nurse sits between the beds of two wounded soldiers in a federal hospital in Nashville, Tennessee, in 1862. Many Northern middle-class women worked in the hospitals as nurses and tried, with the help of the United States Sanitary Commission, to keep the ravages of disease and complications from wounds from claiming the lives of their charges.

company with you as you examine its tents. Do not too much hasten this part of your work, as it will probably be your best opportunity of serving the cause in which you are engaged. . . .

VI.—PREVENTION OF DISEASE POSSIBLE; SUPPRESSION DIFFICULT AND UNCERTAIN

Endeavor by every means in your power to remind the officers of [the USSC's recommendations for sanitary camp conditions] and of the necessity of their strict obedience to them, to the safety and credit of the regiment. Explain to them that they are based upon a universal military experience, that disastrous consequences inevitably follow the neglect of such precautions as they are intended to secure. Let them know that, although the outbreak of malignant or epidemic disease in camps and quarters can be almost certainly prevented, it can seldom be suppressed after having once broken out, by any measure, however energetic, and never without great destruction of life.

VII.—COOKING ARRANGEMENTS

If there is an opportunity, taste the cooked food, and criticise the cooking. Endeavor to stimulate an ambition to make wholesome and palatable food with the existing rations, by a skillful method of cooking with the simple utensils furnished by the Government and the camp fire. . . .

XIV.—AMBULANCES AND AMBULANCE STORES

The surgeon should be prepared for battle duty. If he has an ambulance, has he a trusty driver for it, and an ambulance corps, upon which he can depend under fire? Do they know how to lift and carry a man with shattered bones? Do they know that water is more precious than gold to those who follow the track of a battle, and are they instructed how to secure it and administer it providently?

XX.—SINKS, MANURE AND OFFAL

You will advise that the manure and litter of all horses and cattle be collected, removed from camp and covered with earth, or burned, at short and regular intervals; and also that the offal of cattle slaughtered near any camp or post be buried at once, and at sufficient depth. . . .

Though the lives of Northern soldiers were hard, most historians agree that in general, those of Southern soldiers were even worse. They dealt with severe food and clothing

The officers above the rank of captain knew but little of the hardships of war from personal experience. They had their black cooks, who were out foraging all the time, and they filled their masters' bellies if there was fish or fowl to be had. The regimental wagons carried the officers' clothes, and they were never half-naked, lousy, or dirty. They never had to sleep upon the bare ground nor carry forty rounds of cartridges strapped around their galled hips; the officers were never unshod or felt the torture of stone-bruise.

—Alexander Hunter, *Johnny Reb and Billy Yank*, 1905

shortages and often undertook long marches and hard battles on empty stomachs and bare feet. In the following document, a reporter from the Charleston *Daily Courier* describes the conditions among some Confederate soldiers in August 1862.

I look around me and see men barefooted and ragged, bearing only their muskets and a single blanket each, yet all inspired by the hope of another battle. I have seen some, too, who were hungry—stragglers who would come up to the camp fire, tell a pitiful story of sickness or fatigues, and then ask for a bit of bread and meat. . . . Speaking of bare feet, I suppose that at least forty thousand pairs of shoes are required to-day to supply the wants of the army. Every battle contributes to human comfort in this respect, but it is not every man who is fortunate enough to "foot" himself upon the field. It has become a trite remark among the troops, that "all a Yankee is now worth is his shoes," and it is said, but I do not know how truly, that some of our regiments have become so expert in securing these coveted articles, that they can make a charge and strip every dead Yankee's feet they pass without coming to a halt.

The Battlefield

Camp life and the endless marching were treacherous in their own ways—the exposure to harsh weather, poor diet, and fatigue led to waves of disease that killed more men than the battles themselves. But for many men, it was the battlefield that held the greatest terror, as well as the greatest thrill.

   Soldiers reacted to battle in different ways, but all of them hoped they would display courage. For 19th-century men, courage was a cornerstone of their masculinity, and battle offered them the ultimate chance to prove it. They prayed for their courage to hold fast in the face of enemy fire, and they admired courage in others—even in enemy soldiers. In the following letter, James T. Miller, a private in the 11th Pennsylvania regiment, describes soldiers' efforts to disguise the fear they feel on the battlefield.

[I]f you could only be with us around our camp fires after a fight and listen to the accounts of the hairbreadth escapes that are told of and hear the loud laughs that greet each one's experience and see the gay reckless careless way in which they are told, you

A Confederate quarter guard tries to keep warm by covering his head and shoulders with a blanket. Unlike many Confederate soldiers', his feet are covered.

The ivory grip of this sword is in the form of an ear of corn, and its guard shows a stalk of hemp, a tobacco leaf, and a cotton boll, all symbols of the major crops of the Southern economy. The weapon was awarded to Confederate Gen. Sterling Price by the City of New Orleans after his victories at Wilson's Creek and Lexington, Missouri, in August and September of 1861.

would be very apt to think that we were the happiest set of men you ever saw. But if you should go with us to the battle field and see those that [were] so gay, their faces [now] pale and their nerves trembling, and see anxiety on every countenance almost bordering on fear, you would be very apt to think we were all a set of cowardly potroons—this picture to be taken just before the fight begins, and the enemy is in sight and the dull ominous silence that generally takes place before the battle begins.

In some cases, soldiers were known to stop firing at a particularly brave soldier, or to cheer aloud his actions. In the following selection from his memoirs, Union soldier Frank Wilkeson describes his admiration for the courage displayed by an enemy officer.

I saw an officer on a milk-white horse ride forth from the woods in the rear of the Confederate work. Confident that he would be torn to bits by shells, I dropped my pipe, and glued my glass on him and waited for the tragedy. He trotted briskly over the plain where shell[s] were thickly bursting, and into the fort. I saw him hand a paper to the officer in command of the work. He sat calmly on his horse, and talked and gesticulated as quietly as though he were on dress parade. My heart went out to that man. I hoped he would not be killed. I wished I had the aiming of the guns. He lifted his hand in salute to the visor of his cap. He turned his white horse and rode slowly across the open ground, where shot and shell were thickly coursing. Dust rose above him. Tiny clouds of smoke almost hid him from view. Shot struck the ground and skipped past him, but he did not urge his horse out of a walk. He rode as though lost in meditation and deaf to the uproar that raged around him. He rode into the woods, disappeared in the timber, and was safe. With a "Thank God that brave man was not killed," I rejoined my gun.

Not everyone lived up to this courageous ideal. Charles Harvey Brewster, a young man from Northampton, Massachusetts, wrote home to his mother on July 12, 1862, and described the actions in battle of a man they knew in their neighborhood.

Fred Clark . . . has been lining some for a month trying to get a discharge and playing sick, but he is all together to healthy to lie still long enough to make any kind of a show of sickness in fact there is not a tougher healthier man in the Army of the Potomac and now I see he ranks as wounded in the late battle he was not wounded in the battle one of our wounded wanted to speak to him as he lay behind the company the next thing he was gone. he did not wait to see the end of the battle. he was seen the next day all right and the next thing he sent word that he was accidentally wounded in the hand by a revolver. nobody doubts that he shot himself. I don't want you to say anything about this for I do not want it to come from me, but he is small loss he was a trembling little coward anyway.

There was good reason to be afraid. The aftermath of battle was certain devastation, with almost inconceivable numbers of dead and wounded. In the following recollection written years after the war, Gen. Carl Schurz describes the scene after the battle of Gettysburg, as doctors set to work in the homes surrounding the deadly Pennsylvania battlefield.

At Gettysburg the wounded—many thousands of them—were carried to the farmsteads behind our lines. The houses, the barns, the sheds, and the open barnyards were crowded with moaning and wailing human beings, and still an unceasing procession of stretchers and ambulances was coming in from all sides to augment the number of the sufferers. A heavy rain set in during the day—the usual rain after a battle—and large numbers had to remain unprotected in the open, there being no room left under roof. I saw long rows of men lying under the eaves of the buildings, the water pouring down upon their bodies in streams. Most of the operating tables were placed in the open where the light was best, some of them partially protected against the rain by tarpaulins or blankets stretched upon poles. There stood the surgeons, their sleeves rolled up to the elbows, their bare arms as well as their linen aprons smeared with blood, their knives not seldom held between their teeth, while they were helping a patient on or off the table, or had their hands otherwise occupied; around them pools of blood and amputated arms or legs in heaps, sometimes more than man-high. Antiseptic methods were still unknown at that time. As a wounded man was lifted on the table, often shrieking with pain as the attendants handled him, the surgeon quickly examined the wound and resolved upon cutting off the injured limb. Some ether was administered and the body put in position in a moment. The surgeon snatched his knife from between his teeth . . . wiped it rapidly once or twice across his blood-stained

Two soldiers are forced to wear a shaming sign of "gambler" on their backs and to stand and play dice for valueless pebbles until they collapse from exhaustion. They are being punished for gambling, a popular pastime among soldiers in both armies.

*Confederate soldiers under protection
of a truce remove their dead and
wounded near Blackburn's Ford and
Centreville, Virginia.*

apron, and the cutting began. The operation accomplished, the surgeon would look around with a deep sigh, and then—"Next!"

And so it went on, hour after hour, while the number of expectant patients seemed hardly to diminish. Now and then one of the wounded men would call attention to the fact that his neighbor lying on the ground had given up the ghost while waiting for his turn, and the dead body was then quietly removed. Or a surgeon, having been long at work, would put down his knife, exclaiming that his hand had grown unsteady, and that this was too much for human endurance—not seldom hysterical tears streaming down his face. Many of the wounded men suffered with silent fortitude, fierce determination in the knitting of their brows and the steady gaze of their bloodshot eyes. Some would even force themselves to a grim jest about their situation or about the "skedaddling of the rebels." But there were, too, heart-rending groans and shrill cries of pain piercing the air, and despairing exclamations, "Oh, Lord! Oh, Lord!" or "Let me die!" or softer murmurings in which the words "mother" or "father" or "home" were often heard.

Although soldiers often tried to protect their families from learning too much about the horror of the battlefield, at times they had to share the anguish they were feeling. In this letter to his sister in Boston, James Edward (Ned) Holmes describes his feelings after the Battle of Chancellorsville.

Camp near White Oak Church, Virginia
May 21, 1863

My dear Sister Abbie;
. . . On the 3rd May we moved up in front of the works of Maray's Hill [Marye's Heights] and there laid in line of battle until about

12 M when we were ordered to charge the enemies' works which we did successfully but at a fearful cost to my reg't in particular.

In my company the killed were Cap'n Gray, Serg't Holmes (a Cousin of mine) and privates Fogg and Krive. We had eighteen wounded. On the 4th of May we lost two taken prisoners. Our loss now foots up eighteen wounded and missing. And in all we shall lose permanently sixteen who were wounded so seriously that it hardly probable they will ever be fit for military duty again. At least during their term of service.

Our loss in the two right Co's was much heavier than it would have been if it was not that two Rng'ts on our right broke and fled ignominiously which exposed us to an enfilading fire from the enemy in the rifle pits on our right.

I thought I had become callous having witnessed so much suffering, having seen so many dead and dying of the past years, but I never in the experience of the whole of my misspent life, felt so bad as I did on the ever memorable 3rd of May.

Associated as I have been with many of the men for two years, we had become as one family, we had become endeared to each other by the strong ties which our dangerous occupation will not be likely to weaken.

To see lying around you, your warmest friends and companions, some in excruciating pain from severe wounds, others in the cold embrace of death, who but a few moments before were in robust health, to see them . . . caused me more pain than anything I ever before experienced in life. God grant I may never witness the like again.

With many apologies for this senseless letter and promises to try to do better in my next, and with love to all inquiring friends of which please to take a good share to yourself. I will close.

Write soon and oblige, your aff[ectiona]te Brother, Ned

Ned Holmes asserted that he had *thought* he had become callous to death until he witnessed the Battle at Chancellorsville. Many other soldiers recounted that they did, indeed, become hardened to the sight of so much suffering.

George Allen watched as two stretcher-bearers carried a wounded man off the field. They dug his grave, then sat and smoked, ignoring the man as he lay painfully dying. Once he had died, they dumped him into the fresh hole, and went back for the next man. Allen wrote about his impressions of this seeming callousness.

Anthems

The Civil War spurred a national outpouring of new songs, some written for soldiers and some aimed more at those who lived out the war at home. Sheet music, printed and marketed specifically for domestic use, underwent a dramatic rise in popularity and profitability during the war. In particular, two songs were among the most popular, both with soldiers and with their friends and families, and both came to symbolize loyalty to a particular side of the conflict.

The power of these songs and their symbolism was apparent in the 1960s, when Civil Rights protesters often sang "Battle Hymn of the Republic" and Southern resisters responded with rounds of "Dixie."

"Battle Hymn of the Republic" fuses religious and military images, drawing on the popular Northern notion that God was on the Union's side. Over time it became a kind of Northern and abolitionist anthem, encouraging supporters with its powerful words: "As [Christ] died to make men holy, let us die to make men free!"

By being accustomed to sights which would make other men's hearts sick to behold, our men soon became heart-hardened, and sometimes scarcely gave a pitying thought to those who were unfortunate enough to get hit. Men can get accustomed to everything; and the daily sight of blood and mangled bodies so blunted their finer sensibilities as almost to blot out all love, all sympathy from the heart, and to bring more into prominence the baser qualities of man, selfishness, greed, and revenge.

Frank Wilkeson described his own transformation into someone who not only could witness death carelessly, but even treat it almost as sport. In his memoirs, he described the following scene in the lines outside Petersburg in 1865, the final year of the war:

Thickly scattered among the trees, and grouped at the edge of the open field in the shade, were those cowards, the "coffee boilers." Gangs of officers' servants and many refugee negroes were [also] there. Pack-mules loaded with pots, frying-pans, gripsacks, and bags of clothing stood tied to trees. White-capped army wagons . . . stood at the edge of the woods. The drivers . . . were drinking coffee with friendly "boilers," and they were probably frightening one another by telling blood-curdling tales of desperate but mythical battles they had been engaged in. . . . I could almost smell the freshly made Rio and the broiled bacon. It was as though a huge pic-nic were going on in the woods. The scene angered me. I knew that the "coffee-boilers" were almost to a man bounty-jumping cowards, and I wanted the camp broken up.

Soon the Confederates noticed his battery as it passed to the rear to replenish ammunition and then returned.

I saw the Confederate gunners spring to their cannon. I looked at the camp of the "coffee boilers." They were enjoying life. I leaned forward and clasped my knees with [an] excess of joy as I realized what was about to occur. . . . Clouds of smoke shot forth from the redoubt, and out of these, large black balls rose upward and rushed through the air, and passed, shrieking shrilly, close above us, to descend in the camp of the "boilers." It was a delightful scene. I hugged my knees and rocked to and fro and laughed until my flesh-less ribs were sore. [L]arge trees . . . fell with a crash among the frying-pans and coffee-pots. Teamsters sprang into their wagons . . . and ran for the rear. Men, clad and armed as soldiers,

Fine.

Originally a Northern minstrel song written before the war, "Dixie" took deep root in the South, where it represented loyalty to the Confederacy and the Southern way of life. There were many versions, as soldiers composed their own words to suit their needs and the tenor of the times. This one stresses the Southern way of life and uses a dialect meant to imitate slaves' speech.

2.

Old Missus marry "Will-de-weaber,"
Willium was a gay deceaber;
            Look away! &c—
But when he put his arm around'er,
He smilled as fierce as a 'forty-pound'er.
            Look away! &c—
    Chorus— Den I wish I was in Dixie, &c—

3.

His face was sharp as a butchers cleaber,
But dat did not seem to greab'er;
            Look away! &c—
Old Missus acted de foolish part,
And died for a man dat broke her heart.
            Look away! &c—
    Chorus— Den I wish I was in Dixie, &c—

4.

Now here's a health to the next old Missus,
An all de galls dat want to kiss us;
            Look away! &c—
But if you want to drive'way sorrow,
Come an hear dis song to-morrow.
            Look away! &c—
    Chorus— Den I wish I was in Dixie, &c—

5.

Dar's buck-wheat cakes an 'Ingen' batter,
Makes you fat or a little fatter;
            Look away! &c—
Den hoe it down an scratch your grabble,
To Dixie land I'm bound to trabble.
            Look away! &c—
    Chorus— Den I wish I was in Dixie, &c—
                    4924

skurried as frightened rabbits, hid in holes, lay prone on the earth. . . . Through the dust and smoke and uproar I saw men fall, saw others mangled by chunks of shell, and saw one, struck fairly by an exploding shell, vanish. Enormously pleased, I hugged my lean legs, and laughed and laughed again. It was the most refreshing sight I had seen for weeks.

Chapter Five

Moving Toward Revolution

Just as men were transformed from enthusiastic recruits with romantic visions of battlefield heroism into hardened soldiers weary of the ravages of war, the war itself underwent significant changes over the four years it lasted. These shifts happened at the level of the ultimate goals of the war as well as strategy, and the two were inherently intertwined. Although most Northerners originally considered it a limited fight to preserve the Union, the Civil War gradually evolved into a revolution aimed at overturning the entire economic and social structure of the South. In order to accomplish this purpose, Northern generals began to take aim not only at Confederate soldiers but at the civilian population that supported the Southern army. Unlike any other war fought on U.S. soil, the Civil War became a total war, drawing on the resources and lives of nearly everyone in the country.

The story of the shift in the reason the North fought, from trying to reclaim the Southern states to breaking the bonds of four million slaves, is crucial to understanding the impact of the Civil War. The transformation into a fight for freedom dramatically affected not only the outcome of the war itself, but the course of U.S. history for years to come.

The Crittenden-Johnson Resolutions

In the early days of the war, one of Lincoln's overriding concerns was how to make sure that the Border States remained with the Union. He was afraid that if these slave-owning states felt that slavery was a target of the Northern armies, they might bolt and

This photograph, taken by Alexander Gardner in November 1863, shortly before Lincoln's Gettysburg Address, conveys the President's humanity—in the texture of his hair and beard, for instance—and yet captures the aura of inner strength, moral weightiness, and intellectual depth that has come to be associated with Lincoln the national hero.

Plantation police, with their rifles and dogs at the ready, examine black men's passes, which African Americans had to carry when traveling. During the war Southern whites watched the movements of African Americans, both free and enslaved, even more carefully because African Americans often served as spies and lookouts for the Union army.

join the Confederacy. He therefore repeatedly assured the public that his only aim in the war was to restore the Union, and that he was not interested in abolishing slavery. In July 1861, two resolutions passed Congress reinforcing Lincoln's own pronouncements on this subject. The Crittenden-Johnson Resolutions represent the clearest description of the Union's early war aims. They both refer to the "established institutions" of the Southern states, meaning, of course, slavery.

Resolved. . . . That the present deplorable civil war has been forced upon the country by the disunionists of the Southern States now in revolt against the constitutional Government and in arms around the capital; that in this national emergency Congress, banishing all feelings of mere passion or resentment, will recollect only its duty to the whole country; that this war is not waged upon our part in any spirit of oppression, nor for any purpose of conquest or subjugation, nor purpose of overthrowing or interfering with the rights or established institutions of those States, but to defend and maintain the supremacy of the Constitution and to preserve the Union, with all the dignity, equality, and rights of the several States unimpaired; and that as soon as these objects are accomplished the war ought to cease.

Although federal officials insisted that the war was not to end slavery, African Americans in the South thought and acted otherwise. As the Union armies came through, hundreds and then thousands of slaves began to flee their masters' farms and plantations and seek protection with the Yankee troops. The reactions of officers and soldiers to these

"*My paramount aim in this struggle is to save the Union, and is not either to save or destroy slavery. If I could save the Union without freeing any slaves, I would do it, and if I could save it by freeing all the slaves I would do it; and if I could save it by freeing some and leaving others alone I would also do that.*"

—Abraham Lincoln, in an open letter to *New York Tribune* editor Horace Greeley August 22, 1862 new arrivals were mixed, and the army struggled to figure out how to handle the situation. At first, it was general policy to send the slaves back to their masters. But as more and more blacks sought refuge with the army, and as soldiers witnessed the terrible punishments inflicted on those sent back, this policy became less and less tenable. The fugitive slaves themselves forced Union officials to recognize that, despite the Crittenden-Johnson Resolutions, the war was, in fact, destroying slavery.

On July 30, 1861, from his camp in Hampton, Virginia, Gen. Benjamin F. Butler wrote to Secretary of War Simon Cameron for advice. By this time, 900 escaped slaves had been living and working with his army, and Butler wanted to know how to treat them. Earlier he had proposed that slaves be treated as contraband of war, that is, property confiscated in order to prevent its use by the enemy. In this letter, he writes about the practical, political, and philosophical ramifications of this policy.

In the village of Hampton there were a large number of negroes, composed in great measure of women and children of the men who had fled thither within my lines for protection, who had escaped from marauding parties of rebels who had been gathering up able-bodied blacks to aid them in constructing their batteries on the James and York Rivers. I had employed the men in Hampton in throwing up intrenchments, and they were working zealously and efficiently at that duty, saving our soldiers from that labor under the gleam of the mid-day sun. The women were earning substantially their own subsistence in washing, marketing, and taking care of the clothes of the soldiers, and rations were being served out to the men who worked for the support of the children. But by the evacuation of Hampton, rendered necessary by the withdrawal of troops, leaving me scarcely 5,000 men outside the Fort, including the force at Newport News, all these black people were obliged to break up their homes at Hampton, fleeing across the creek within my lines for protection and support. Indeed it was a most distressing sight to see these poor creatures, who

Hundreds of fugitive slaves, including mothers with young children, seek entrance to Fortress Monroe at Hampton, Virginia, and the protection of Gen. Benjamin Butler in June 1861. By forcing Butler to recognize both the dangers they faced and the services they could provide the Union army, African Americans pushed Butler to declare them "contraband of war" and to reverse the policy of sending them back to their masters.

had trusted to the protection of the arms of the United States, and who had aided the troops of the United States in their enterprise, to be thus obliged to flee from their homes, and the homes of their masters who had deserted them, and become fugitives from fear of the return of the rebel soldiery, who had threatened to shoot the men who had wrought for us, and to carry off the women who had served us, to a worse than Egyptian bondage. I have, therefore, now within the Peninsula, this side of Hampton Creek, 900 negroes, 300 of whom are able-bodied men, 30 of whom are men substantially past hard labor, 175 women[,] 225 children under the age of 10 years, and 170 between 10 and 18 years, and many more coming in. The questions which this state of facts presents are very embarrassing.

First, What shall be done with them? And, *Second,* What is their state and condition?

Upon these questions I desire the instructions of the Department.

The first question, however, may perhaps be answered by considering the last. Are these men, women and children, slaves? Are they free? Is their condition that of men, women, and children, or of property, or is it a mixed relation? What their *status* was under the Constitution and laws, we all know. What has been the effect of rebellion and a state of war upon that *status?* When I adopted the theory of treating the able-bodied negro fit to work in the trenches as property liable to be used in aid of rebellion, and so contraband of war, that condition of things was in so far met, as I then and still believe, on a legal and constitutional basis. But now a new series of questions arises. Passing by women, the children, certainly, cannot be treated on that basis; if property, they must be considered the incumbrance rather than the auxiliary of an army, and, of course, in no possible legal relation could be treated as contraband. Are they property? If they were so, they have been left by their masters and owners, deserted, thrown away, abandoned, like the wrecked vessel upon the ocean. Their former possessors and owners have causelessly, traitorously, rebelliously, and to carry out the figure, practically abandoned them to be swallowed up by the winter storm of starvation. If property, do they not become the property of the salvors? But we, their salvors, do not need and will not hold such property, and will assume no such ownership: has not, therefore, all propriety relation ceased? Have they not become, thereupon, men, women, and children? No longer under ownership of any kind, the fearful relics of fugitive masters, have they not by their masters' acts, and the state of war, assumed the condition, which we hold to be the normal one, of those made in God's image. Is not every constitutional, legal, and moral requirement, as well to the runaway master as their relinquished slaves, thus answered? I confess that my own mind is compelled by this reasoning to look upon them as men and women. If not born free, yet free, manumitted, sent forth from the hand that held them never to be reclaimed. . . .

Pardon me for addressing the Secretary of War directly upon this question, as it involves some political as well as propriety of military action. I am, sir, your obedient servant,

Benjamin F. Butler

In his response to Butler, dated August 8, 1861, Cameron made clear that he supported Butler's decision, but that he still considered the war to be a fight to preserve the Union, not a struggle for freedom.

You will, however, neither authorize nor permit any interference by the troops under your command with the servants of peaceful citizens, in house or field; nor will you, in any way, encourage such servants to leave the lawful service of their masters; nor will you, except in cases where the public safety may seem to require it, prevent the voluntary return of any fugitive to the service from which he may have escaped.

Just two days before Cameron's letter to Butler, the U.S. Congress passed the First Confiscation Act. This legislation proclaimed that any slaveholder whose slaves were used by the Confederate army lost all rights to those slaves. However, if fugitive slaves could not prove they had been forced to labor for the Confederate army, they were still supposed to be returned to their masters. In some cases Union soldiers cooperated with this policy, but in other cases they did not. The following affidavit was collected along with others by a delegation of Maryland legislators and sent to Edwin M. Stanton, the new secretary of war, protesting Union soldiers refusing to turn slaves over to their masters.

State of Maryland Chs. County 1st Mach [sic] 1862

On or about the 14th of november last I proceeded to Camp Fenton near Port Tobacco to get three of my servants viz a man about Twenty four years of age a boy about seventeen years of age and a boy some 13 or 14 years of age who had left their home and taken up their abode with the soldiers at the above named camp[.] Col. Graham who was in command at the time gave me an order to the officer of the day to search the camp for my servants but at the same time intimated I might meet with some difficulty as a portion of his troops were abolitionist[.] I learned by some of the soldiers my servants were in Camp and soon as my mission became general known a large crowd collected and followed me crying shoot him, bayonet him, kill him, pitch him out, the nigger Stealer the nigger driver[.] at first their threats were accompanied with a few stones thrown at me which very soon became an allmost continued shower of stones a number of which struck me, but did me no serious damage. Seeing the officer who accompanied me took no notice of what was going on and fearing that some of the soldiers would put their threats of shooting me into execution I informed him that I would not proceed any farther, about this time Lieutenant Edmund Harrison came to my assistance and swore he would shoot the first man who threw a stone at me, the soldiers hooted at him and continued throwing. I returned to Col. Grahams quarters but was not permitted to see him again. I left the camp without getting my servants and have not been favored to get them yet.

J. Smoot

Slavery Must Die

Most African Americans and many white abolitionists strongly disagreed with Lincoln's resistance to making the abolition of slavery an overt Union war aim. One of Lincoln's most outspoken critics in this matter was the orator and newspaper publisher Frederick Douglass, who had escaped from slavery 20 years earlier. As the war dragged on and the South won victory after bloody victory, Douglass repeatedly admonished Lincoln for refusing to emancipate the slaves and arm black men. The following editorial from his newspaper, the *Douglass Monthly*, was published in September 1862, just a few weeks after Lincoln's letter to the *New York Tribune*.

Notwithstanding the apparent determination of the Government and of Generals commanding in the field, to preserve slavery and save the Union at the same time, notwithstanding the exaltation of proslavery over antislavery commanders, and the steady purpose of the Government to check and arrest all anti-slavery measures and tendencies in the army and country, it is evident that the idea that this horrible slaveholding rebellion can only be speedily and successfully put down by suppressing its cause, in the entire abolition of slavery, has gained decided ground during the last few weeks among the loyal people.—The defeats and disasters on the field which have visibly thinned the ranks of the loyal army, and the call for six hundred thousand more men, and the prospect of heavily increased national debt, and grinding taxation, are doing their legitimate work among the people, however little they may seem to affect the Government at Washington. . . . A few weeks more of sufferings, disasters, defeats and ruin of the slaughter of our country's first born, a few weeks more of successful rebellion and threatened intervention from abroad, a few weeks more of gloomy prostration of business and of earnest protest on the part of the suffering people will, we trust, arouse the Government to a just and wise sense of the demands of the age and of the hour. We are to be saved as by fire. . . .

By some, it is even now thought too late. We have . . . bowed so low to the dark and bloody spirit of slavery that it is doubted whether we have the requisite moral stamina to save our country from destruction, whether we shall not at last give up the contest, patch up a deceitful peace and restore the slave power to more than its former power and influence in the republic. . . .

Nevertheless we have yet strong grounds of hope. The rebels are firm, determined, enthusiastic and wonderfully successful. They have beaten off McClellan, hold Richmond securely, and are menacing Washington, and all the Border States. With slavery undisturbed they can prolong the war indefinitely. . . . Considerations of this character will make the South slow to listen to any compromise, and will, we still hope, compel the Federal Government to take at last *the* step, which it ought to have taken at the first, i.e. destroy this slaveholding contagion, by destroying the filthy cause which produced it. Than this there is no other way, slavery must die if the nation lives, and the nation must die if slavery lives.

Douglass was right that the Southern victories outside of Richmond, Virginia, in the summer of 1862 were trying the patience of Northern politicians and civilians. Because Southerners used slave labor to do agricultural work that supplied the army with food, build fortifications, drive army wagons, haul supplies, and perform much of the military's menial labor, many came to believe that only by freeing the

Through recruitment posters and speeches Frederick Douglass and other black leaders urged African-American men to join the Union army as a way to prove their loyalty to the country and to prove their fitness for full citizenship rights. But Douglass became disillusioned with the way black soldiers were treated in the army and stopped recruiting men to fill the ranks.

slaves would the North be able to cripple the Confederacy enough to win the war. Lincoln eventually reached this conclusion as well. In his memoir, Francis C. Carpenter, a portraitist, remembered visiting Lincoln in order to paint a picture of him signing the Emancipation Proclamation. The president described to the artist how he had reached his decision on when to release the proclamation and how to announce it.

The appointed hour found me at the well-remembered door of the official chamber—that door watched daily, with so many conflicting emotions of hope and fear, by the anxious throng regularly gathered there. The President had preceded me, and was already deep in Acts of Congress, with which the writing-desk was strewed, awaiting his signature. He received me pleasantly, giving me a seat near his own armchair . . . he took off his spectacles, and said, "Well, Mr. C——, we will turn you in loose here, and try to give you a good chance to work out your idea." Then, without paying much attention to the enthusiastic expression of my ambitious desire and purpose he proceeded to give me a detailed account of the history and issue of the great proclamation.

"It had got to be," said he, "midsummer, 1862. Things had gone on from bad to worse, until I felt that we had reached the end of our rope on the plan of operations we had been pursuing; that we had about played our last card, and must change our tactics, or lose the game! I now determined upon the adoption of the emancipation policy; and, without consultation with, or the knowledge of the Cabinet, I prepared the original draft of the proclamation, and, after much anxious thought, called a Cabinet meeting upon the subject. This was the last of July, or the first part of the month of August, 1862." (The exact date he did not remember.) "This Cabinet meeting took place, I think, upon a Saturday. All were present, excepting Mr. Blair, the Postmaster-General, who was absent at the opening of the discussion, but came in subsequently. I said to the Cabinet that I had resolved upon this step, and had not called them together to ask their advice, but to lay the subject-matter of a proclamation

In this lithograph based on an allegorical painting, Lincoln sits with the Bible on his knee, the scales of justice hanging in the background, surrounded by posters and declarations of protest by every group from the Quakers to the Peace Democrats. The President seems to be weighing the various influences as he tries to draft the Emancipation Proclamation.

before them; suggestions as to which would be in order, after they had heard it read. . . .

Various suggestions were offered. Secretary Chase wished the language stronger in reference to the arming of the blacks. Mr. Blair, after he came in, deprecated the policy on the ground that it would cost the Administration the fall elections. Nothing, however, was offered that I had not already fully anticipated and settled in my own mind, until Secretary Seward spoke. He said in substance: 'Mr. President, I approve of the proclamation, but I question the expediency of its issue at this juncture. The depression of the public mind, consequent upon our repeated reverses, is so great that I fear the effect of so important a step. It may be viewed as the last measure of an exhausted government, a cry for help; the government stretching forth its hands to Ethiopia, instead of Ethiopia stretching forth her hands to the government.' His idea," said the President, "was that it would be considered our last shriek, on the retreat." (This was his precise expression.) "'Now,' continued Mr. Seward, 'while I approve the measure, I suggest, sir, that you postpone its issue, until you can give it to the country supported by military success, instead of issuing it, as would be the case now, upon the greatest disasters of the war!'"

Mr. Lincoln continued: "The wisdom of the view of the Secretary of State struck me with very great force. It was an aspect of the case that, in all my thought upon the subject, I had entirely overlooked. The result was that I put the draft of the proclamation aside, as you do your sketch for a picture, waiting for a victory. From time to time I added or changed a line, touching it up here and there, anxiously watching the progress of events. Well, the next news we had was of Pope's disaster, at Bull Run. Things looked darker than ever. Finally, came the week of the Battle of Antietam. I determined to wait no longer. The news came, I think, on Wednesday, that the advantage was on our side. I was then staying at the Soldiers' Home (three miles out of Washington). Here I finished writing the second draft of the preliminary proclamation; came up on Saturday; called the Cabinet together to hear it, and it was published the following Monday."

The Battle of Antietam

The battle of Antietam may have justified Lincoln's Emancipation Proclamation, but it was hardly a stunning victory for the North. The Union commander was Gen. George McClellan, the most controversial of Lincoln's officers. He won the

Not a Fool

In the summer of 1862, thousands of Native Americans in Minnesota nearly starved because of poor hunts that winter and crop failures in 1861. Rumors had spread that the government was going to pay them only half of the money that they normally received as a yearly annuity. Tempers ran high, and when government agents suggested that they would pay the Indians in paper money called "greenbacks" instead of in the usual gold specie, the Indians were infuriated. On August 17, 1862, several young Dakota men killed some white men and women in Acton, Minnesota. They returned to their village and asked Little Crow, a warrior who lived nearby, to lead them into battle against the whites. At first he refused and went back inside his house. The angry young men called him a coward. Grabbing the headdress off the man who had offended him, Little Crow made the following speech. He refers to himself as Taoyateduta, his personal name, which means "His (Strong) Red Nation."

Taoyateduta is not a coward, and he is not a fool! When did he run away from his enemies? When did he leave his braves behind him on the warpath and turn back to his tepees? When you retreated from your enemies, he walked behind you on your trail with his face to the Ojibways, and covered your backs as a she-bear covers her cubs.

Is Taoyateduta without scalps? Look at his war feathers! Behold the scalp locks of his enemies hanging there on his lodge poles! Do they call him a coward? Taoyateduta is not a coward and he is not a fool.

Braves, you are like little children; you know not what you are doing. You are full of the white man's devil water. You are like dogs in the hot moon, when they run and snap at their own shadows. We are only little herds of buffalo left scattered; the great herds that once covered the prairies are no more. See! The white men are like locusts when they fly so thick that the whole sky is a snowstorm. . . .

[T]hey fight amongst themselves a way off. Do you hear the thunder of their big guns? . . . [B]ut if you strike at them they will all turn on you and devour you and your women and little children just as the locusts in their time fall on the trees and devour all the leaves in one day.

You are fools. You cannot see the face of your chief; your eyes are full of smoke. You cannot hear his voice; your ears are full of roaring waters. Braves, you are little children, you are fools. You will die like rabbits when the hungry wolves hunt them in the Hard Moon. Taoyateduta is not a coward. He will die with you!

hearts and loyalty of the Union soldiers by brilliantly train-ing them and raising their morale after the chaos and demor-alization of their early losses. But when it came to actually fighting the war, McClellan appeared inherently flawed. A Democrat, he disagreed politically with many of the Republi-cans' aims, and seemed to want to fight the war without hurting the South too much. He usually found excuses to avoid battles; he overestimated the enemy's numbers, or underestimated his men's preparedness.

Antietam, fought on September 16, 1862, was the blood-iest single day of the Civil War. By nightfall, the battlefied was strewn with 2,100 dead Yankees and 2,700 dead rebels. Another 18,000 soldiers lay wounded, 2,500 of whom would later die. Whole units on both sides were virtually wiped out. By comparison, U.S. forces suffered only 6,000 casualties on D-Day in World War II, about one-fourth the number at Anti-etam. More than twice as many Americans were killed or mortally wounded in combat in one day at Antietam as in the War of 1812, the Mexican War, and the Spanish-American War combined.

Rufus Dawes, a soldier with a Wisconsin regiment that lost 152 of its 314 men, describes his experience during the Battle at Antietam Creek.

Another line of our men came up through the corn. We all joined together, jumped over the fence, and again pushed out into the open field. There is a rattling fusilade [sic] and loud cheers.

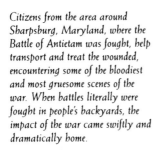

Citizens from the area around Sharpsburg, Maryland, where the Battle of Antietam was fought, help transport and treat the wounded, encountering some of the bloodiest and most gruesome scenes of the war. When battles literally were fought in people's backyards, the impact of the war came swiftly and dramatically home.

"Forward" is the word. The men are loading and firing with demonaical fury and shouting and laughing hysterically, and the whole field before us is covered with rebels fleeing for life, into the woods.

In stark contrast to Dawes's description of chaos and hysteria, commanding officer McClellan emphasizes his troops' "gallantry" and determination.

The whole of the brigade . . . now advanced with gallantry, driving the enemy before them in confusion into the cornfield beyond the sunken road. . . . Our troops on the left part of this line having driven the enemy far back, they, with reinforced numbers, made a determined attack directly in front. To meet this, Col. Barlow brought his two regiments to position in line, and drove the enemy through the cornfield into the orchard beyond.

The Emancipation Proclamation

The Union win at Antietam furnished Lincoln with his chance to announce the Emancipation Proclamation, but also made clear McClellan's ineptitude as a commanding officer. McClellan was roundly criticized by the President and by many Northern civilians for failing to crush Gen. Robert E. Lee's Confederate army after his victory at Antietam. Robert Gould Shaw, a white officer who would later lead the 54th Massachusetts Regiment of African-American soldiers, wrote to his mother about his thoughts on the announcement of the Emancipation Proclamation, as well as why he believed the criticisms of McClellan were misplaced. ("Harry" is Shaw's cousin, and "Effie," his younger sister.)

So the "Proclamation of Emancipation" has come at last, or rather, its forerunner. I suppose you are all very much excited about it. For my part, I can't see what practical good it can do now. Wherever our army has been, there remain no slaves, and the Proclamation will not free them where we don't go. Jeff Davis will soon issue a proclamation threatening to hang every prisoner they take, and will make this a war of extermination. I would give anything to have had Harry free before Lincoln issued that; I am so afraid it will go hard with him. The condition of the slaves will not be ameliorated certainly, if they are suspected of plotting insurrection, or trying to

A few weeks after the Battle of Antietam, President Lincoln visited Gen. George B. McClellan on the field and expressed his frustration that McClellan had not crushed the Southern army or even actively pursued the retreating General Lee and his men.

*"King Abraham" Lincoln removes
a mask of his face, revealing the
Devil, in this cartoon from the
Southern Illustrated News.
After he issued the Emancipation
Proclamation, Southerners felt
Lincoln proved himself to be not
only a tyrant but evil incarnate.*

run away; I don't mean to say that it is not the right thing to do, but that, as a war measure, the evil will overbalance the good for the present. Of course, after we have subdued them, it will be a great thing. . . .

I have just got a letter from Effie of 14th inst. She walks into McClellan for not following up the Rebels; but I don't sympathize with her a bit. If he is not a very great general, he is the best we have, I fully believe, and the same men who didn't behave well at Manassas, fought without faltering, the other day, under him. The men place the most implicit faith in him, and he never appears without being received with cheers.

Those who talk of rapid pursuit, don't know that there were, and are, about five thousand stragglers between here and Alexandria; a march made by easy stages. In my opinion, the individuals to be walked into are our rulers, who, after fifteen months' experience, continue a military system by which it is impossible to form a well-disciplined army, and account of which thousands and thousands of lives have been thrown away. They not only continue the old system, but they neglect to fill up old regiments who have been through a long campaign, and have some esprit de corps, and desire to distinguish themselves, and send out new ones which are perfectly unmanageable and useless. . . . Marching is as important as fighting, but, if the sun is a little hot or we don't halt before dark, our new brethren in arms take matters into their own hands, halt at a convenient place, and go to housekeeping. I don't say they are not just as brave men, and I know they are physically far superior to the first levies, but there is no discipline, and without it a soldier is not a soldier. There is little enough of it in the old regiments, but they are inured to hardship, and accustomed to the sound of battle. Then they have learnt, in a great measure, that safety and honour depend on obedience to orders, and many come to it from their natural good sense. Recruits mixed in with old men do well; that's our experience.

While Robert Gould Shaw supposed that the Emancipation Proclamation would make no practical difference, others, both black and white, saw it very differently. Many Southern whites greatly feared January 1, the day that the proclamation would take effect, and worried that it would bring with it a slave uprising that might threaten their lives. One planter in Louisiana, Pierre Soniat, wrote to Gen. Nathaniel P. Banks, a Union military commander, expressing his fear.

Parish of St. Charles [Louisiana] December 20, 1862

General my advanced age, my position as a planter, and my perfect knowledge of the country, make it my duty to present a few remarks which I hope you will receive favorably. We have suffered greatly during this unfortunate war, and we undoubtedly will have much more to suffer before order is restored and peace smiles again on this country. So far we have, to regret in most instances, only the ruin and desolation which have extended to crops & farms; but the evil that threatens us is far more terrible than the loss of fortunes; our very lives are at stake! As far as the memory of man can go, there has existed among the negro population a tradition which has caused us many a sleepless night. They imagine that they are to be freed by Christmas. Vague reports are spread about that they intend, taking whatever weapons they can find, to come in vast numbers and force the federal government to give them their freedom. Having been deceived in their expectation, great crimes might be committed by them. The negro regiments, in particular, being organized and armed are especially to be feared. General I have no conduct to dictate to you, but if I were allowed to make a suggestion, I would tell you to disarm the negroes at least for the present and place white men, to see to their behavior Respectfully

Pre. Soniat

While slave owners worried about armed uprisings, slaves and free blacks planned to celebrate what would become known as the Day of Jubilee. In New Orleans, blacks who had formed a union association wrote to General Banks asking permission for the observances they had planned.

In obedience To Th High chift an Command of Th Head quarters Department of Th Gulf Maggo Gen N P Bank We Th members of Th union association Desir Th & Respectfully ask of you The privirliges of Salabrating The first Day of January th 1863 by a Large procesion on that Day & We Wish to pass th Head quarters of th union officers High in a authority that is if it Suit your approbation & We also Wish to Give a Grand union Dinner on th Second Day of January that is if it so pleas you & th profit of th Dinner Will Go To th poor people in th Camp th Colour Woman & children Your Most Homble obedien servant
J M Marshall th president of th union association
Henry Clay th Superintendent of th Dinner

Although in practical terms the Emancipation Proclamation did not free every slave at once and forever, it did mark a major turning point for both the war and the country. The Civil War officially became a struggle for freedom, and when it was finally over, slavery would be dead. On January 1, 1863, the Emancipation Proclamation, which follows, went into effect.

Whereas, on the twenty-second day of September, in the year of our Lord one thousand eight hundred and sixty-two, a proclamation was issued by the President of the United States, containing, among other things, the following, to wit:

That on the first day of January, in the year of our Lord one thousand eight hundred and sixty-three, all persons held as slaves within any State, or designated part of a State, the people whereof shall then be in rebellion against the United States, shall be then, thenceforward, and forever free; and the Executive Government of the United States, including the military and naval authority thereof, will recognize and maintain the freedom of such persons, and will do no act or acts to repress such persons, or any of them, in any efforts they may make for their actual freedom.

That the Executive will, on the first day of January aforesaid, by proclamation, designate the States and parts of States, if any, in which the people thereof respectively, shall then be in rebellion against the United States; and the fact that any State, or the people thereof, shall on that day be in good faith represented in the Congress of the United States by members chosen thereto at elections wherein a majority of the qualified voters of such State shall have participated, shall in the absence of strong countervailing testimony, be deemed conclusive evidence that such State, and the people thereof, are not then in rebellion against the United States.

Now, therefore, I, Abraham Lincoln, President of the United States, by virtue of the power in me vested as commander-in-chief of the Army and Navy of the United States, in time of actual armed rebellion against authority and government of the United States, and as a fit and necessary war measure for suppressing said rebellion, do, on this first day of January, in the year of our Lord one thousand eight hundred and sixty-three, and in accordance with my purpose so to do, publicly proclaimed for the full period of one hundred days from the day first above mentioned, order and designate as the States and parts of States wherein the people thereof, respectively, are this day in rebellion against the United States, the following, to wit:

Arkansas, Texas, Louisiana (except the parishes of St. Bernard, Plaquemines, Jefferson, St. John, St. Charles, St. James, Ascension, Assumption, Terrebonne, Lafourche, St. Mary, St. Martin, and Orleans, including the city of New Orleans), Mississippi, Alabama, Florida, Georgia, South Carolina, North Carolina, and Virginia (except the forty-eight counties designated as West Virginia, and also the counties of Berkley, Accomac, Northampton, Elizabeth City, York, Princess Ann, and Norfolk, including the cities of Norfolk and Portsmouth), and which excepted parts are, for the present, left precisely as if this proclamation were not issued.

And by virtue of the power and for the purpose aforesaid, I do order and declare that all persons held as slaves within said designated States and parts of States are, and henceforward shall be, free; and that the Executive government of the United States, including the military and naval authorities thereof, will recognize and maintain the freedom of said persons.

And I hereby enjoin upon the people so declared to be free to abstain from all violence, unless in necessary self-defense; and I recommend to them that, in all cases when allowed, they labor faithfully for reasonable wages.

And I further declare and make known, that such persons of suitable condition, will be received into the armed service of the United States to garrison forts, positions, stations, and other places, and to man vessels of all sorts in said service.

And upon this act, sincerely believed to be an act of justice, warranted by the Constitution, upon military necessity, I invoke the considerate judgment of mankind and the gracious favor of Almighty God.

In witness whereof, I have hereunto set my hand, and caused the seal of the United States to be affixed.

Done at the city of Washington, this first day of January, in the year of our Lord one thousand eight hundred and sixty-three, and of the Independence of the United States of America the eighty-seventh.

Prejudice Overturned

African Americans everywhere rejoiced at the news of the Emancipation Proclamation. Among other things, they welcomed the opportunity it gave black men to join the army and fight for freedom. Many whites, though, still doubted that blacks had the courage or discipline to do so. In three battles

Black troops in full uniform stand outside their barracks. Although they fought in segregated regiments and faced a variety of humiliations, offenses, and dangers, many African-American men believed that it was particularly important for black men to serve in the Union army.

in the summer of 1863, at Port Hudson, Louisiana, Miliken's Bend, Mississippi, and Fort Wagner, South Carolina, valiant black soldiers proved their courage and their ability as soldiers. In the following letter to the chief recruiter of black troops in southern Louisiana, Elias D. Strunke, a Union officer, reported on the actions of the black troops at Port Hudson, many of whom had come to the army as contrabands.

Baton Rouge May 29th/63

General. feeling deeply interested in the cause which you have espoused, I take the liberty to transmit the following, concerning the colored Troops engaged in the recent battles at Port Hudson.

I arrived here the evening of the 26th Inst, was mustered and reported to Maj. Tucker for duty—

During the night I heard heavy cannonadeing [sic] at Port Hudson. Early next morning I obtained permission and went to the front. But was so much detained, I did not reach our lines until the fighting for the day had nearly ceased—There being no renewal of the engagement the following day—I engaged in removing and administering to the wounded, gathering meantime as much information as possible concerning the battle and the conduct of our Troops. My anxiety was to learn all I could concerning the Bravery of the Colored Reg. Engaged, for their good conduct and bravery would add to your undertakings and make more popular the movement. Not that I am afraid to meet unpopular doctrins [sic], for I am not. But that we may show our full strength, the cause should be one of general sanction.

I have ever believed, from my idea of those traits of character which I deemed necessary to make a good soldier, together with their history, that in them we should find those characteristics necessary, for an effective [sic] army. And I rejoice to learn, in the late engagements the fact is established beyond a doubt.

The following is (in substance) a statement personally made to me, by 1st Lt. Co. F. 1st R[egiment]. La. Native Guard who was wounded during the engagement.

"We went into action about 6 A.M. and was under fire most of the time until sunset.

The very first thing after forming line of battle we were ordered to charge—My Co. was apparrently [sic] brave. Yet they are mostly contrabands, and I must say I entertained some fears as to their pluck. But I have none now—The moment the order was given, they entered upon its execution. Valiantly did the heroic descendants of Africa move forward as cool as if Marshaled for dress parade, under a most murderous fire from the enemy guns, until we reached the main ditch which surrounds the Fort. finding it impassible we retreated under orders to the woods and deployed as shirmishers—In the charge we lost our Capt. And Colored sergeant, the latter fell wrapped in the flag he had so gallantly borne—Alone we held our position until 12. O'clock when we were relieved—

At two o'clock P. M. we were again ordered to the front where we made two separate charges each in the face of a heavy fire from the enemies Battery of seven guns—whose destructive fire would have confuse and almost disorganized the bravest troops. But these men did not swerve, or show cowardice. I have been in several engagements, and I never before beheld such coolness and darring—

Their gallantry entitles them to a special praise. And I already observe, the sneers of others are being tempered into eulogy—"

It is pleasant to learn these things, and it must be indeed gratifying to the General to know that his army will be composed of men of almost unequaled coolness & bravery—

The men of our Reg. Are very ready in learning the drills, and the officers have every confidence in their becoming excellent soldiers.

Assureing you that I will always, both as an officer of the U. S. Army and as a man, endeavor to faithfully & fully discharge the duties of my office, I am happy to Subscribe Myself, Very Respectfully, Your Most Obt. Servt,

Elias D. Strunke

Old Tactics, New Guns

One reason for the Civil War's terrible loss of life was that officers' strategy had not caught up with changes in military technology. Before the Civil War, the most common military weapon was a smoothbore musket. These long, straight guns were not very accurate, because the bullet did not spin as it left the barrel. A bullet might travel up to 250 yards, but a soldier could hit a target at a range of only about 80 yards. A new kind of rifle—a musket that was grooved on the inside and took a new type of bullet that spun through the air—could shoot more than 1,000 yards and had an accuracy range of about 400 yards.

Most of the army officers on both sides had been trained at the famous military academy West Point, where they learned tactics that dated back to the Napoleonic Wars earlier in the century and were based on the old, inaccurate weapons. In this game plan, large masses of men standing close together would march forward slowly, firing at the enemy, and when reaching them, would fight hand-to-hand combat with their bayonets. The new rifles, however, made a bloody mockery of this tactic, because entire lines of men could be cut down as they marched in. Even as late as the summer of 1863, generals on both sides clung to these old tactics at the cost of thousands of lives.

General Lee is the most successful general of the age. His exploits are brilliant almost beyond example. When we say this of a man who commands an immense army, it is supererogatory to say anything of his talents. Nothing but genius of the highest order can conceive the combinations necessary to insure the uninterrupted success of so large a host, over an enemy greatly superior in force. In all departments of science his acquirements are great, and has besides an uncommon stock of general information. His judgment is as quick as his military glance, and it rarely deceives. Withall he is one of the most unpretending men in the world—a thorough gentleman in his manner—very affable to all who approach him—and extremely amiable in private life. He is about five feet ten inches high, was eminently handsome in his youth, is still one of the finest looking men in the army, rides like a knight of the old crusading days, is indefatigable in business, and bears fatigue like a man of iron.

—from *The War and Its Heroes,*
published in Richmond, Virginia, 1865

The Battle of Gettysburg

The months just before and after the Emancipation Proclamation went into effect were long and bloody, with many costly battles. Perhaps one of the most famous of these terrible assaults was Confederate Gen. George Pickett's charge at Gettysburg. The Battle of Gettysburg, which occurred from July 1 to 3, 1863, marked a significant turning point in the war. The Union army, under the command of George Gordon Meade, stopped Lee's advance into Pennsylvania, effectively ending the Confederacy's offensive move into the North. It was the most massive and bloody battle of the war, with 23,000 Union and 28,000 Confederate casualties. The tremendous losses at Gettysburg put a terrible drain on the South's manpower, and it was never able to completely recover.

Gen. James Longstreet was blamed by many on the Confederate side for this loss, and in this description, written after the war, he tries to deflect the burden onto others. Many military historians agree, though, that his own slowness in bringing forward his two divisions contributed to the disaster. In the following excerpt from his report on the battle, Longstreet describes the night before the battle began.

The eve of the great battle was crowded with events. Movements for the concentration of the two vast armies went on in mighty force, but with a silence in strong contrast to the swift-coming commotion of their shock in conflict. It was the pent quiet of the gathering storm whose bursting was to shake the continent and suddenly command the startled attention of the world.

Longstreet's portrayal of the battle reveals the popular romanticization of battle as well as the dramatic reality and tragedy of this specific fight. Here he describes the moments leading up to the tragedy of Pickett's charge.

In the absence of orders, I had scouting parties out during the night in search of a way by which we might strike the enemy's left, and push it down towards his center. I found a way that gave some promise of results, and was about to move the command when [Gen. Robert E. Lee] rode over after sunrise and gave his orders. His plan was to assault the enemy's left center by a column to be composed of McLaws's and Hood's divisions reinforced by Pickett's brigades. I thought that it would not do; that the point had been

Perhaps the single most famous assault of the Civil War, Pickett's Charge was Gen. Robert E. Lee's futile attempt to break through the Union line at Gettysburg on July 3, 1863. Thousands of Southern soldiers marched across the fields to their deaths, and with them died any hope for the Confederacy's ability to prevail.

fully tested the day before, by more men, when all were fresh; that the enemy was there looking for us, as we heard him during the night putting up his defenses; that the divisions of McLaws and Hood were holding a mile along the right of my line against twenty thousand men, who would follow their withdrawal, strike the flank of the assaulting column, crush it, and get on our rear towards the Potomac River; that thirty thousand men was the minimum force necessary for the work; that even such force would need close cooperation on other parts of the line; that the column as he proposed to organize it would have only thirteen thousand men (the divisions having lost a third of their numbers the day before); that the column would have to march a mile under concentrating battery fire, and a thousand yards under long-range musketry; that the conditions were different from those in the days of Napoleon, when field batteries had a range of six hundred yards and musketry about sixty yards.

He said the distance was not more than fourteen hundred yards. . . . He then concluded that the divisions of McLaws and Hood could remain on the defense line; that he would reinforce by divisions of the Third Corps and Pickett's brigades, and stated the point to which the march should be directed. I asked the strength of the column. He stated fifteen thousand. Opinion was then expressed that the fifteen thousand men who could make successful assault over that field had never been arrayed for battle; but he was impatient of listening, and tired of talking, and nothing was left but to proceed. General Alexander was ordered to arrange the batteries of the front of the First and Third Corps. . . .

The director of artillery was asked to select a position on his line from which he could note the effect of his practice, and to advise General Pickett when the enemy's fire was so disturbed as to call for the assault. . . .

General Pickett rode to confer with Alexander, then to the ground upon which I was resting, where he was soon handed a slip of paper. After reading it he handed it to me. It read:

> If you are coming at all, come at once, or I cannot give you proper support, but the enemy's fire has not slackened at all. At least eighteen guns are still firing from the cemetery itself.
>
> ALEXANDER

Pickett said, "General, shall I advance?"

The effort to speak the order failed, and I could only indicate it by an affirmative bow. He accepted the duty with seeming confidence of success, leaped on his horse, and rode gaily to his command. I mounted and spurred for Alexander's post. He reported that the batteries he had reserved for the charge with the infantry had been spirited away by Lee's chief of artillery; that the ammunition of the batteries of position was so reduced that he could not use them in proper support of the infantry. He was ordered to stop the march at once and fill up his ammunition chests. But, alas! there was no more ammunition to be had.

The order was imperative. The Confederate commander had fixed his heart upon the work. Just then a number of the enemy's batteries hitched up and hauled off, which gave a glimpse of unexpected hope. Encouraging messages were sent for the columns to hurry on—and they were then on elastic springing step. The officers saluted as they passed, their stern smiles expressing confidence. Confederate batteries put their fire over the heads of the men as they moved down the slope, and continued to draw the fire of the enemy until the smoke lifted and drifted to the rear, when every gun was turned upon the infantry columns. The batteries that had been drawn off were replaced by others that were fresh. Soldiers and officers began to fall, some to rise no more, others to find their way to the hospital tents. Single files were cut here and there, then the gaps increased, and an occasional shot tore wider openings, but, closing the gaps as quickly as made, the march moved on. . . . The big gaps in the ranks grew until the lines were reduced to half their length. I called [General Fremantle's] attention to the broken, struggling ranks. Trimble mended the battle on the left in handsome style, but on the right the massing of the enemy grew stronger and stronger. Brigadier Garnett was

Gen. George E. Pickett's ringlets of hair, drooping moustache, and goatee reflect his romantic image of the hero. He is most famous, however, for leading the doomed charge at Gettysburg that marked the beginning of the end for the Confederacy.

killed, Kemper and Trimble were desperately wounded; Generals Hancock and Gibbon were wounded. . . .

Pickett's lines being nearer, the impact was heaviest upon them. Most of the field officers were killed or wounded. . . .

General Pickett, finding the battle broken, while the enemy was still reinforcing, called the troops off. There was no indication of panic. The broken files marched back in steady step. The effort was nobly made, and failed from blows that could not be fended. . . .

General Lee was soon with us, and with staff officers and others assisted in encouraging the men and getting them together. . . . When engaged collecting the broken files after the repulse, General Lee said to an officer who was assisting, "It is all my fault."

Sherman's March to the Sea

The Civil War changed not only in its weapons—from smoothbore to rifled muskets—and in its aim—from preserving the Union to freeing the slaves—but also in its targets. As the South fought desperately in the later years of the war, the North decided that only by completely destroying the Southern civilians' will and ability to support the Confederate army could they attain victory. The following is an excerpt from a letter from Gen. William T. Sherman to the mayor and other council members of Atlanta. Sherman had just captured the city, and the council had petitioned him not to force an evacuation of the residents. In his reply, the general outlined his understanding of the new realities of war.

I have your letter of the 11th, in the nature of a petition to revoke my orders removing all the inhabitants from Atlanta. I have read it carefully, and give full credit to your statements of the distress that will be occasioned, and yet shall not revoke my orders, because they were not designed to meet the humanities of the case, but to prepare for the future struggles in which millions of good people outside of Atlanta have a deep interest. We must have peace, not only at Atlanta, but in all America. To secure this, we must stop the war that now desolates our once happy and favored country. To stop war, we must defeat the rebel armies which are arrayed against the law and Constitution that all must respect and obey. To defeat the armies, we must prepare the way to reach them in their recesses, provided with the arms and instruments which enable us to accomplish our purpose. . . .

For four hours I hurried forward on my way to the front of the wagon train and in all that time I was never out of hearing of the groans and cries of the wounded and dying. Scarcely one in a hundred had received adequate surgical aid. . . . Many . . . had been without food for thirty-six hours. Their torn and bloody clothing, matted and hardened, was rasping the tender, inflamed and still oozing wounds. Very few of the wagons even had a layer of straw in them, and all were without springs. The road was rough and rocky. . . . From near every wagon . . . came cries such as these:

"Oh my God, why can't I die?"

"My God, will no one have mercy and kill me?"

"Stop! Oh! For God's sake, stop just one minute, take me out and leave me to die by the roadside. . . ."

No heed could be given to any of their appeals. . . . On! on! We must move on. . . . During this one night I realized more of the horrors of war than I had in the preceding two years.

—Confederate officer's description of the aftermath at Gettysburg, July 1863

Gen. William Tecumseh Sherman, sitting on his horse, reviews his troops as they march by in a demonstration of their strength and victory, under the Union flag they have hung in Savannah, Georgia. Sherman's troops occupied Savannah after laying waste to the Southern countryside in a 175-mile march from Milledgeville aimed at destroying the Southern people's will and ability to support the Confederate army.

You cannot qualify war in harsher terms than I will. War is cruelty, and you cannot refine it; and those who brought war into our country deserve all the curses and maledictions a people can pour out. I know I had no hand in making this war, and I know I will make more sacrifices to-day than any of you to secure peace. But you cannot have peace and a division of our country. If the United States submits to a division now, it will not stop, but will go on until we reap the fate of Mexico, which is eternal war. . . . Once admit the Union, once more acknowledge the authority of the national Government, and, instead of devoting your houses and streets and roads to the dread uses of war, I and this army become at once your protectors and supporters, shielding you from danger, let it come from what quarter it may. . . .

You might as well appeal against the thunder-storm as against these terrible hardships of war. They are inevitable, and the only way the people of Atlanta can hope once more to live in peace and quiet at home, is to stop the war, which can only be done by admitting that it began in error and is perpetuated in pride.

We don't want your negroes, or your horses, or your houses, or your lands, or any thing you have, but we do want and will have a just obedience to the laws of the United States. That we will have, and if it involves the destruction of your improvements, we cannot help it. . . .

But, my dear sirs, when peace does come, you may call on me for any thing. Then will I share with you the last cracker, and watch with you to shield your homes and families against danger from every quarter.

Now you must go, and take with you the old and feeble, feed and nurse them, and build for them, in more quiet places, proper habitations to shield them against the weather until the mad passions of men cool down, and allow the Union and peace once more to settle over your old homes at Atlanta. Yours in haste,

W. T. Sherman, Major-General commanding.

Sherman's famous March to the Sea put his ideas about warfare into practice. Northern soldiers set out to take or destroy the crops and property of Southern civilians as they marched from Atlanta to the coast. In her diary, revised after the war for publication, Dolly Lunt Burge, a widow running her own plantation, describes her encounter with Sherman's army.

[November] 17th [1864]

Have been uneasy all day. At night some of those neighbors called who went to town. Said it was a large force but could not tell what or where they were going. They moved very slow. What shall I do? Where go—

[November] 18th [1864]

Slept very little last night. Went out doors several times. Could see large fires like burning buildings. Am I not in the Hands of a merciful God Who has promised to take care of the widow & the orphan—Sent off two of my mules in the night. Mr. Ward & Frank took them away & hid them. In the morning took a barrel of salt which cost me two hundred dollars into one of the black womens gardens put a paper over it & then on the top of that leached ashes fixed it on a board as a leach tub daubing it with ashes. [This was the old-fashioned way of making lye for soap] Had some few pieces of meat taken from my smoke house Henry & James Around assisting & carried to the old place & hid under some fodder. bid them hide waggon & gear & then go on to ploughing told them to hide all of their things. Went to packing up my & Sadais [Sadai is her daughter] clothes fear that we shall be homeless.

[November] 19th [1864]

Slept in my clothes last night as I heard the Yankees went to neighbor Montgomerys Thursday night at one o clock & searched his house drank his wine took his money &c. &c. As we were not disturbed I after breakfast with Sadai walked up to Mr. Jo Perrys my nearest neighbors where the Yankees were yesterday to learn something of their movements. . . . Accidentally I turned & looked behind me & saw some "blue coats" coming down the hill by old Mrs. Perrys. Said I "I believe there are some now. ". . . I . . . ran

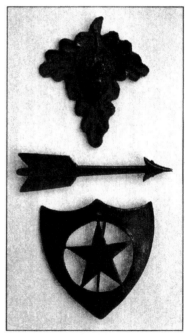

In order to help identify members of the enormous force that he led across the Southern countryside to Atlanta, Georgia, in 1864, Gen. Sherman ordered the men to wear corps badges like these. Members of the 14th Corps of the Army of the Cumberland wore the acorn badge and that army's 20th Corps wore the star. The arrow identified members of the Army of Tennessee's 17th Corps.

"I beg to present you, as a Christmas gift, the city of Savannah, with 150 heavy guns and plenty of ammunition, and also about 25,000 bales of cotton."
—General Sherman, in a telegram to Lincoln, December 21, 1864

home as fast as I could with Sadai. I could hear them holla [holler] Halt, Halt, & their guns in quick succession. Oh God the time of trial has come. . . . I hastened back to my frightened servants & told them they had better hide & then went back to the gate to claim protection & a guard—

But like Demons they rush in. My yards are full. To my smoke house, my Dairy, Pantry, kitchen & cellar like famished wolves they come, breaking locks & whatever is in their way. The thousand pounds of meat in my smoke house is gone in a twinkling my flour my meal, my lard, butter, eggs, pickles of various kinds, both in vinegar & brine. Wine, jars, & jugs, are gone. My eighteen fat turkeys, my hens, chickens & fowls. My young pigs are shot down in my yard, & hunted as if they were the rebels themselves. Uttlerly powerless I came to appeal to the guard. I cannot help you Madam it is the orders. . . . Sherman with a greater portion of his army passed my house all day. All day as its sad moments rolled on were they passing, not only in front of my house, but they came up behind tore down my garden palings, made a road through my back yard & lot field, driving their Stock & riding through tearing down my fences and desolating my home. Wantonly doing it when there was no necessity for it. Such a day if I live to the age of Methusela may God spare me from ever seeing again—.

[November] 20 [1864]
I had watched all night & the dawn found me watching for the moving of the Soldiers that were encamped about us. Oh how I dreaded those that were to pass as I suppose they would complete the ruin that the others had commenced. As I had been repeatedly told that they would burn everything as they passed. . . . They marched directly on none scarcely breaking ranks. A bucket of water was called for & they drank without coming in. About ten o clock they had all passed save one who came in & wanted coffew made which was done & he too went on. A few minutes elapsed & two couriers riding rapidly passed back again they came & this ended the passage of Shermans army by my place leaving me poorer by thirty thousand dollars than I was yesterday morning. And a much stronger rebel.

Although Dolly Burge claimed that Sherman's March strengthened her resolve, for many in the South it marked a gloomy and demoralizing end to their hope for the Confederacy. Indeed, the end was near. Sherman captured Savannah in December 1864.

From there, Sherman marched through the Carolinas, wreaking even more destruction than he had in Georgia. Charleston, the very heart of the Confederacy, fell to Sherman on February 18, 1865. A black regiment reached the city first, to the cheers of the local African-American population. Petersburg, Virginia, went down on April 2, and then, on April 3, the Confederates evacuated their capital, Richmond, leaving the victorious Union army to march in.

Thomas M. Chester was a reporter for the *Philadelphia Press* who was with the first Union regiments to enter Richmond. He described the events as follows.

. . . Every regiment tried to be first. All cheerfully moved off with accelerated speed. The pickets which were on the line during the night were in the advance.

Brevet Brigadier General Draper's brigade of colored troops, Brevet Major General Krautz's division, were the first infantry to enter Richmond. . . .

Along the road which the troops marched, or rather double quicked, batches of negroes were gathered together testifying by unmistakable signs their delight at our coming. Rebel soldiers who had hid themselves when their army moved came out of the bushes, and gave themselves up as disgusted with the service. The haste of the rebels was evident in guns, camp equipage, telegraph wires, and other army property which they did not have time to burn. . . .

There were many persons in the better-class houses who were peeping out of the windows, and whose movements indicated that they would need watching in the future. There was no mistaking the curl of their lips and the flash of their eyes. . . .

The citizens stood gaping in wonder at the splendidly-equipped army marching along under the graceful folds of the old flag. Some waved their hats and women their hands in token of gladness. The pious old negroes, male and female, indulged in such expressions: "You've come at last"; "We've been looking for you these many days"; "Jesus has opened the way"; "God bless you"; "I've not seen that old flag for four years"; "It does my

African-American residents rejoice as the 55th Massachusetts Colored Infantry, a regiment of black Union soldiers, marches into what remains of Charleston after retreating Confederate soldiers set the city ablaze. Some of the black soldiers had been slaves in Charleston not long before, and they marched in singing "John Brown's Body."

eyes good"; "Have you come to stay?"; "Thank God", and similar expressions of exultation.

Samuel Cormany, a Union soldier from Pennsylvania, wrote in his diary about the final days of the war. After the fall of Richmond, his cavalry regiment was ordered to pursue Lee's fleeing troops in order to prevent them from joining up with Gen. Joseph Johnston's army.

April 9, 1865 Sunday. We had a late supper about midnight—good fresh mutton, and potatoes—biscuit—milk & Coffee—Slept til about 6 AM and had a dandy breakfast akin to supper—and at 8 A.M. mounted and moved out, and soon met the Enemy in force—A general engagement seemed pending—The rebel Cavalry fell back before us, and on our right, our Infantry and Artillery seemed to be forming into line. . . . The enemy cavalry disappeared from our front, and our regiment was ordered to dismount. . . . So our dismounted men . . . formed in line of battle our right connecting with the Infantry line—our men lying on the open ground about 4 or 5 feet apart—each one capable to shoot 13 times without re-loading—and instructed to hold his place at all hazzards—we were to hold our line by all means. . . .

I heard the enemys coming—one could see their double line—with steady tread, but they saw us not—lying on the ground—but a quick Attention! Fire at Will! Rang out, and our line opened—with deadly aim—and volley after volley was poured into the approaching lines with terrible effect—

In vain their Officers tried to hold their men—and keep advancing—Too many fell, and too many others wounded fell back—and then too, the lay of the ground would occasion all but well taught & drilled shooters to shoot too high—overshoot. This was their failure—But they came on—in some fashion—til some were quite close—The cloud of smoke was blinding—our men knew no faltering—but with a yell, as if to Charge—many arose—using their revolvers, and

Using broadsides like this, Confederate commissary chief Gen. Isaac St. John launched a campaign to bring in more food for Lee's army, which faced possible starvation in the last months of the war. Officials reported that the campaign brought immediate results, but the rebels' lack of supplies was too serious to fix with deliveries of corn and beans.

TO THE CITIZENS OF
LYNCHBURG AND CAMPBELL CO.

→ • ••• ←

LYNCHBURG, February 28th, 1865.

The undersigned, by authority of the Commissary General, solicits IMMEDIATE supplies for the army, of BACON, PORK, BEEF, FLOUR, WHEAT, CORN, CORN MEAL, BEANS, PEAS and DRIED FRUIT—either as donations, loans or sales. The department gives assurance that loans will be returned in kind as soon as practicable, and all purchases will be paid for in Government Certificates which, by a recent and special act of Congress, are redeemable in taxes.

The undersigned have full authority to fix the prices of all articles delivered in their district, which will be determined in reference to the fair market and not schedule rates. They are prepared to make contracts for future as well as present deliveries.

OUR ARMY IS IN WANT—Nothing further need be said to a Virginian.

JOHN ROBIN McDANIEL,
BOLING CLARK,
RICHARD MORGAN.

now the scattering enemy broke to the rear, across the little rise of ground—leaving many dead wounded and dying I ran along our line ordering "Men! Load up quickly—Carbines first—Bully! Boys! You never flinched a bit. You may have to do it again, but you Cant do it better"—I returned to the Captain—reported what I had done and he fairly flooded us with praise "Bully!" was his word—We could now hear the enemy on the job of rallying—and could easily understand how difficult was their task. Again, I ran along the line with "They'll come again—Do as before. Don't fire til you have the command, but remember the lay of the land—and just exactly where the chests of the bodies are and aim there &c" and soon, on they came—steadily—over the rise—and into view—next again the Command—and the boys poured in as before, and the enemy overshot as before—and their retreat again was as much or more of a skedaddle and our boys fairly followed them but were commanded to re-load to the limiit—as they may obtain reinforcements—and try us harder—"But Boys we must hold at all hazzards". . . now our Regiment is soon mounted again, and in Column of fours, moving towards the left. . . .

The Command now given to our Brigade was "Prepare to Charge!" "Draw Saber." Every Sabre was bare. Just then! Away! Far! Off! To our right our ears caught the sound of Cheering—But the command came "Forward—Guide Right—March!" and the brigade—en masse moves steadily—slowly—men clasp the hilt of the sword tensely—awaiting the final "CHARGE!" to be given But a moment and it was given a great line of the enemy now appeared out from the woods—a few shots were being fired by 1st Maine— The cheering on our right became plainer. The Brigade Charge started—Now a staff officer, on a black Horse—came dashing up towards the Brigade Head Q[uarters] Flag exclaiming "For Gods sake Stop that Charge!"—an occasional shot still goes off—The Rebels show the white flag, and Their Bugle blows "Cease firing" and Ours blows the HALT! And all is quiet in an instant—

O what a lull! What a wondering Why?—Flags of Truce meet—What's up? The News! "Generals Grant and Lee are counselling"—Next Comes the Cry, "LEE SURRENDERS!"

"Ye Gods!" What cheering comes along in waves from far off to the right, becoming more intense as taken up by those commands nearer to us. Now our Brigade lets loose more fully as the news is confirmed. Hats and caps uplifted on the points of Sabers are whirled and waved overhead—and with tearful voices—Scores of overjoyed men exclaim "Now I can go home to Wife Babies Mother Sister Sweetheart, and our Country is forever safe—"

Stonewall Jackson

Thomas "Stonewall" Jackson of Virginia was one of the Confederacy's most famous generals. He acquired his nickname at the first Battle of Bull Run, when his troops were holding well against a strong Union attack, and Gen. Barnard Bee, trying to rally his own failing South Carolinian brigade shouted "Look! There is Jackson standing like a stone wall! Rally behind the Virginians!" At the Battle of Chancellorsville in May 1863, a Confederate company—mistaking Jackson in nighttime darkness for an attacking Union force—wounded him. Jackson's left arm was amputated, and Lee, upon hearing the fate of his star commander, said "He has lost his left arm; but I have lost my right arm." A few days later, Jackson died of pneumonia. His obituary in the Southern Illustrated News read:

Day before yesterday, at Lexington, in the very heart of Virginia, there was committed to the earth the inanimate remains of one of the most remarkable men of his time. Many beautiful and affecting tributes have been rendered to his lofty character and his immeasurable services, which are yet but a most inadequate expression of the public grief; and we might well hesitate, when the pens of ready writers have failed to set forth the genius and worth of the hero and the love and sorrow which have followed him to the tomb, to write one line upon an event at once so august and so appalling as that single death. But we can write of nothing else. The wailing music of the funeral dirge is still sounding in our ears; we still see the ghastly plumes nodding above the bier; and when we endeavor to direct our thoughts to subjects such as ordinarily engage us in these columns, the mournful calamity, in all its weight of woe, rushes back upon us, and excludes every other consideration. . . .

He followed no star, he sought no throne, he asked no earthly guerdon, was guided by no selfish consideration, and lured by no vulgar ambition. Duty, and duty alone, was the principle of his conduct. He recognized a call to fight for Virginia in her hour of agony, and he obeyed it.

Chapter Six

This Sad War Is a Bad Thing

When soldiers went off to war, the world they left behind inevitably changed. Families lost fathers, husbands and sons, who were also their primary breadwinners. Businesses lost employees and customers. Entire towns lost large portions of their male populations. Both the North and the South dealt with steep inflation and record numbers of newly indigent families. Communities everywhere did their best to help feed, clothe, and care for their soldiers, but this soon represented a major strain on their resources, particularly in the South.

The war's impact on the Southern home front was far more dramatic overall. Armies marched through plantations and killed each other in farmers' backyards. As slaves fled to Union lines, the Northern army destroyed not only farmland and men, but the entire social structure of each community it passed through. For whites it was a time of upheaval, uncertainty, and great bitterness, while for African Americans the chaos of the moment was entwined with the joy of their newfound freedom.

The war changed the lives of just about everyone who remained at home, but in some ways the impact on women was most profound. In both the North and the South, thousands of women suddenly had to support their families and run the family farm or business. They faced loneliness and near constant worry about their loved ones in the army. When the dreaded message of a relative's death reached them, they struggled to accept and make sense of their loss.

The Civil War drew on the resources and the strength of those who remained at home. As many contemporaries commented, their efforts were nearly as essential to the war as those of the soldiers themselves. Some women garnered a sense of accomplishment and pride in the work they did for the army or in maintaining their family through the country's crisis. Others were simply grateful to return as much as

Black and white residents of Richmond huddle through the night in the capitol square after Lee evacuates the city and leaves it in flames on April 2, 1865. The despondency on the faces of the whites reflects their knowledge that the fall of the capital marks the end of the Confederacy.

possible to the way things were before the war, once the fighting was over. For some, the destruction of family, friends, home, and property overwhelmed any sense of pride and precluded any return to normalcy. For many white Southerners, the bitterness of defeat left them filled only with a sense of desperation, disappointment, and failure.

Letters Home

Men who joined the army, especially after the first Battle of Bull Run, knew that they might never see their families again. Nevertheless, they tried to maintain as much normalcy as they could in their relationships by writing letters as often as possible. Today, historians treasure letters between soldiers and their families as one of the best sources for understanding what it was like to live through the Civil War. Soldiers described their life in camp, and tried to convey what it felt like to be in a battle. Wives and mothers and children wrote about the changes in their lives at home, asked for advice about farming or money, and reassured the soldiers that they were not being forgotten. The following selection of letters between L. Merrit Anderson, his wife, Melissa, and their children, Clark and Lodema, during his year of service from 1864 until the end of the war, reveal the good humor and love that one family managed to maintain through the trial of their separation.

Sept 25, 1864

Well Merrit I supose you will expect a few lines from me but you know my failings . . . it has bin the lonesomost two weeks that I ever experienced but little did I know what my feelings would be till I was deprived of your company I feel I am alone although surrounded with friends and home but I must try and [resign] myself to my lot it is a great comfort to me to take your likeness and sit down and could they speak they would say old woman dry up those tears. it is now Monday morning and we are all alive I have commenced my spining but I dont know how fast I shall get along. Br Smiths folks have bin to make me a visit and Monroes folks Mother Malvina and Melinda was here soon after you left they thought you would bee to home on a furlow but wer dissapointed well I must close for it is time for breakfast I wish you was here to eat with us but keep good courage serve good and we shall meet again rite as often as you can Melissa

Home from the war after his initial three-month enlistment has expired, a soldier father informs his young son that he will "jest have a cup of tea and be off again!" to reenlist in the army for a three-year stint. Many families faced severe hardships during these long separations.

Oct 2, 1864

. . . I have bin gone from home a bout one month and I have got but one letter I shall have to punch you up with a sharp stick if you do not do bet[ter] I want to here from home twice a weke not because I am home sick but because it is natural (that is what) a word to the wise is sufficient. . . . tell me about the meeting and the new preachers and whare the old ones are and all the news how are pola-ticks their I should like to read a paper from home . . . keepe things strait have you found whare you will live this winter I want the Children to go to school with out fail. . . .

Oct 11, 1864

How do you do old woman to day what are you doing stubing around I supose as usual bare footed with your sleeves roled up it seams as if I could see you going out to milk or to feede the pigs how do you get along with your spinning have you bin up to Monroes since I left do not stay at home to close I am a fraid you will grow poor and run dow[n] but do not work to hard keepe good courage time is passing soon I shall be at home if the good lord is willing then we will get a little home and take comfort and spend our remaining day to the honor and glory of God and in the enjoyment of each other society you may want to know how I like soldiering I will tell you I have had a little experience in it I like it as well as I expected I never thought it was verry nice and I am not disapointed. . . . I want you to answer evry letter I send will you not pray for mee.

Oct 14, 1864

dear pa I write evry chance that I can get I am so anxious to write that I do write very often lizzy is here she has come to stay you must nd think it strange of my writing so often it is friday night and we are all in uncle Alansons room all but ma and aunt merit is in your room uncle Alanson has gone to town byron me and lizzie are all writing byron is writing to you lizzie is writing to one of her friends i do not know his name is that she is a riting to i spoke a peace to day at school it was the lamb in my lulaby book ma has been diging potatoes to dry . . . and she is pretty tired to night to pay for it thats what my shoes sqeak so loud that i am

"The Soldier's Vision," a wartime song, helped give voice to the feelings of sol-diers longing for home. Published sheet music formed the basis for a widespread form of entertainment as families and friends gathered around pianos to sing, providing each other with support in hard times and gaiety in better ones.

ashamed of their squeaking . . . ma is pounding salt to salt her butter squated down on the flore and aunt Dorit is siting by the stove kniting and pa i want to here you you had better believe that but i have one of your photographs and i half to kiss it it does me a good deal of good but still it is nd you nor near it hey pa . . . but it has to do . . . Lodema.

Feb 17, 1865

. . . Lodema I have sent you a paper and two little Books which I hope you will get you must bee a good girl and help ma all you can and write to me often tell me how billey and the cows get a long and the Pig if you keep him yet and the hens do they lay write often and all tell all the news. my love to all

. . . Lodema you want a new Dress wall I think you must have one if this Letter reaches you I will send you two Dollars I am a fraid it will not get you one but if it does not I will send you more. . . . Attend to it old woman and get her a Dress . . . .

April 16, 1865

it is with feelings of intense anxiety old man that I sit down to pen a few lines to you not knowing where you are or wat your situation may be but I hope and pray that you are all write if you are I shall feel it is in answer to prayer we have heard that the boys from around heare was all write but I fear it is to good news I hope the ware is about done and the soldiers return home in Peace. . . . I have not mutch news to rite but if I could see you we could find enough to talk about it seems as though I could not wait till I can see you O may the time soon come write soon

April 18, 1865

my good old woman a short chat with you you must keepe up good Courage and not get down harted do not worry about me but let us look up from whence cometh all our help I am glad their is help their and just what we need. . . . [H]ow long they will keep us here I cannot tell. . . . [A]t all events the fighting is over I expect in these parts try and keepe up good Courage how is that humor in your blood have you got it checked do not neglect to attend to it and write all you can find time to write. . . . Lodema, . . . take good Cair of the hens so I can have some eggs when I get home.

[No Date]

Absent but not forgotten companion and friend with me through the rough journey of life I am again seated to have a short chat with you. . . . [Y]ou wrote in your last leter you thought you would soon be at home I hope it will be so for it would be a happy time to us I dare not let my animated feelings rise to high for fear they will fall in dissapointment I hope not I dreamed last night I got the news that they had sent you futher south and I was crying so hard that I awoke O may it not be a reality but let us keep up good courage hoping soon to meet again. I have bin very busy this week geting things settled in our new house it is a pleasant place to live in if you were here we could take comfort I hope the day will soon come when the oft repeated wish that Pa was here will be granted and the presence of one whose absence has long bin felt will again make mery and glad hearts. . . . I must close when I get to writing I dont now when to stop it is some comfort to write if I cant see you forget me not till death.

Evidence suggests that L. Merrit Anderson made it home later that summer. In other, more tragic cases, the family eagerly awaiting another letter from their brother, husband, or son at war would receive one like the following, from Thomas Nickerson to Mrs. Bullock, the mother of his friend John, a fellow soldier from a Rhode Island regiment. John Bullock had apparently been illiterate.

Fort Seward, Bay Point, South Carolina
January 19, 1862

From a Friend,
Dear Woman I now set down with a broken heart to inform you of your Dear unfortunate Son, which died on Saturday January 18th. 1862. he had been sick about three weeks and at the time we shifted our quarters a crossed the river we were oblidge to leave him on acount of his being so lo. but we took it very hard in leaving him for we thought every thing of him. he was as nice and as good hearted a young man as we had in our Regiment. and i do not think i would of missed one of my own Brothers anymore than i do him for he always was willing to divied the last mouthfull of any thing he had among his friends or even his enimys. he was a deedful good hearted fellow and our offesers thought every thing of him and i myself has roat him a great many letters to send to you. and he used to bring me his letters which he recived from you and have me to read them, and by the letters which i have seen that came from you i take you to bee a very nice Woman and it apears that you are a poor Woman as well as my own Mother and a great many others and therefore i made a motion last night for

This anonymous young couple posed together for the photographer just before the husband went off to war. Husbands and wives faced inevitable changes in their relationships when the men left, and the strong possibility that the men would never return.

our Company to put in one dollar a piece and have a head stone put to the head of his grave and what ever there is left to bee sent to you and use it as you think proper. in the first place i made a motion to have a head and foot stone but out Capt. and the Col. thought as he was a going to buried so far from home that a nice board with letters painted in grand stile would answer full as well as if it were stone and it would not cost near so much.

now Mrs. Bullock i am agoing to tel you and i am a going to do just the same by your Son as i would if it was eather of my Brothers which i have got here. in the first place perhaps we shall raise to the amount of $75. dollars or more. well if we should send to New York or some other place which would bee far from here and get a head and foot stone it would perhaps take the most part of the Money, but if we get some man right a round here to make a nice head board and have the letters painted in good shape it would not cost more that $10. dollars and what ever would be left it would do you a great deal more good aspecialy such times as we are haveing at present. John was a great friend of myne and i would do every thing i could for him, and i hope that you will not take so hard as to make you sick, for i think and earnestly pray to the lord that he has got out of this hard life and got into a far better world. we have not got our pay yet and do not know how soon we shall but we are a going to draw up a paper and sign our names to it and when our pay day comes we are to let our Capt have one dollar a peice. it is true that the most of our own folks are poor and needy, but still we are willing to do all we can towards this matter and i for one am shure it will do me $50 dollars worth of good to put in the sum of one dollar, and i hope that nothing will happen but every man in the Co will put his dollar in when our pay days comes. Mr. Simmons is well at present and is one of our cooks. there is but few that are sick in our Co, and i hope that there will not be an other such a thing to occur in our Co or even in the Regiment while i am in the service for it creates a dredful bad feeling amoung us, and another thing it is impossible to send a corps from here to R.I.

my Father has turned out quite a number of soldiers out of his family and he has also come himself i went out in the first R.I. Regt. and i had a Brother in the same Co. also one in the second R.I. Regt and three cousins and we were in the fight at Bulls Run. no one got hirt exsept my Brother in the second R.I. he had a small piece shot of the end of his finger. then i came home and took my Father and two of my Brothers and came out in the Co which i am now in a present. i have also got a Brother in law and a cousin in the same Co. with me. so you see if we have a battle that we stand a narrow chance to all get of[f] without some of us being hirt.

i am in hopes that this war will soon be over and we poor soldiers return to our homes where our folks are now sheding teers for us. i will now close by saying this is from a friend of your Son.

Mr. Thomas O. Nickerson

Soldiers' Families Struggle

Sometimes families found it too difficult to support themselves without the men who usually ran the farm or family business. While white soldiers were supposed to be paid $13 per month, their pay was often delayed, sometimes for many months. In other cases soldiers spent or gambled most of their money away, and so had little to send home. Occasionally the money they did send home through the mail never made it, being either lost or stolen on the way. Often cities and towns set up relief funds for the families of soldiers, but these never provided very generous amounts, and thousands of families struggled. Many women wrote letters to various officials, including the secretary of war and the President, outlining their troubles and asking or demanding help. Most often what they wanted was a discharge, or at least a furlough, for their husband or son.

The following letter from Hattie Carr of North Evans, New York, to President Lincoln is such a request. She refers to the law that said that if a son had enlisted in the army without the knowledge or consent of his parents, and he was under 18, his parents could request a discharge for him. Carr is careful to paint herself as a patriot who supports the war, but as a woman who needs her husband back nonetheless.

January 29, 1864

Abraham Lincoln, Honored Sir,

I come with a request trusting that out of the goodness of your heart you will grant it. It is but a breath with you. While to me [it is] as life and death. I beg you for the discharge of my Husband. . . . He has faithfully served our common cause for eighteen long months, while I have struggled with sickness and poverty at times[.] I can do that no longer, for I am sick—dying, for the sight of that dear face[.] I can labor no more and I could starve I am alone and friendless. . . . I know there is no law in my favor—

This envelope, sent at Christmastime, is decorated with symbols of Union patriotism and military strength. A well-dressed soldier stands armed and at attention before artillery. The Stars and Stripes tops an army tent in the background.

allows a mother a right to her only son, why can I not have my only friend? My Husband to support me and comfort me, the little time I have to stay. . . . I am a Loyal woman. I love our Dear old flag—I bade my Husband go forth and support it. Now I would beg that he may come to me and that I may live. Will you turn a deaf ear to my prayer, or will your kind heart bid you help me. Hoping and trusting that you will be kind to me,

    I am truly a daughter of the old Flag,

    Hattie L. Carr

In response to Hattie Carr's letter, Lt. Col. John Higgins wrote the President:

I can see no reason why the man should be discharged. We probably have a great many men in the regiment whose families are no better provided for than this man's and should you commence discharging men for such reasons I think there would be no end to it and would cause us a great deal of trouble and injury.

Women Join the Workforce

For many women, the loss of their family's main breadwinner meant that for the first time ever they entered the paid workforce. In both the North and the South prior to the war, it was generally believed that women should not work outside the home. Of course this applied mainly to white middle- and upper-class women. Southern whites certainly had no qualms about black women working, and Northerners did not hesitate to hire white and black women to work as servants. During the war, many women who had not worked for wages before found it impossible to remain housewives because their families were starving. But there were very

few jobs that were considered acceptable for women. The majority of women who worked for wages during the war became seamstresses, sewing uniforms for the soldiers. At first the federal government hired them directly. Over time, middlemen began buying up large lots of material from the government and hiring women to sew it into uniforms. These middlemen, or contractors, usually paid the women just half of what the government had originally offered. As wartime inflation made these wages less and less valuable, sewing women began to protest. They petitioned the government for higher wages, and some even formed unions.

The following is an excerpt from "Song of the Working-women," a poem by Mrs. Ann S. Stephens that appeared in *Fincher's Trades Review*, a newspaper aimed at the working classes. She draws a sharp picture of the subcontractors from the perspective of the starving women they employed.

Then we plead that as gold goes higher
Our fuel is rising too—
That our hearths lack warmth and fire;
And the sewing that we can do
With all our weary, toilsome stitching,
With all our tears and pain,
With our desolate midnight watching,
Is worse, oh worse, than in vain.
Work! Work! Work! is still the answering cry,
'Heap coal and wine in our cellars—
    poor women were born to die.'

In this letter to her brother William, Mary Cooper of Philadelphia describes how she earned money by sewing "soldier coats" while her grandmother watched her baby, Annabella.

Bill you gave me fits for not writing to you before but I have been so busy that i have not had time to write to any body I am at work on the Soldier Coats and we have to work day and night on them until the contract is filled and that will not be for three months yet so the foreman says I make out first-rate at them I made nearly three dollars last week and last Sunday and Thanksgiving day. I have a good bit of work in the house to do besides and I set up at night late to do it. . . . Grandmother has just come in with the baby she has had her out all the evening. . . . Annnabella is kicking and laughing so that she shakes me so I cant write.

Some husbands did not approve of their wives working. Samuel Alexander realized the necessity of his wife Agnes's income, but he made clear his opposition to her employment, and his frustration that the Union government was not providing more assistance to the families of soldiers.

I am Sorry to the Heart that a wife of mine should have to sew or do any kind of work for other People if I had some of them Abolitionists by the neck I would make them keep there promises about keeping the Soldiers' wives.

Some men worried that, as their wives learned to take care of themselves and their families, they would not need them as much when the men returned home. While they admired their wives for their strength and resilience, they sometimes felt uncertain what their own role would be when they got home. In this letter to his wife, Albert Rake reveals that, beneath his teasing tone, he is experiencing some of this unease.

June 15th, 1863

O Dear, My Darling dumpling but you must of bin mad by the way you sent that letter back again with the two dollars in well my Dear Honney I am verry much oblige to you for your kindness but you shouldn't get so spunky or I shall be afraid to come home again I had thought some of coming home next monnth but if you rave and pich [sic] so I shall be afraid to come but I guess you will not be so verry dangerous after all if I should stay here til then I shall try it enny how well my dear Darling I have left Arlington Lane. . . . I will close by sending you a grate big kiss my Dear little spunky wife.

The Volunteer Effort

Women who did not have to worry about earning their daily bread still wanted to help the war effort, and many of them did so by joining ladies' aid societies. These voluntary associations formed in villages, towns, and cities all across the North and South as soon as the war began. Some were small, informal gatherings of women who came together in the first heady weeks, to can a few peaches and knit some socks before disbanding. Others grew into grand institutions like the Ladies Aid Society of Philadelphia, which by 1863

estimated that it had received and distributed more than $60,000 worth of goods. It was through the work of ladies' aid societies that the U.S. Sanitary Commission raised a large proportion of its money and gathered the necessary supplies for hospitals and soldiers.

In September 1861, Ellen Orbison Harrison, the secretary of the Ladies' Aid Society of Philadelphia, drafted the following "Appeal to the Ladies of Pennsylvania, New Jersey, and Delaware" to encourage women in those states to prepare food and supplies for the soldiers. She also wanted to make relief efforts more organized and efficient, and therefore urged women to send their goods through her organization, rather than sending them directly to the soldiers themselves.

The Ladies' Aid of Phila[delphia] after a personal inspection by its Officers of the Hospitals in and near Washington, find there a pressing and needful work, which cannot be demanded or expected from the regular authorities, but is especially adapted to the sphere of woman's attention.

Rooms have been furnished them at Washington by the Government as a Depository of such Hospital stores as may be entrusted to their care—the Apt. Secretary of war; the Surgeon General, and the Surgeons of the different Hospitals have

Merchants ran magazine advertisements for products such as artificial limbs, packets of stationery, "segars" and tobacco, and needles, buttons, and thread—all important items to soldiers during the war.

Sailors play backgammon on the deck of the Monitor. *Some soldiers gambled away their earnings, leaving their families in dire circumstances.*

engaged to assist their benevolent efforts. The superintendence of ladies of undoubted loyalty and efficiency, and the aid of kind and judicious nurses has been secured; and every facility afforded them for reaching those who are suffering from wounds and diseases incurred in the defence of our Government.

We ask the Ladies of Penna. and adjacent states to form themselves into local committees for the purpose of making or collecting such things as are needful for wounded or sick soldiers, and notify us accordingly, that they may become a part of our organization. They will then be furnished with a detailed account of our operations and any interesting incidents connected therewith.

Messages and enquiries from Parents, wives, and sisters to their loved ones will secure attention; for the kindly influence of such home remembrances cannot but prove beneficial to mind and body.

Donations for particular regiments will, so far as practicable, be applied to their benefit.

A regard for those who are now found in the Hospitals should secure for this appeal a prompt and cheerful response; and in view of impending conflicts, when thousands more will be thrown upon beds of suffering and death, every day's inaction in the quiet of our homes, seems like criminal neglect. . . .

The services of all connected with this work are voluntary and without remuneration.

Contributions of food or clothing such as Woolen Clothes of all kinds, feather pillows and bed clothing, jellies, dried fruits, apple butter, crackers, white sugar, tea, chocolate, butter (well prepared) farinaceous preparations, spices, pickles, dried beef, hams, oil of lemons, etc. etc., should be marked "Ladies Aid, Hospital Stores" and send freight prepaid to the care of John. P. Rhoads, no. 701 Walnut Street, Philadelphia.

Donations of money, which can be sent to any of the officers, will be applied with care and economy to the purchase of such things as may be found serviceable.

Inflation

While many people in the North suffered undeniably during the war, through loss of income and family members, in general their lot was not as harsh as those of men and women in the South. The Union had set up a naval blockade at the beginning of the war that effectively isolated the South from the rest of the world. This meant that the Confederacy had difficulty importing goods from the North or Europe. Although blockade runner's ships specially designed to evade the Northern navy continued to bring in some goods, shortages and steep inflation plagued the South during the course of the war. In the three months after Gettysburg and Vicksburg, prices rose 58 percent. While the very wealthy could, in some cases, maintain their standard of living for a while, for most simply finding the necessities for everyday living became a struggle.

In her diary, young Sarah Morgan Dawson of Louisiana revealed the effort involved in finding a pair of shoes in the spring of 1862.

May 21st 1862

I have had such a search for shoes this week that I am disgusted with shopping. I am triumphant now, for after traversing town in every direction and finding nothing, I finally discovered a pair of *boots* just made for a little negro to go fishing with, and only an inch and a half too long for me, besides being unbendable; but I seized them with avidity, and the little negro would have been outbid if I had not soon after discovered a pair more seemly, if not more serviceable, which I took without further difficulty. Behold my tender feet cased in crocodile skin, patent-leather tipped, low-quarter boy's shoes, No. 2! "What a fall was there, my country," from my pretty English glove-kid, to sabots made of some animal closely connected with the hippopotamus!

Before the Civil War, Sarah Morgan was accustomed to wearing fine clothes. Like many other wealthy Southern women, Morgan would soon have to adjust her wardrobe to the harsh realities brought on by shortages and inflation.

For many people, though, the lack of stylish shoes was the least of their problems; they faced near-starvation. All across the South, people lost patience and took matters into their own hands. A series of food riots shocked observers in the Confederacy.

One of the largest took place in the Confederate capital, Richmond, Virginia. By 1863 refugees and other people seeking factory work had swelled Richmond's population from 38,000 to approximately 100,000. There was not enough food to go around, and what was available was outrageously expensive. Defying Southern expectations that women be apolitical, submissive, and quiet, white working-class women (many of whom were married to Confederate soldiers) marched through the city on April 2 and, demanding government aid, broke into warehouses and stores and took food and clothing. The riot was squelched when Confederate President Jefferson Davis ordered the public guard to shoot the women if they did not disperse in five minutes. But in Richmond and many other cities, the women succeeded in forcing the government to take more notice of the problems of poor people and to set up a better system for dispersing food, fuel, and clothing to the needy.

Sara Agnes Rice Pryor included the following letter from her friend Agnes, dated April 4, 1863, in a book called *Reminiscences of Peace and War*, published in 1905. In the letter, Agnes describes her impressions of the scene in Richmond during the bread riot.

Something very sad has just happened in Richmond—something that makes me ashamed of all my jeremiads over the loss of the petty comforts and conveniences of life—hats, bonnets, gowns, stationery, books, magazines, dainty food. . . .

Yesterday, upon arriving [at the Capitol Square] I found within the gates a crowd of women and boys—several hundreds of them, standing quietly together. I sat on a bench near, and one of the number left the rest and took the seat beside me. She was a pale, emaciated girl, not more than eighteen. . . . 'I could stand no longer,' she exclaimed. . . . As she raised her hand to remove her sunbonnet, her loose calico sleeve slipped up, and revealed a mere skeleton of an arm. She perceived my expression as I looked at it, and hastily pulled down her sleeve with a short laugh. 'This is all that's left of me!' she said. 'It seems real funny don't it?' . . . I was encouraged to ask: 'What is it? Is there some celebration?'

Mr. Davis mounted the dray . . . and made a brief address to the formidable crowd of both sexes, urging them to abstain from their lawless acts. He reminded them of how they had taken jewelry and finery instead of supplying themselves with bread, for the lack of which they claimed they were suffering. He concluded by saying: "You say you are hungry and have no money. Here is all I have; it is not much, but take it." He then, emptying his pockets, threw all the money they contained among the mob, after which he took out his watch and said: "We do not desire to injure anyone, but this lawlessness must stop. I will give you five minutes to disperse, otherwise you will be fired on." The order was given for the company to prepare for firing, and the grim, resolute old Captain . . . gave his men the command: "Load!" The muskets were then loaded with buck and ball cartridges, with strict observance of military usage, and everyone could see that when this stern commander received orders to fire he intended to shoot to kill. The mob evidently fully realized this fact, and at once began to disperse, and before five minutes had expired the trouble was over, and the famous misnamed bread riot was at an end.

—Varina Howell Davis, on Jefferson Davis's speech to the bread rioters, in *Jefferson Davis, Ex-President of the Confederate States of America: A Memoir by His Wife*, 1890

'There is,' said the girl, solemnly; 'we celebrate our right to live. We are starving. As soon as enough of us get together we are going to the bakeries and each of us will take a loaf of bread. That is little enough for the government to give us after it has taken all our men.'. . .

The girl turned to me with a wan smile, as she rose to join the long line that now formed and was moving, she said simply, 'Good-bye! I'm going to get something to eat!'. . .

The mob now rapidly increased, and numbered, I am sure, more than a thousand women and children. It grew and grew until it reached the dignity of a mob—a bread riot. They impressed all the light carts they met, and marched along silently and in order. They marched through Cary Street and Main, visiting the stores of speculators and emptying them of their contents. Governor Letcher sent the Mayor to read the Riot Act, and as this had no effect he threatened to fire on the crowd. The city battalion came up. The women fell back with frightened eyes, but did not obey the order to disperse. The President then appeared, ascended a dray, and addressed them. It is said that he was received at first with hisses from the boys, but after he had spoken some little time with great kindness and sympathy, the women quietly moved on, taking their food with them. . . . While I write women and children are still standing in the streets, demanding food, and the government is issuing them rations of rice.

This is a frightful state of things. I am telling you of it because *not one word* has been said in the newspapers about it. . . .

Although the Confederacy tried to censor newspaper coverage of the Richmond bread riots, this image made it into Frank Leslie's Illustrated News. *The depiction of the women combines condemnation of them as violent, crazed figures and a hint of sympathy for their plight, showing them as thin, ragged, barefoot, and in one case, carrying a baby.*

The Peculiar Institution Falls Apart

What often upset slaveholders about the chaos of the war, even more than the loss of property, was the loss of their accustomed sense of superiority and safety. From the very beginning of the war, as slaves fled to Union lines, and especially after the Emancipation Proclamation took effect, Southern whites watched hopelessly as the whole structure of their

Richmond, April 2, 1863
To the Richmond Press:

GENTLEMEN: The unfortunate distur-
bance which occurred today in this city is
so liable to misconstruction and misrepresenta-
tion abroad that I am desired by the Secretary
of War to make a special appeal to the editors
and reporters of the press at Richmond, and
earnestly request them to avoid all reference
directly or indirectly to the affair. The reasons
for this are so obvious that it is unnecessary to
state them, and the Secretary indulges the
hope that his own views on this connection
will be approved by the press generally. Any
other course must tend to embarrass our cause,
and to encourage our enemies in their inhu-
man policy.

Very respectfully, &c.,
Jno Withers
Assistant Adjutant-General

society fell apart. Having deluded themselves for so long that blacks were happy as slaves and loyal and devoted to their white families, many whites were genuinely shocked and thoroughly embittered when these same slaves took the first opportunity to escape to freedom. In many cases, whites tried to send their slaves far away from the approaching armies, especially to Texas where they would be far from the fighting, in order to keep them from being freed by the Yankees.

This letter from W. D. Branford, a slave-owning Mississip-pi captain in the Confederate army, reveals the impact of the approaching U.S. army on his hometown. His plea for a 30-day furlough was granted, demonstrating the Confederacy's recognition of his desire to safeguard his property, as well as his suggestion that he might be able to recruit new soldiers. While his wife may have rejoiced at his homecoming, his slaves probably grieved at their lost chance to escape to the Union lines.

Camp French [Va.] Dec[ember] 13th, 1862

General, I have the honor to ask for thirty days leave of
absence, to visit the Town of Pontotoc in the state of Mississippi,
for the following reasons: viz,

I. I reside at Pontotoc Miss, and have just been informed by letters from my family that the enemy is encamped within 18 miles of
that place, and is expected to take possession of it, in a Short time,
and that most of the citizens have removed their families, and
property, in order to avoid their being captured; leaving that Section of Country, almost entirely to the mercy of Runaway Slaves,
and reckless Straglers from our army, and that the enemy is devastating the country wherever they go, taking all of the male slaves
by force, if they do not accompany them willingly. All of the above
Statements are *true* or they would not have been made to me, for
they are the first words of complaint, that I have heard from my
home since I last saw it, (on the 26th day of August 1861).

My family is a helpless one, (consisting of a mother, and five
little children) and has now, to rely *alone*, on the labor of fifteen or
twenty Slaves for its support, without any person (except my wife,
who is *entirely unaccustomed* to *such things*) to controll them; (My overseer having volunteered in the army long since). I have no rela-
tives, to whom my wife can apply for advice or assistance, as they
are all in the army, or too distant to render aid. If the enemy takes
the place; they will certainly *Rob* me of all I have, and [raise] the

very foundation of my house, for *many* of them *know me*. I have been in the Service, since the 26th day of August 1861. and have not visited, my home, or been absent one single day from my command, except on special duty by orders from my Superiors.

II. I require Fifty two (52) privates to fill the ranks of my company, and if permitted to go home I think, perhaps, I may net some if not all of them. Very Respectfully Your obt. Servt.

W. D. Branford

In the following excerpt from her diary, Kate Stone, the daughter of slaveholders, records her experience in the spring of 1863, when the Union army besieged Vicksburg, across the river from her home in Louisiana. As the soldiers spread the word about the Emancipation Proclamation, Kate Stone and her family, like many around them, were terrified by the thought of what ex-slaves might do with their new freedom. Her account describes what happened when the Yankees came through her neighborhood. The sight of black soldiers defied Stone's entire perspective on the world. A group of local slaves was apparently angry with one slave owner, Mr. Hardison, because of his efforts to remove two of his slaves, perhaps thereby splitting up families.

On Thursday, March 26, hearing that Mr. Hardison had returned from Monroe, Sister and I walked up in the afternoon to hear what news he had brought. As we approached the house it struck me that something was wrong. As we were going through the garden, George Richards came out and told us a party of Yankees and armed Negroes had just left, carrying with them every Negro on the place, most of Mrs. Hardison's and the children's clothes, and all the provisions they could manage. They were led by Charles, Mr. Hardison's most trusted servant, and they were all vowing vengeance against Mr. Hardison. They said they would shoot him on sight for moving two of his Negroes a few days before. Mr. Hardison had fortunately seen them coming and, knowing he would be arrested or perhaps killed as a conscript officer, he escaped to the woods.

We walked in and found Mrs. Hardison and the children all much excited and very angry, with flaming cheeks and flashing eyes. The Negroes had been very impertinent. The first armed Negroes they had ever seen. Just as we were seated someone called out the Yankees were coming again. It was too late to run. All we could do was to shut ourselves up together in one room, hoping they would not come in. George Richards was on the gallery. In a minute we heard the gate open and shut, rough hoarse voices, a volley of oaths, and then a cry: "Shoot him, curse him! Shoot him! Get out of the way so I can get him."

Looking out of the window, we saw three fiendish-looking, black Negroes standing around George Richards, two with their guns leveled and almost touching his breast. He was deathly pale but did not move. We thought he would be killed instantly, and I shut my eyes that I might not see it. But after a few words from George, which we could not hear, and another volley of curses, they lowered their guns and rushed into the house "to look for guns." they said, but only to rob and terrorize us. The Negroes were completely armed and there was no white man with them. We heard them ranging all through the house, cursing and laughing, and breaking things open. Directly one came bursting into our room, a big black wretch, with the most insolent swagger, talking all the time in a most insulting manner. He went through all the drawers and wardrobe taking anything he fancied, all the time with a cocked pistol in his hand. Cursing and making the most awful threats against Mr. Hardison if they ever caught him, he lounged up to the bed where the baby was sleeping. Raising the bar, he started to take the child, saying as he waved the pistol, "I ought to kill him. He may grow up to be a jarilla. Kill him." Mrs. Hardison sprang to his side, snatched the baby up, and shrieked: "Don't kill my baby. Don't kill him." The Negro turned away with a laugh and came over where I was sitting with Little Sister crouched close to me holding my hand. He came right up to us standing on the hem of my dress while he looked me slowly over, gesticulating and snapping his pistol. He stood there about a minute, I suppose. It seemed to me an age. I felt like I would die should he touch me. I did not look up to move, and Little Sister was as still as if petrified. In an instant more he turned away with a most diabolical laugh, gathered up his plunder, and went out. I was never so frightened in my life. Mrs. Hardison said we were both as white as marble, and she was sure I would faint. What a wave of thankfulness swept over us when he went out and slammed the door. In the meanwhile, the other Negroes were rummaging the house, ransacking it from top to bottom, destroying all the provisions they could not carry away, and sprinkling a white powder into the cisterns and over everything they left. We never knew whether it was poison or not.

The Negroes called and stormed and cursed through the house, calling each other "Captain" and "Lieutenant" until it nearly froze the blood in our veins, and every minute we expected them to break into our room again. I was completely unnerved. I did not think I could feel so frightened.

Mrs. Alexander went into her room hoping to prevent their robbing her bed, when one of them pointed his pistol at her head and said: "I told you once before, old woman, to keep out of here and stop your jaw." Mr. McPherson and George were all the time on the gallery with Negroes guarding them with leveled guns.

After carrying on this way about two hours they lit matches, stuck them about the hall, and then leisurely took themselves off, loaded down with booty. We rushed around, put out all the matches, gathered up the few little articles left, and started at once for home. Since the Negroes declared as they moved off that they were coming back in a little while and burn every house on the place, I took the baby, and Mrs. Hardison, Mrs. Alexander, and the children with George and Mr. McPherson gathered up everything of any value left, and we hurried home, reaching there spent with excitement. Mrs. Hardison was almost crazy. . . .

The next evening the Negroes from all the inhabited places around commenced flocking to Mr. Hardison's, and they completely sacked the place in broad daylight, passing our gate loaded down with plunder until twelve at night. That more than anything else frightened Mamma and determined her to leave, though at the sacrifice of everything we owned.

For some slaves, the approach of the Union army brought not only freedom but, ironically, the loss of whatever property they had managed to save up while they were slaves. When Sherman and his forces ravaged the land outside Atlanta, they did not always differentiate between the belongings of

A poor woman yesterday applied to a merchant in Carey Street to purchase a barrel of flour. The price he demanded was $70. "My God!" exclaimed she, "how can I pay such prices? I have seven children; what shall I do?" "I don't know, madam," said he, coolly, "unless you eat your children."

—a Richmond resident's diary entry, October 22, 1863

slaveholders and those of their slaves. First of all, the soldiers were hungry and ragged and took whatever they could get. In addition, they sometimes suspected that slave masters tried to protect their property by passing it off as belonging to their slaves. Finally, they did not always understand that some slaves could in fact earn money and might actually own goods.

In 1871, the federal government set up the Southern Claims Commission to hear claims from ex-slaves and white Unionists for property the army had taken. The following testimony comes from Nancy Johnson in support of her husband's claim. She is responding to a series of questions aimed at determining just how much property she had lost, and also proving that she and her husband were, indeed, the owners. (The questions themselves have not been preserved.) Her testimony (signed with an "x" because she could not write) reveals the kinds of aid that slaves were able to give the Union army, the mixed emotions Johnson felt during her encounter with Sherman's troops, and the significant amount of property that she and her husband had managed to accumulate.

[Savannah March 22, 1873]

General Interrogatories by Special Com'r—My name is Nancy Johnson. I was born in Ga. I was a slave and became free when the army came here. My master was David Baggs. I live in Canoochie Creek. The claimant is my husband. He was a good Union man during the war. He liked to have lost his life by standing up for the Union party. He was threatened heavy. There was a Yankee prisoner that got away & came to our house at night; we kept him hid in my house a whole day. He sat in my room. White people didn't visit our house then. My husband slipped him over to a man named Joel Hodges & he conveyed him off so that he got home. I saw the man at the time of the raid & I knew him. He said that he tried to keep them from burning my house but he couldn't keep them from taking everything we had. I was sorry for them though a heap. The white people came hunting down this man that we kept over night; my old master sent one of his own grandsons & he said if he found it that they must put my husband to death, & I had to tell a story to save life. My old master would have had him killed. He was bitter. This was my master David Baggs. I told him that I had seen nothing of him. I did this to save my husbands life. Some of the rebel soldiers deserted & came to our house & we fed

A "contraband" fugitive slave informs federal cavalry officers about the movements of Confederate troops. African Americans in the South often provided the Union army with invaluable information.

them. They were opposed to the war & didn't own slaves & said they would die rather than fight. Those who were poor white people, who didn't own slaves were some of them Union people. I befriended them because they were on our side. I don't know that he ever did any thing more for the Union; we were way back in the country, but his heart was right & so was mine. I was served mighty mean before the Yankees came here. I was nearly frostbitten: my old Missus made me weave to make clothes for the soldiers till 12 o'clock at night & I was so tired & my own clothes I had to spin over night. She never gave me as much as a bonnet. I had to work hard for the rebels until the very last day when they took us. The old man came to me then & said if you won't go away & will work for us we will work for you; I told him if the other colored people were going to be free that I wanted to be. I went away & then came back & my old Missus asked me if I came back to behave myself & do her work & I told her no that I came to do my own work. I went to my own house & in the morning my old master came to me & asked me if I wouldn't go and milk the cows: I told him that my Missus had driven me off—well said he you go and do it—then my Mistress came out again & asked me if I came back to work for her like a "nigger"—I told her no that I was free & she said to be off then & called me a stinking bitch. I afterwards wove 40 yds. Of dress goods for her that she promised to pay me for; but she never paid me a cent for it. I have asked her for it several times. I have been hard up to live but thank God, I am spared yet. I quit then only did a few jobs for her but she never did anything for me except give me a meal of victuals, you see I was hard up then, I was well to do before the war.

Second set of Interrogatories by Spec'l Com'r

1 I was present when this property was taken

2 I saw it taken

3 They said that they didn't believe what I had belonged to me & I told them that I would swear that it belonged to me. I had tried to hide things. They found our meat, it was hid under the house & they took a crop of rice. They took it out & I had some cloth under the house too & the dishes & two fine bed-quilts. They took them out. These were all my own labor & night labor. They took the bole [bolt] of cloth under the house and the next morning they came back with it made into pantaloons. They were starved & naked almost. It was Jan & cold, They were on their way from Savannah. They took all my husbands clothes, except what he had on his back.

These things were taken from David Bagg's place in Liberty County. The Yankees took them. I should think there were thousands of them. I could not count them. They were abut a day & a night.

There were present my family, myself & husband & this man Jack Walker. He is way out in Tatnal Co. & we can't get him here.

There were what we called officers there. I don't know whether they ordered the property taken. I put a pot on and made a pie & they took it to carry out to the head men. I went back where the officers camped & got my oven that I cooked it in back again. They must have ordered them or else they could not have gone so far & they right there. They said that they stood in need of them. They said that we ought not to care what they took for we would get it all back again; that they were obliged to have something to eat. They were mighty fine looking men.

They took the mare out of the stable; they took the bacon under the house, the corn was taken out of the crib, & the rice & the lard. Some of the chickens they shot & some they run down; they shot the hogs.

They took it by hand the camp was close by my house.

They carried it to their camps; they had lots of wagons there.

They took it to eat, bless you; I saw them eating it right there in my house. They were nearly starved.

I told one of the officers that we would starve & they said no that we would get it all back again come & go along with us; but I wouldn't go because the old man had my youngest child hid away in Tatnal Co: he took her away because she knew where the gold was hid & he didn't want her to tell. My boy was sent out to the swamp to watch the wagons of provisions & the soldiers took the wagons & the boy, & I never saw him anymore. He was 14 yrs. Old. I could have got the child back but I was afraid my master would kill him; he said that he would & I knew that he would or else make his children do it: he made his sons kill 2 big tall men like you. The Lord forgive them for the way they have treated me. The child could not help them from taking the horses. He said that Henry (my boy) hallooed for the sake of having the Yankees find him; but the Yankees asked him where he was going & he did-n't know they were soldiers & he told them that he was going to Master's mules.

I didn't ask for any receipt.

It was taken in the day, not secretly. . . .

Item No. 3 I had half a barrel of lard. It was in gourds, that would hold half a bushel a piece. We had this hid in the crib. This was lard from the hogs.

Item No. 4 I could not tell exactly how much corn there was but there was a right smart. We had 4 or 5 bushels ground up into meal & they took all the corn besides. They carried it off in bags and my children's undershirts, tied them like bags & filled them up. My husband made baskets and they toted some off that way. They toted some off in fanners & big blue tubs.

Item No. 5 I don't know exactly how much rice there was; but we made a good deal. They toted it off in bundles, threshed out— It was taken in the sheaf. They fed their horses on it. I saw the horses eating it as I passed there. They took my tubs, kettles &c. I didn't get anything back but an oven.

Item No. 7 We had 11 hogs. They were 2 or 3 years old. They were in pretty good order. We were intending to fatten them right next year—they killed them right there.

Item No. 8 I had 30 or 40 head of chickens. They took the last one. They shot them. This property all belonged to me and my husband. None of it belonged to Mr. Baggs. I swore to the men so, but they wouldn't believe I could have such things. My girl had a changable silk dress & all had [talanas?] & they took them all—It didn't look like a Yankee person would be so mean. But they said if they didn't take them the whites here would & they did take some of my things from their camps after they left.

her

Nancy X Johnson

Mark

Lost Interest in the "Cause"

As the South's fortunes declined and they faced repeated defeats on the battlefield, many people lost their faith in their government, in their army, and in their cause. They grew angry and disillusioned, and simply tired of all the death and destruction. Many women wrote to their husbands in the army begging them to desert and come home, which thousands of Confederate soldiers did.

In the 1864 edition of her children's schoolbook *The Dixie Speller*, Marinda Branson Moore included a new passage that reveals the depth of Southern disaffection for the war. While her earlier editions had been full of patriotic messages for young readers, the following text reflects her new perspective.

This sad war is a bad thing.
My pa-pa went, and died in the army.
My big broth-er went too and got shot. A bomb shell took off his head.
My aunt had three sons, and all have died in the army. Now she and the girls have to work for bread.
I will work for my ma and my sis-ters.
I hope we will have peace by the time [I] am old enough to go to war.
If I were a man, and had to make laws, I would not have any war, if I could help it.
If little boys fight old folks whip them for it; but when men fight, they say "how brave!"

Assassination of Lincoln

The news of Lee's surrender on April 9, 1865, filled the North with jubilation, and the South with a mixture of despair and relief that at least the ordeal was over. Less than a week later, on April 14, the entire country was stunned by the news that Abraham Lincoln had been shot by an assassin, John Wilkes Booth, as he watched a play at Ford's Theater in Washington.

Wealthy New York Unionist George Templeton Strong recorded in his diary the events of that tumultuous day. Not

only was Lincoln killed, but Secretary of State William Seward was also attacked by an accomplice of Booth's, who cut his throat. Seward survived, but the President died the next day.

April 15th, Saturday. Nine o'clock in the morning. LINCOLN AND SEWARD ASSASSINATED LAST NIGHT!!!!

The South has nearly filled up the measure of her iniquities at last! Lincoln's death not yet certainly announced, but the one o'clock despatch states that he was then dying. . . . Poor Ellie [his wife] is heartbroken, though never an admirer of Lincoln's. We shall appreciate him at last.

Up with the Black Flag now!

Ten P.M. What a day it has been! Excitement and suspension of business even more general than on the 3rd instant [when Richmond was captured]. Tone of feeling very like that of four years ago when the news came of Sumter. This atrocity has invigorated national feeling I the same way, almost in the same degree. People who pitied our misguided brethren yesterday, and thought they had been punished enough already, and hoped there would be a general amnesty, including J. Davis himself, talk approvingly today of vindictive justice and favor the introduction of judges, juries, gaolers, and hangmen among the dramatis personae.

Augusta, Sunday, April 30th, 1865
My Dearest Mother,

. . . We are almost paralyzed here by the rapid succession of strange and melancholy incidents that have marked the last few weeks—the sudden collapse of our tried and trusted General Lee and his army, about which, sad as it is, I can feel no mortification, for I know he did all that mortal man could do; then the rumors of peace, so different from the rapturous delight of a *conquered peace* we all looked forward to; then the righteous retribution upon Lincoln. One sweet drop among so much that is painful is that he at least cannot raise his howl of diabolical triumph over us. . . .

Most affectionately your daughter,
Caroline Jones.

Images of War

We often seek in photographs from the Civil War era a record of the truth, a picture of what it was really like to be a part of this country's most dramatic time. And indeed there is a great deal of information to be found in these artifacts; photographs can convey eloquently the youthfulness of a soldier, the grandeur of a regiment, the horror of a battlefield death. As we scrutinize a nurse's face or observe the gruesome images of wounded soldiers, we often find ourselves relating to the subjects with more emotional intensity than we feel reading a description of hospitals or battles. But photographs can conceal as much as they reveal, and in order to "read" them accurately, we need to take into account many other pieces of information.

Today we can capture both the mundane and the exciting events of everyday life with automatic focus cameras that we carry on a string around our neck, or handheld video cameras. In 1861, though, photography was still new in the United States, and required far clumsier equipment and more complicated techniques than it does today. First the photographer or an assistant, working in the dark, coated a piece of glass with a liquid called collodion, let it dry until it was sticky, and then bathed it in silver nitrate for a few minutes. Then, after placing the plate in a lightproof holder, he ran to the camera, which he had previously set up on a tripod, and inserted the plate. When the picture was taken, the plate needed to be exposed to light for about 10 seconds. If the subject moved at all, he or she would turn out blurry in the photograph. After the exposure, the photographer took the plate out and ran back to the darkroom to develop the image. The whole process had to be completed within about 20 minutes or the photograph would be ruined.

During the Civil War, this process usually involved two men, working from a horse-drawn wagon that had been specially outfitted as a photographer's darkroom. These conditions were far from ideal— a change in the weather could ruin a picture—nevertheless these wagons allowed photographers to travel with the army. They could document soldiers' lives and record their deaths. But they could not capture

Civil War photographer Alexander Gardner sits with a camera lens in his hand. The camera was often set up near the tent or wagon in which the chemicals were stored in order to save time in the hurried process of taking and processing a photograph.

the battles themselves because the flying bullets and charging men would have shown up only as blurs and streaks.

Technology limited photographers in other ways as well. The supplies were expensive, and very few in the South could afford them because of the North's naval blockade. Most Civil War photographs extant today, therefore, tend to represent a Northerner's perspective. Pictures could not be taken in the rain or on cloudy days, or in very hot or freezing weather, so the photographic record of the war does not convey the worst conditions. It was impossible for photographers to reach certain battles, and they had to remain at a safe distance from most others.

The photographers themselves made important decisions that shaped their products, and thus the way we imagine the war looked. Any time a photographer looks into a camera to take a picture, he or she makes choices about what to include in the frame, which object to focus on, and what the central image should be. Civil War photographs were meant to convey messages—about the glory or the horror of war, about the bravery or the vulnerability of men, about the nobility of the cause or the futility of the whole endeavor. In choosing their subjects, posing them against particular backdrops, and framing them in certain compositions, photographers aimed to convey these messages to their audiences. Even after the photographs were developed, they could take on new meanings when they were marketed. A photograph's caption in an exhibit or a book, for example, could have a tremendous impact on how viewers interpreted what they were seeing.

The impact of wartime photographs was immense. Most people, including the photographers themselves, had never seen war up close, and the images of wounded men, starving prisoners of war, and dismembered corpses were shocking to those who had long romanticized the warrior ideal. Originally influenced by the heroic, large-scale celebratory paintings of the Revolutionary War and glorious portraits of high-ranking generals, Civil War photographers slowly switched their focus to the hardships endured by the common soldiers themselves, the sacrifices they made, and their weary adherence to duty.

Perhaps the most cherished kind of photograph was the portrait of a soldier, taken for friends and family back home. Loved ones held on to these mementos, hoping that they would not be all that remained of their son or husband or brother. Soldiers sent them home to sweethearts, parents, wives, and children to show off their uniforms, prove their manliness, or give the folks back home a sense of what soldiering was all about.

Sometimes, in order to boost the drama of their portraits, men held weapons borrowed from the photographer's trunk of props. This young man is holding a rifle. It may have been his own gun, but this type of weapon was rare in the army.

Some soldiers stopped at photography studios in the cities through which they traveled. At formal studios they might pose in front of a painted backdrop, like this man. He is from the Rhode Island Zouaves, known for their colorful uniforms.

We stare at a face—like this 12-year-old boy's—and wonder what was going through his mind at this moment. His presence in the army demonstrates the country's idealized notions of war as glorious and exciting, something no young man would want to miss. Thousands of boys ran off without their parents' consent to join the armies—some were sent home again, but others served, fought, and were killed. Toward the end of the war in the South, boys this age and old men were all that were left to fill the companies of soldiers.

Just as newspapers and television reports today rely on images to prove the truth of their stories, photographers in the 19th century documented unusual people or events in order to demonstrate that they really existed. Some historians estimate that a total of about 600 women served the Union and Confederate armies. Many were only discovered when they were wounded or became sick and had to go to the doctor. This woman chose to document her transformation from Frances Clalin of Maine (left) into a private in the 13th Maine Cavalry regiment.

Sometimes soldiers visited the photography studios that were set up in tents in military camps or even near battlefields. They often went in pairs, and some brought their sense of humor—as did these two men, who are demonstrating how to eat hardtack, the staple of many military meals.

Even in what appears to be a candid shot of soldiers relaxing with a game of cards, the photographer had to obtain his subjects' cooperation while he set up and focused his camera, and then they had to stay perfectly still for the length of time—generally about 10 seconds—it took to expose the plate. While families were undoubtedly glad to see these men alive and doing well, images like these worried many strictly religious civilians who feared their sons and husbands would be corrupted by the card playing, gambling, and other sinful activities that went on in camps.

Obviously, some photographs were posed. These Union officers and their young black servant strike a remarkably formal stance, highly reminiscent of the history paintings with which 19th-century audiences would be familiar. The eye is drawn first to the young boy, and we follow his gaze into the center of the picture. Perhaps his relative ease is meant to highlight the fact that he is not a slave in the Union army. On the other hand, his function in the composition of the picture is the same one that animals often served in 19th-century paintings—drawing the viewer's attention to a cute and accessible image, and then leading the eye to the real focus of the picture.

These Confederate soldiers are resting on the fortifications the Southern army built to impede the movement of Union troops. The man sitting in front appears to be petting a two-headed dog; the animal must have moved while the photograph was being taken.

This is the kind of action scene that photographers could not capture with their technology. In order to get a sense of what battle looked like (in this case Shiloh), Northern audiences relied on artists who followed the armies and hurriedly drew sketches while the fighting was taking place. Many of these drawings were then sent north to the offices of newspapers, such as *Frank Leslie's Illustrated Newspaper,* published weekly in New York City and distributed widely throughout the war. Leslie employed 130 craftsmen who copied the sketches onto blocks of wood and then cut out the uninked sections. In order to speed up the usually laborious process, Leslie had the blocks cut into many smaller squares, which he then distributed to individual engravers. While a single craftsman might take weeks to produce a woodcut, Leslie's engravers could have an important image ready for publication within 48 hours. Sometimes the woodcut engravers cleaned up the sketches by removing images of dead soldiers or adding in generals who actually had not been near the front. Although not always completely accurate, they do allow an eyewitness account that would otherwise be unavailable.

Most 19th-century Americans had never seen a battlefield, nor had they witnessed the destruction of war up close. Images like this one, taken by Timothy O'Sullivan and showing dead soldiers scattered across the battlefield, brought home the true cost of war. This photograph was published in Alexander Gardner's *Photographic Sketchbook of the War* in 1866. Gardner had worked for Mathew Brady but had left to start up his own gallery and studio in 1863. The *Sketchbook* contained 100 actual photographs taken by Gardner and others in his employ, including O'Sullivan, pasted into place on the pages. The book was expensive to produce and very few copies were ever made or sold. In addition, after the war, many people wanted to forget, not remember, the carnage of the war. The book was a financial failure. Gardner wrote captions for each of the photographs in his *Sketchbook*, and his words reveal the Northern bias of his perspective. The caption to this photograph described the corpses as Union dead who "wore a calmed and resigned expression, as though they had passed away in the act of prayer." Photographed from a different angle, the very same soldiers—who were indeed Northern—were identified as Confederates who had "paid with life the price of their treason."

There were other instances when photographs actually lied. In one of the most famous cases, Gardner and his assistants took a picture of a young soldier, and titled it "A Sharpshooter's Last Sleep." One historian of Civil War–era photography has argued that, based on where he is on the battlefield, this soldier was probably not a sharpshooter, but instead an ordinary infantryman. In a move far more brazen than mislabeling the soldier, Gardner and his men actually dragged the body 72 yards and placed him in a more dramatic setting. They propped a rifle against the wall (a gun that shows up in several of Gardner's photographs, and not the kind that a sharpshooter would use), and put a knapsack under his head. Then they again took his picture. When he published this photograph in his *Sketchbook*, Gardner made up a story for the caption about how the young man had been wounded, and, using his knapsack as a pillow, lay down to await his death.

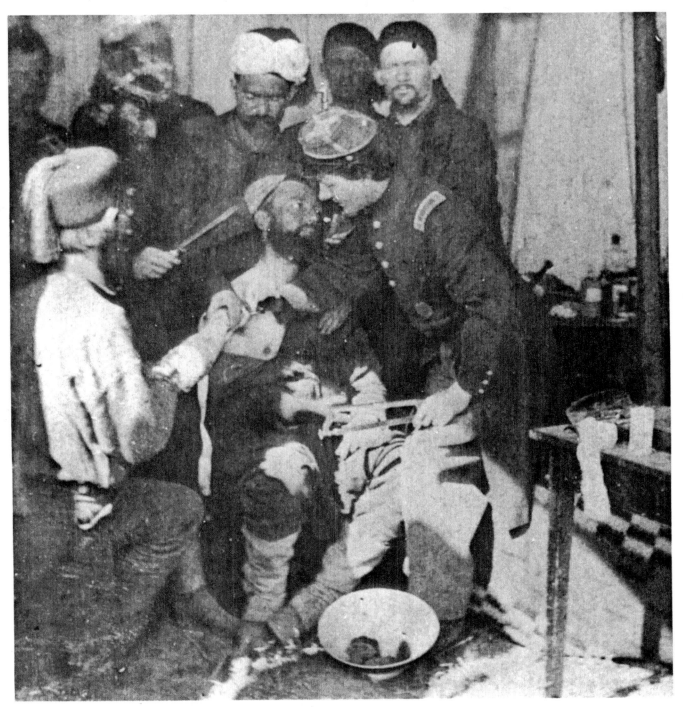

In order to convey some of the horror
of the military hospitals, this photographer staged a mock amputation.

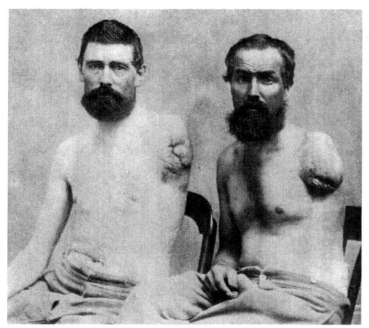

There was no need to embellish the real results of the war on men's bodies or surgeons' limited ability to repair them. Photographs such as this were meant to record the results of surgery for medical practitioners, as well as to demonstrate the very real sacrifices men made for their country.

Perhaps the most shocking images from the war document the condition of the prisoners released from some of the most notorious prison camps. These men were released from Belle Isle, a Southern camp, in 1864, having been reduced to living skeletons. Other similar photographs documented the horrors of the prison camp near Andersonville. Images like these prompted outrage among Northerners, but Southern prisoners of war sometimes starved as well.

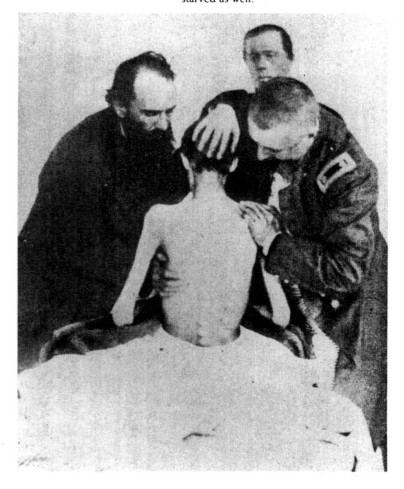

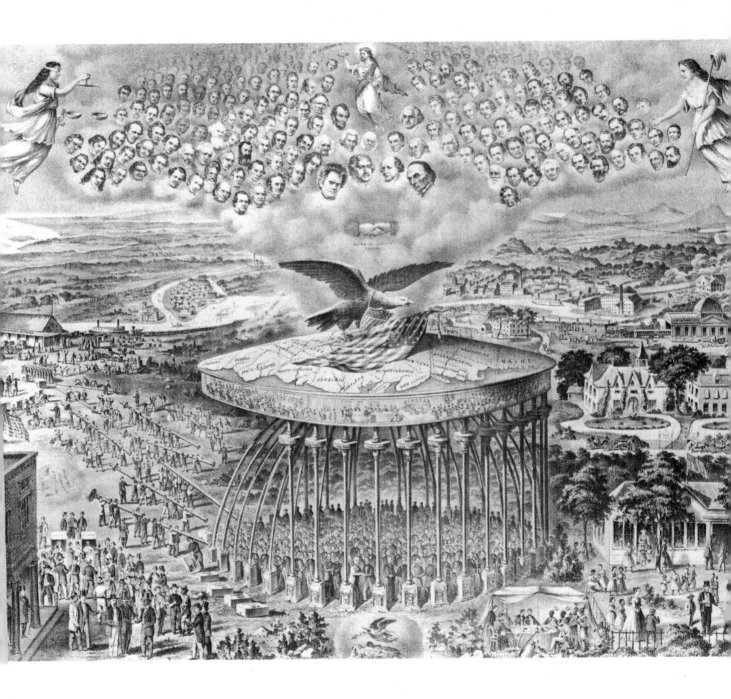

Chapter Eight

A Fool's Errand?

The word "Reconstruction" literally means the process of building again. After the Civil War much of the South lay in ruins—not only the physical buildings, railroads, and farmlands, but the fabric of everyday life for millions of people, both black and white. One way or another, both the material world and the social world had to be rebuilt. But how would this be done? Who would make the decisions, and how would they be enforced? How much would change, and how much would remain the same?

For a dozen years, from 1865 to 1877, these questions gripped Americans as they looked to see what result the horrible carnage of the war would bring. Some, particularly ex-slaves, rejoiced in the chance to completely restructure society and hoped the changes would represent a long-lasting revolution in their lives. Others, especially ex-slaveholders, faced the new world with bitterness and a desperate determination to regain their old power. Meanwhile, the Northerners who observed and took part in the process were likewise divided between those who wanted to see radical shifts in the Southern culture and those who would be satisfied with more moderate changes.

Inevitably the Reconstruction era was one of severe upheaval and contention, and the outcome had immense implications not only for the political structure of the country, but also for the lives of individual Americans. Historians have viewed Reconstruction differently over the years. For many decades, white Southerners and historians argued that Reconstruction had been a series of terrible mistakes and grotesque injustices inflicted upon Southern whites by blacks, Northerners, and the Republican Party. They celebrated the fact that Southern white Democrats finally "redeemed" their states by regaining control of their governments.

More recently, especially since the 1960s, this image has been challenged and overturned by historians who present Reconstruction

Political leaders, statesmen, and even Jesus Christ and Joan of Arc watch over the work of rebuilding the postwar nation, represented by a colossal pavilion in this idealistic drawing. The columns of the Confederate states, or the "Foundations of Slavery," are being replaced with "Justice," "Liberty," and "Education." Trailing a banner that says "All men are born free and equal," an eagle flies over a black and a white child asleep in their baskets.

The crowds, dignitaries, and marching bands in the procession to Cemetery Hill, Gettysburg, for the dedication of the cemetery were in for a long ceremony. Lincoln's address, however, was as eloquent as it was brief.

as a profound time in U.S. history, in which the country faced the possibility of remaking itself for the better. Some important strides were made, they argue, but in the end, it can only be viewed as a tragic failure to overcome racism and injustice toward the newly freed African Americans. Many today point to this failure as the root cause for the racial tensions that still plague our country. The following documents trace the myriad implications of the Reconstruction era for both blacks and whites in the South. They raise the sticky questions of what the goals ought to have been and how they might have been reached, and they demonstrate not only what happened but also what it meant for the United States.

Planning for Reconstruction

Although Reconstruction is generally considered the period after the Civil War ended, in fact the process of remaking Southern society started during the war itself. As we have seen, slavery began to unravel as the Union army marched southward and slaves fled to the Yankees and gained their freedom as contraband of war. Likewise, as the Union gained control of Southern states in the fighting, Northern politicians started debating how to reconstitute their governments. President Lincoln had been working out his ideas on Reconstruction as early as 1862, once Louisiana and Tennessee were in the hands of his military. On November 19, 1863, he gave a brief but moving speech at a ceremony dedicating a cemetery for the soldiers who had died on the battlefield at Gettysburg. In his remarks, known today as the Gettysburg Address, Lincoln eloquently outlined his general hope for the outcome of the war.

Four score and seven years ago our fathers brought forth on this continent, a new nation, conceived in Liberty, and dedicated to the proposition that all men are created equal.

Now we are engaged in a great civil war, testing whether that nation or any nation so conceived and so dedicated, can long endure. We are met on a great battle-field of that war. We have come to dedicate a portion of that field, as a final resting place for those who here gave their lives that that nation might live. It is altogether fitting and proper that we should do this.

But, in a large sense, we cannot dedicate—we cannot consecrate—we cannot hallow—this ground. The brave men, living and dead, who struggled here, have consecrated it, far above our poor power to add or detract. The world will little note, nor long remember what we say here, but it can never forget what they did here. It is for us the living, rather, to be dedicated here to the unfinished work which they who fought here have thus far so nobly advanced. It is rather for us to be here dedicated to the great task remaining before us—that from these honored dead we take increased devotion to that cause for which they gave the last full measure of devotion—that we here highly resolve that these dead shall not have died in vain—that this nation, under God, shall have a new birth of freedom—and that government of the people, by the people, and for the people, shall not perish from the earth.

On December 8, 1863, less than a month after the Gettysburg Address, Lincoln announced his specific plan for Reconstruction. Later known as the 10 Percent Plan, it allowed a former Confederate state back into the Union once a group of men equal to one-tenth of the state's population that voted in 1860 swore an oath of allegiance to the Union and promised to uphold the Emancipation Proclamation.

Whereas in and by the Constitution of the United States it is provided that the President "shall have power to grant reprieves and pardons for offenses against the United States, except in cases of impeachment"; and

Whereas a rebellion now exists whereby the loyal state governments of several states have for a long time been subverted, and many persons have committed and are now guilty of treason against the United States; and

Whereas, with reference to said rebellion and treason, laws have been enacted by Congress declaring forfeitures and confiscation of property and liberation of slaves, all upon terms and conditions therein stated, and also declaring that the President was thereby authorized at any time thereafter, by proclamation, to extend to persons who may have participated in the existing rebellion in any state or part thereof of pardon and amnesty, with such exceptions and at such times and on such conditions as he may deem expedient for the public welfare; and

Whereas, with reference to said rebellion, the President of the United States has issued several proclamations with provisions in regard to the liberation of slaves; and

Whereas it is now desired by some persons heretofore engaged in said rebellion to resume their allegiance to the United States

On examination of this proclamation it will appear, as is believed, that nothing will be attempted beyond what is amply justified by the Constitution. True, the form of an oath is given, but no man is coerced to take it. The man is only promised a pardon in case he voluntarily takes the oath. The Constitution authorizes the executive to grant or withhold the pardon at his own absolute discretion; and this includes the power to grant on terms, as is fully established by judicial and other authorities.

—Abraham Lincoln, State of the Union address, defending the 10 Percent Plan, 1863 and to reinaugurate loyal state governments within and for their respective states:

Therefore, I, Abraham Lincoln, President of the United States, do proclaim, declare, and make known to all persons who have, directly or by implication, participated in the existing rebellion, except as hereinafter excepted, that a full pardon is hereby granted to them and each of them, with restoration of all rights of property, except as to slaves and in property cases where rights of third parties shall have intervened and upon the condition that every such person shall take and subscribe an oath and thenceforward keep and maintain said oath inviolate, and which oath shall be registered for permanent preservation and shall be of the tenor and effect following, to wit:

I, ___ ___ ___, do solemnly swear, in presence of Almighty God, that I will henceforth faithfully support, protect, and defend the Constitution of the United States and the Union of the states thereunder; and that I will in like manner abide by and faithfully support all acts of Congress passed during the existing rebellion with reference to slaves, so long and as far as not repealed, modified, or held void by Congress or by decision of the Supreme Court; and that I will in like manner abide by and faithfully support all proclamations of the President made during the existing rebellion having reference to slaves, so long and so far as not modified or declared void by decision of the Supreme Court. So help me God.

The persons excepted from the benefits of the foregoing provisions are all who are or shall have been civil or diplomatic officers or agents of the so-called Confederate government; all who have left judicial stations under the United States to aid the rebellion; all who are or shall have been military or naval officers of said so-called Confederate government above the rank of colonel in the Army or of lieutenant in the Navy; all who left seats in the United States Congress to aid the rebellion; all who resigned commissions in the Army or Navy of the United States and afterward aided the rebellion; and all who have engaged in any way in treating colored persons, or white persons in charge of such, otherwise than lawfully as prisoners of war, and which persons may have been found in the United States service as soldiers, seamen, or in any other capacity.

And I do further proclaim, declare, and make known that whenever, in any of the states of Arkansas, Texas, Louisiana, Mississippi, Tennessee, Alabama, Georgia, Florida, South Carolina and North Carolina, a number of persons, not less than one-tenth in number of the votes cast in such state at the presidential election of the year A.D. 1860, each having taken oath aforesaid, and not having since violated it, and being a qualified voter by the election law of the state existing immediately before the so-called act of secession, and excluding all others, shall reestablish a state government which shall be republican and in nowise contravening said oath, such shall be recognized as the true government of the state, and the state shall receive thereunder the benefits of the constitutional provision which declares that "the United States shall guarantee to every state in this Union a republican form of government and shall protect each of them against invasion, and, on application of the legislatures, or the executive (when the legislature cannot be convened), against domestic violence."

And I do further proclaim, declare, and make known that any provision which may be adopted by such state government in relation to the freed people of such state which shall recognize and declare their permanent freedom, provide for their education, and which may yet be consistent as a temporary arrangement with their present condition as a laboring, landless, and homeless class will to be objected to by the national executive.

And it is suggested as not improper that in constructing a loyal state government in any state the name of the state, the boundary, the subdivisions, the constitution, and the general code of laws as before the rebellion be maintained, subject only to the modifications made necessary by the conditions herein before stated, and such others, if any, not contravening said conditions and which may be deemed expedient by those framing the new state government.

To avoid misunderstanding, it may be proper to say that this proclamation, so far as it relates to state governments, has no reference to states wherein loyal state governments have all the while been maintained. And for the same reason it may be proper to further say that whether members sent to Congress from any state shall be admitted to seats constitutionally rests exclusively with the respective houses and not to any extent with the executive. And, still further, that this proclamation is intended to present the people of the states wherein the national authority has been suspended and loyal state governments have been subverted a mode in and by which the national authority and loyal state governments may be reestablished within said states or in any of them;

"What McClellan was on the battle-field—'Do as little hurt as possible!'—Lincoln is in civil affairs—'Make as little change as possible!'"
—Wendell Phillips,
March 27, 1864

and while the mode presented is the best the executive can suggest, with his present impressions, it must not be understood that no other possible mode would be acceptable.

Radical Reconstruction

Lincoln's plan angered Radical Republicans, who believed most thoroughly in rights for African Americans, for two reasons. First, it assumed that he, as President, had the right to decide which states would be readmitted to the Union and which would not, whereas the Radicals believed that this right belonged to Congress. Second, they thought Lincoln's 10 Percent Plan made it too easy for Confederate states to reenter the Union and did not do enough to protect the freedom of ex-slaves. In the summer of 1864, Rep. Henry Winter Davis and Sen. Benjamin Wade presented a bill outlining the ideas their wing of the party had about Reconstruction. Their bill placed control of Reconstruction with Congress, and made it far more difficult for Southern states to reenter the Union. Instead of just 10 percent, a majority of voters had to take the oath of allegiance to the United States. No former Confederate officials would be allowed to vote, and some provisions protecting the rights of African Americans were included. The Wade-Davis Bill passed Congress, but Lincoln pocket vetoed it, infuriating the Radicals. On August 5, 1864, the New York Tribune printed the following manifesto by Davis, explaining the radicals' view of Reconstruction.

To the Supporters of the Government:

We have read without surprise, but not without indignation the proclamation of the President of the 8th of July, 1864 [explaining why he vetoed the Wade-Davis Bill]. . . . A more studied outrage on the legislative authority of the people has never been perpetrated. Congress passed a bill, the President refused to approve it; and then, by proclamation, puts as much of it in force as he sees fit, and proposes to execute those parts by officers unknown to the laws of the United States and not subject to the confirmation of the Senate. . . . The bill provided for the civil administration of the laws of the State till it should be in a fit temper to govern itself, repealing all laws recognizing slavery, and making all men equal before the law. These beneficent provisions the President has annulled. People will die, and marry, and transfer property, and buy and sell, and to these acts of civil life courts and officers of the law are necessary. Congress legislated for these necessary things, and the President deprives them of the protection of the law. It was the solemn resolve of Congress to protect the loyal men of the nation against three great dangers: (1) the return to power of the guilty leaders of the rebellion; (2) the continuance of slavery; and (3) the burden of the rebel debt. Mark the contrast! The bill requires a majority, the proclamation is satisfied with one tenth; the bill requires one oath, the proclamation another; the bill ascertains votes by registering, the proclamation by guess, the bill extracts adherence to existing territorial limits, the proclamation admits others; the bill governs the rebel States *by law*, equalizing all before it, the proclamation commits them to the lawless discretion of military governors and provost-marshals; the bill forbids electors for President, the proclamation and defeat of the bill threaten us with civil war for the admission or exclusion of such votes; the bill exacted exclusion of dangerous enemies from power, and the relief of the nation from the rebel debt, and the prohibition of slavery forever, so that the suppression of the rebellion will double our resources to bear or pay the nation debt, free the masses from the old domination of the rebel leaders, and eradicate the cause of the war; the proclamation secures neither of these guarantees.

The President has greatly presumed on the forbearance which the supporters of his administration have so long practiced, in view of the arduous conflict in which we are engaged, and the reckless ferocity of our political opponents.

But he must understand that our support is of a cause, and not of man; that the authority of Congress is paramount, and must be respected; that the whole body of the Union men of Congress will not submit to be impeached by him of rash and unconstitutional legislation; and if he wishes our support, he must confine himself to his executive duties—to obey and execute—not to make the laws; to suppress by arms armed rebellion, and leave political reorganization to the Congress.

The 13th Amendment

After the war ended, politicians continued to argue over who should control Reconstruction, and how it should proceed. One thing that most in the North agreed on was that a primary goal ought to be legal freedom for all slaves still in bondage.

Pennsylvania Rep. Thaddeus Stevens of the Republican Party was one of the most powerful and outspoken radical voices in the government: "I am for negro suffrage in every rebel state. If it be just, it should not be denied; if it be necessary, it should be adopted; if it be a punishment to traitors, they deserve it."

"My vocation, as an Abolitionist, thank God, is ended."
—William Lloyd Garrison, upon passage of the 13th Amendment

While the Emancipation Proclamation had been a major step toward freeing the slaves, it was limited in scope. Because he justified it as a military measure, President Lincoln had applied his proclamation only to those states that were in rebellion and had been taken under Union control; it did not apply to states still under Confederate control, nor did it apply to the Border States. Most of the Border States had abolished slavery shortly after the Emancipation Proclamation, but Kentucky had not. Toward the end of the war, in order to prevent Kentucky from keeping slavery and to make sure that freedom everywhere remained permanent, Congress passed the 13th Amendment, guaranteeing that no human beings would ever again be bought and sold as property in the United States.

This powerful law left certain things unsaid; it did not determine whether the former slaves were citizens, it did not decide whether they could vote, and it did not protect them from oppressive working conditions. Although many were frustrated by its limitations, most newly freed people welcomed the profound shift the 13th Amendment represented in their status as Americans.

Section 1. Neither slavery nor involuntary servitude, except as a punishment for crime whereof the party shall have been duly convicted, shall exist within the United States, or any place subject to their jurisdiction.

Section 2. Congress shall have power to enforce this article by appropriate legislation.

The Black Codes

While the 13th Amendment guaranteed former slaves' freedom, African Americans and whites had yet to work out exactly what freedom would mean. Because the 13th Amendment left this very important question unanswered, more controversy was inevitable. Deepening the problem was the personality of Vice President Andrew Johnson, the man who had assumed the Presidency after Abraham Lincoln's assassination. Johnson lacked Lincoln's political skill and farsightedness. He identified strongly with the poor white farmers of the South, and while he had supported emancipation and despised the old planter aristocracy, at the same time he was deeply racist.

"Slavery is not abolished until the black man has the ballot."
—Frederick Douglass, in response to Garrison

Johnson instituted his own version of Reconstruction after he took office, beginning the period known as Presidential Reconstruction, which lasted from 1865 to 1867. He offered to pardon all Southern whites who would take an oath of allegiance. While he excepted Confederate leaders and wealthy planters, he granted most of them individual pardons soon afterward. He appointed governors and ordered Southern states to hold conventions in which only whites could vote, and he gave them a great deal of leeway in managing their own affairs.

Southern whites returned the old planter elites to power in many of the new state governments. And in order to retain as much of their old control over African Americans as possible, the state constitutional conventions passed a series of laws known collectively as the Black Codes. These codes gave freedpeople certain rights that they had not had previously, such as the right to own property or sue in court, but they also endeavored to force blacks into a kind of involuntary labor system that seemed little removed from slavery. The following are excerpts from the Black Codes of Mississippi, which included some of the most severe regulations in the South.

1. Civil Rights of Freedmen in Mississippi

Sec. 1. Be it enacted . . . That all freedmen, free negroes, and mulattoes may sue and be sued, implead and be impleaded, in all the courts of law and equity in this State, and may acquire personal property . . . and may dispose of the same in the same manner and to the same extent that white persons may; Provided, That the provisions of this section shall not be so construed as to allow any freedman, free negro, or mulatto to rent or lease any lands or tenements except in incorporated cities or towns, in which places the corporate authorities shall control the same. . . .

Sec. 3. . . . All freedmen, free negroes, or mulattoes who do now and have herebefore lived and cohabited together as husband and wife shall be taken and held in law as legally married . . . it shall not be lawful for any freedman, free negro, or mulatto to intermarry with any white person; nor for any white person to intermarry with any freedman, free negro, or mulatto; and any person who shall so intermarry, shall be deemed guilty of felony, and on conviction thereof shall be confined in the State penitentiary for life. . . .

Sec. 6. . . . All contracts for labor made with freedmen, free negroes, and mulattoes for a period longer than one month shall

Freedpeople thresh rice on a plantation on the banks of Cape Fear near Wilmington, North Carolina. Although slavery ended after the Civil War, many African Americans continued to labor in the same fields they had worked as slaves.

be in writing, and in duplicate, attested and read to said freedman, free negro, or mulatto by a beat, city or county officer, or two disinterested white persons of the county in which the labor is to be performed . . . and said contracts shall be taken and held as entire contracts, and if the laborer shall quit the service of the employer before the expiration of his term of service, without good cause, he shall forfeit his wages for that year up to the time of quitting.

Sec. 7. . . . Every civil officer shall, and every person may, arrest and carry back to his or her legal employer any freedman, free negro, or mulatto who shall have quit the service of his or her employer before the expiration of his or her term of service without good cause; and said officer and person shall be entitled to receive for arresting and carrying back every deserting employee aforesaid the sum of five dollars, and ten cents per mile from the place of arrest to the place of delivery; and the same shall be paid by the employer, and held as a set-off for so much against the wages of said deserting employee: Provided, that said arrested party, after being returned, may appeal to the justice of the peace or member of the board of police of the county . . . either party shall have the right of appeal to the county court. . . .

Sec. 9. . . . If any person shall persuade or attempt to persuade, entice, or cause any freedman, free negro, or mulatto to desert from the legal employment of any person before the expiration of his or her term of service, or shall knowingly employ any such deserting freedman, free negro, or mulatto, or shall knowingly give or sell to any such deserting freedman, free negro, or mulatto, any food, raiment, or other thing, he or she shall be guilty of a misdemeanor, and, upon conviction, shall be fined not less than twenty-five dollars and not more than two hundred dollars and the costs.

Despite the Northern public's outrage over the Black Codes, Johnson announced in December 1865 that because loyal governments were operating in all the Southern states, Reconstruction was no longer needed. Radical Republicans were livid, and wanted to overturn all the Southern governments. Instead, though, they joined with more moderate Republicans in refusing to seat the representatives and senators that the new governments had sent to Washington, and they set up a joint committee to work out how to proceed with Reconstruction.

The tensions between the Republican Party and President Johnson continued to escalate. In 1866 Congress passed two bills, the Freedmen's Bureau Bill and the Civil Rights Bill. The Freedmen's Bureau Bill extended the life of the Freedmen's Bureau, an organization created in March 1865 that had been approved for only one year. The bureau's purpose was to distribute food, clothing, and fuel, and to generally oversee ex-slaves' transition to freedom. It was also authorized to distribute confiscated lands in 40-acre plots for rent to freedpeople and loyal whites, who might eventually buy them. The Civil Rights Bill defined all persons born in the United States, black or white, as citizens, and specifically granted them a series of fundamental rights that it required the Southern governments to recognize. The Civil Rights Bill undid years of discrimination embedded in not only the Black Codes, but also in the Supreme Court's Dred Scott decision, which had declared that no black person, free or slave, could be an American citizen.

Johnson vetoed both of these bills. The Republicans were dumbfounded. Moderates and radicals banded together and for the first time in history Congress passed a law over the President's veto. Then, having given up on Johnson, the Republicans proceeded to institute their own plan for Reconstruction. Their first move was to pass the 14th Amendment.

This amendment, considered by many to be the most important in the U.S. Constitution, made equality before the

law a basic right for all American citizens. It declared the federal government, not the states, responsible for protecting the rights of its citizens. While it did not grant African American men the right to vote outright, it reduced a state's representation in Congress if it did not give black men that right.

Section 1. All persons born or naturalized in the United States, and subject to the jurisdiction thereof, are citizens of the United States and of the State wherein they reside. No State shall make or enforce any law which shall abridge the privileges or immunities of citizens of the United States; nor shall any State deprive any person of life, liberty, or property, without due process of law; nor deny to any person within its jurisdiction the equal protection of the laws.

Section 2. Representatives shall be apportioned among the several States according to their respective numbers, counting the whole number of persons in each State, excluding Indians not taxed. But when the right to vote at any election for the choice of electors for President and Vice President of the United States, Representatives in Congress, the Executive and Judicial officers of a State, or the members of the Legislature thereof, is denied to any of the male inhabitants of such State, being twenty-one years of age, and citizens of the United States, or in any way abridged, except for participation in rebellion, or other crime, the basis of representation therein shall be reduced in the proportion which the number of such male citizens shall bear to the whole number of male citizens twenty-one years of age in such State.

Section 3. No person shall be a Senator or Representative in Congress, or elector of President and Vice President, or hold any office, civil or military, under the United States, or under any State, who, having previously taken an oath, as a member of Congress, or as an officer of the United States, or as a member of any State legislature, or as an executive or judicial officer of any State, to support the Constitution of the United States, shall have engaged in insurrection or rebellion against the same, or given aid or comfort to the enemies thereof. But Congress may by a vote of two-thirds of each House, remove such disability.

Section 4. The validity of the public debt of the United States, authorized by law, including debts incurred for payment of pensions and bounties for services in suppressing insurrection or rebellion, shall not be questioned. But neither the United States nor any State shall assume or pay any debt or obligation incurred in aid of insurrection or rebellion against the United States, or any

A sympathetic portrayal of African American men casting their first vote in 1867, after the passage of the Reconstruction acts allowed for black suffrage. In the foreground the artist represents men who symbolize respectable, responsible citizens worthy of the vote, including an artisan, with his tools in his pocket, and a Union soldier.

claim for the loss or emancipation of any slave; but all such debts, obligations and claims shall be held illegal and void.

Section 5. The Congress shall have power to enforce, by appropriate legislation, the provisions of this article.

Ex-Slaves Build New Lives

Johnson encouraged Southern states to vote against ratification of the 14th Amendment, and many of them did. His continued resistance led to the downfall of Johnson's control over Reconstruction, and the start of the period known as Congressional or Radical Reconstruction. Moderate Republicans joined Radicals in their disgust with Johnson and, over his veto, passed the Reconstruction Act. This bill implemented sweeping changes in the South. It disbanded the Southern governments, divided the South into five military districts, barred many Confederates from voting, and called for elections for new governments, but this time with black men voting alongside white Unionists. Furthermore, these new governments were not to be allowed back into the Union until they ratified the 14th Amendment.

While politicians argued over who should control the process of reconstructing the South, newly freed blacks set about undoing as much of the legacy of slavery as they could. In defining freedom for themselves, they sought as much control over their personal lives as possible. Because they had been tied to the plantation as slaves, for many blacks the first act upon gaining their freedom was to leave their master and mistress and seek a new life in one of the Southern cities. For others, first and foremost, freedom meant the ability to reconstitute their families. Thousands of men and women who had been married under slavery without any legal protection flocked to chaplains who could legally wed them again. Others sought desperately to find family members who had been sold away during slavery. Black newspapers throughout the country were filled with ads like those that follow, seeking information about loved ones who had never been forgotten.

Information Wanted of Caroline Dodson, who was sold from Nashville, Nov. 1st, 1862, by James Lumsden to Warwick (a trader then in human beings), who carried her to Atlanta, Georgia, and she was last heard of in the sale pen of Robert Clarke, (human

Woman Suffrage

The 14th Amendment infuriated women's rights activists. Long allied with abolitionists, many were severely disappointed that the Republican Party refused to use the 14th and 15th Amendments to grant women the vote as well as African-American men. Not only did the amendments ignore their hopes, but the 14th, for the first time ever, included the word "male" in the Constitution. Women's rights activists Elizabeth Cady Stanton and Susan B. Anthony sent a series of petitions to Congress urging the members to include "universal suffrage" in any changes to the Constitution—that is, grant both women and black men the vote. One prominent abolitionist, Gerrit Smith, refused to sign the petition, and Stanton wrote the following response. Stanton's reference to "every type and shade of degraded manhood" reflects the increasingly class- and race-based arguments for woman suffrage that she used over time.

[Gerrit Smith] does not clearly read the sign of the times, or he would see that there is to be no reconstruction of this nation, except on the basis of Universal Suffrage, as the natural, inalienable right of every citizen to its exercise. . . .

As the aristocracy of this country is the "male sex" and as Mr. Smith belongs to the privileged order, he naturally considers it important, for the best interests of the nation, that every type and shade of degraded, ignorant manhood should be enfranchised, before even the higher classes of womanhood should be admitted to the polls.

This does not surprise us. Men always judge more wisely of objective wrongs and oppressions, than of those in which they themselves are involved. Tyranny on a southern plantation is far more easily seen by white men . . . [in] the north than the wrongs of women of their own households. . . .

Although those who demand "Women's Suffrage" on principle are few, those who would oppose "Negro Suffrage" from prejudice are many, hence the only way to secure the latter is to end all this talk of class legislation, bury the Negro in the citizen, and claim suffrage for all men and women as a natural, inalienable right.

trader in that place), from which she was sold. Any information of her whereabouts will be thankfully received and rewarded by her mother. Lucinda Lowery, Nashville.

$200 Reward. During the year 1849, Thomas Sample carried away from this city, as his slaves, our daughter, Polly, and son, Geo. Washington, to the State of Mississippi, and subsequently, to Texas, and when last heard from they were in Lagrange, Texas. We will give $100 each for them to any person who will assist them, or either of them, to get to Nashville, or get word to us of their whereabouts, if they are alive. Ben & Flora East.

Freed men and women who had been forbidden to learn to read or write recognized the immense power of literacy and focused much of their energy on getting an education for their children and themselves. With their own strong belief in the importance of education, many Northerners, both white and black, came down South to open schools for the ex-slaves. They brought with them a combination of courage, dedication, and goodwill—as well as paternalistic and sometimes outright prejudiced ideas about blacks. No matter what their own motivations, many teachers were amazed by the determination of their students.

Many of the negroes . . . common plantation negroes, and day laborers in the towns and villages, were supporting little schools themselves. Everywhere I found among them a disposition to get their children into schools, if possible. I had occasion very frequently to notice that porters in stores and laboring men in warehouses, and cart drivers on the streets, had spelling books with them, and were studying them during the time they were not occupied with their work. Go into the outskirts of any large town and walk among the negro inhabitants, and you will see children and in many instances grown negroes, sitting in the sun alongside their cabins studying.

Many blacks strongly believed that their freedom would mean nothing if they did not have the right to vote. Frederick Douglass, the escaped slave who had gained fame as a great orator and prominent newspaper editor, voiced his opinion on the subject in "What the Black Man Wants," a speech that was then published in the abolitionist newspaper the Liberator, in February 1865.

Freedmen, boys, and wounded Union soldiers celebrate the passage of the Civil Rights Act of 1866. The new law defined blacks as United States citizens, overturning the Dred Scott decision, and guaranteed their rights to own or rent property, make contracts, and have access to the courts as parties and witnesses.

It may be objected, however, that this pressing of the negroes' right to suffrage is premature. Let us have slavery abolished, it may be said, let us have labor organized, and then, in the natural course of events, the right of suffrage will be extended to the negro. I do not agree with this. This is the hour. Our streets are in mourning, tears are falling at every fireside, and under the chastisement of this rebellion, we have almost come up to the point of conceding this great, this all-important right of suffrage. I fear that if we fail to do it now, if Abolitionists fail to press it now, we may not see, for centuries to come, the same disposition that exists at this moment. (Applause.) Hence, I say, now is the time to press this right.

It may be asked, "Why do you want it? Some men have got along very well without it. Women have not this right." Shall we justify one wrong by another? That is a sufficient answer. Shall we at this moment justify the deprivation of the negro of the right to vote because some one else is deprived of that privilege? I hold that women as well as men have the right to vote (applause), and my heart and my voice go with the movement to extend suffrage to woman. But that question rests upon another basis than that on which our right rests. We may be asked, I say, why we want it. I will tell you why we want it. We want it because it is our *right*, first of all. (Applause.) No class of men can, without insulting their own nature, be content with any deprivation of their rights. We want it, again, as a means for educating our race. Men are so constituted

Children listen to a teacher at a school set up for freedpeople in Charleston, South Carolina. Many African Americans considered education a foundation block of freedom, and they flocked to the thousands of schools established after the war.

that they derive their conviction of their own possibilities largely from the estimate formed of them by others. If nothing is expected of a people, that people will find it difficult to contradict that expectation. By depriving us of suffrage, you affirm our incapacity to form an intelligent judgment respecting public men and public measures; you declare before the world that we are unfit to exercise the elective franchise, and by this means lead us to undervalue ourselves, to put a low estimate upon ourselves, and to feel that we have no possibilities like other men. Again, I want the elective franchise, for one, as a colored man, because ours is a peculiar government, based upon a peculiar idea, and that idea is universal suffrage. . . . What I ask for the negro is not benevolence, not pity, not sympathy, but simply *justice.* (Applause.) The American people have always been anxious to know what they shall do with us. . . . Everybody has asked the question, and they learned to ask it early of the abolitionists: "What shall we do with the negro?" I have had but one answer from the beginning. Do nothing with us! Your doing with us has already played the mischief with us. Do nothing with us! If the apples will not remain on the tree of their own strength, if they are worm-eaten at the core, if they are early ripe and disposed to fall, let them fall! I am not for tying, or fastening them on the tree in any way, except by nature's plan, and if they will not stay there let them fall. And if the negro cannot stand on his own legs, let him fall also. All I ask is, give him a chance to stand on his own legs! Let him alone! If you see him on his way to school, let him alone,—don't disturb him! If you see him going to the dinner table at a hotel, let him go! If you see him going to the ballot box, let him alone!—don't disturb him! (Applause.) If you see him going into a workshop, just let him alone,—your interference is doing him positive injury. . . . Let him live or die by that. If you will only untie his hands, and give him a chance, I think he will live.

African Americans Enter Politics

Whereas the Reconstruction Acts of 1867 extended voting rights to black men in the former Confederate states, free black men in most Northern and Border States were, ironically, denied suffrage. In 1868, in order to correct that inconsistency and to protect freedmen's rights in the South in case Southern Democrats regained power, Republicans drafted the 15th Amendment.

There were a variety of ideas about what the 15th Amendment should contain. Some radicals pressed for a broad statement of rights that would prohibit any limits on suffrage such as literacy, property, or nativity requirements. Women's rights activists strongly urged leaders to include woman suffrage. In the end the amendment encompassed a relatively moderate vision. It prohibited disenfranchisement "on account of race, color, or previous condition of servitude." But stipulations that voters had to be native-born still allowed whites to prevent Chinese immigrants in the West and Irish and Germans in the North from voting. It did not grant women the vote, and its lack of protection against literacy requirements would prove disastrous for blacks when Democrats eventually regained control of state legislatures in the South.

Section 1. The right of citizens of the United States to vote shall not be denied or abridged by the United States or by any State on account of race, color, or previous condition of servitude.

Section 2. The Congress shall have power to enforce this article by appropriate legislation.

This commemorative print marking the enactment of the 15th Amendment features a celebratory parade in Baltimore. Several vignettes decorate the border, including President Ulysses S. Grant in the upper left corner, Frederick Douglass flanked by two other black leaders in the top center, and, at the bottom, scenes celebrating former slaves' new rights to institutions such as marriage and education.

In this 1868 cartoon by Currier and Ives, a former slave holds onto the "tree of liberty" and offers to help the white man, whom he calls "master," who is about to go over a waterfall. The white man refuses, and President Ulysses S. Grant, on the riverbank, suggests that he is being foolhardy. Northerners held white Southerners in contempt for not seeming to understand the precariousness of their position and refusing to recognize the new realities of the postwar South. Blacks were seen as willing to work with whites, as long as they could hold on to their rights and liberty.

RE·CONSTRUCTION,

Ex-slaves exercised their new right to vote with a combination of eagerness and solemnity. Almost without exception, those who could register to vote did so. Nearly unanimously they supported the Republican Party and represented that party's main constituency in the South. With their newfound political power, they voted themselves into office. While they never reached representation proportional to their population, African Americans served at every level of the government during Reconstruction. A total of 14 served in the U.S. House of Representatives and two became senators from Mississippi, while close to 700 served in state legislatures. There was one black governor, P. B. S. Pinchback of Louisiana, and others across the South served as lieutenant governors, treasurers, and superintendents of education. Almost overnight, towns found themselves being served by black sheriffs, justices of the peace, policemen, and tax assessors.

Southern whites were horrified by what they viewed as a spectacle in their state legislative halls. They hated all Republicans—the "carpetbaggers," Northerners who came south after the war, and the "scalawags," Southerners who supported the Union and the Republican Party—but they had a special scorn for black politicians. Northerners, too, worried that blacks were not capable of holding public office. In

1873 the *New York Tribune* sent James J. Pike, a Maine Republican, on a tour of South Carolina. Although he had supported abolishing slavery, Pike did not believe in equal rights for blacks, and he had advocated deporting freed slaves or placing them on reserves similar to Indian reservations. In the reports he sent back to the newspaper, published later that year as a book, *The Prostrate State*, Pike described his impressions of South Carolina's legislature. His writing influenced Northern opinions and convinced many that the experiment with democratic government in the South had been a failure.

Columbia, the capital of South Carolina, is charmingly situated in the heart of the upland country, near the geographical centre of the State. It has broad, open streets, regularly laid out, and fine, shady residences in and about the town. . . .

Yesterday, about 4 P.M., the assembled wisdom of the State, whose achievements are illustrated on that theatre, issued forth from the State-House. About three-quarters of the crowd belonged to the African race. They were of every hue, from the light octoroon to the deep black. They were such a looking body of men as might pour out of a market-house or a court-house at random in any southern State. Every negro type and physiognomy was here to be seen, from the genteel serving-man to the rough-hewn customer from the rice or cotton field. Their dress was as varied as their countenances. There was the second-hand black frock-coat of infirm gentility, glossy and threadbare. There were the stove-pipe hat of many ironings and departed styles. There were also to be seen a total disregard of the proprieties of costume in the coarse and dirty garments of the field; the stub-jackets and slouch hats of soiling labor. In some instances, rough woolen comforters embraced the neck and hid the absence of linen. Heavy brogans, and short, torn trousers, it was impossible to hide. The dusky tide flowed out into the littered and barren grounds, and issuing through the coarse wooden fence of the inclosure, melted away into the street beyond. These were the legislators of South Carolina. . . .

Let us approach nearer and take a closer view. We will enter the House of Representatives. Here sit one hundred and twenty-four members. Of these, twenty-three are white men, representing the remains of the old civilization. Deducting the twenty-three members referred to, who comprise the entire strength of the

I ask the country, I ask white men, I ask Democrats, I ask Republicans whether the Negroes have presumed to take improper advantage of the majority they hold in [South Carolina] by disregarding the interests of the minority? They have not. Our [constitutional] convention which met in 1868, and in which the Negroes were in a large majority, did not pass any proscriptive or disfranchising acts, but adopted a liberal constitution, securing alike equal rights to all citizens, white and black, male and female, as far as possible. Mark you, we did not discriminate, although we had a majority. Our constitution towers up in its majesty with provisions for the equal protection of all classes of citizens. Notwithstanding our majority there, we have never attempted to deprive any man in that State of the rights and immunities to which he is entitled under the Constitution of this Government. You cannot point me to a single act passed by our Legislature, at any time, which had a tendency to reflect upon or oppress any white citizen of South Carolina. You cannot show me one enactment by which the majority in our State have undertaken to crush the white men because the latter are in a minority.

—South Carolina Rep. Joseph H. Rainey, speech to the House of Representatives, 1872 opposition, we find one hundred and one remaining. Of this one hundred and one, ninety-four are colored, and seven are their white allies. Thus the blacks outnumber the whole body of whites in the House more than three to one. . . . But the reader will find almost any portraiture inadequate to give a vivid idea of the body, and enable him to comprehend the complete metamorphosis of the South Carolina Legislature, without observing its details. The Speaker is black, the Clerk is black, the door-keepers are black, the little pages are black, the chairman of the Ways and Means is black, and the chaplain is coal-black. At some of the desks sit colored men whose types it would be hard to find outside of Congo; whose costume, visages, attitudes, and expression, only befit the forecastle of a buccaneer. It must be remembered, also, that these men, with not more than half a dozen exceptions, have been themselves slaves, and that their ancestors were slaves for generations. . . . One of the things that first strikes a casual observer in this negro assembly is the fluency of debate, if the endless chatter that goes on there can be dignified with this term. The leading topics of discussion are well understood by the members, as they are of a practical character, and appeal directly to the personal interests of every legislator, as well as to those of his constituents. When an appropriation bill is up to raise money, to catch and punish the Ku-klux, they know exactly what it means. They feel it in their bones. So, too, with educational measures. The free school comes right home to them; then the business of arming and drilling the black militia. They are eager on this point. Sambo can talk on these topics and those of a kindred character, and their endless ramifications, day in and day out. There is no end to his gush and babble. The intellectual level is that of a bevy of fresh converts at a negro camp-meeting.

In Washington, Frederick Douglass and his sons published a weekly newspaper, the *New Era*, in which they reported on the election of black officials to Congress. Their attitude toward black legislators, not surprisingly, is different from Pike's.

February 3, 1870

Senator Revels called at the editorial rooms of the *New Era* on Monday last, immediately after his arrival. We were with him at the Capitol and were pleased to know that Democrats were as cordial in receiving him as a prospective member of the Senate as Republicans.

December 22, 1870

Hon. Joseph H. Rainey, Representative of the First Congressional District of South Carolina was sworn in and took his seat Monday last, being the first colored man who has held such a position in this country. He was born in Georgetown, D.C. in 1832 from humble parentage, his father and mother both having been slaves. Mr. Rainey's early education was limited, never having attended school in his life, but he took every opportunity to acquire knowledge of books and improved rapidly. His parents having purchased their freedom, he removed with them to Charleston, S.C.

January 19, 1871

Georgia is represented today in the House of Representatives by one of her long-despised sons. Hon. Jefferson Long of the Fourth Congressional District is an American citizen of African descent and has in the old era been inventoried as property in the very district he now represents as a man. And he is a man—a gentleman. Mr. Long is about thirty-five years of age, of a light brown complexion and gives the impression of a man actuated by a high sense of duty and of the position he occupies.

March 13, 1873

We have in the 43rd Congress, [eight] colored members, Pinchback, Lynch, Elliott, Rainey, Rapier, Walls, Cain, Ransier. This is an increase of three members and a decided advance as to ability. Pinchback, Rapier and Cain are all men of mind, of nerve and fidelity, who will be seconded in their labors by the experience of parliamentary life gained in the last two years by Elliott, Walls and Rainey. In the presence of such men our cause ought not to suffer.

February 19, 1874

All hail Mississippi! The brightest star of the galaxy of Reconstructed states! Hon B. K. Bruce was elected yesterday for the long term in the U.S. Senate with scarcely an effort. The first ballot in each house wrought the victory. No flinching, no dodging, no wincing by white Republicans because their Bruce is a Negro.

White Southern Democrats are shown holding their noses against the supposed stench of the Republican freedman, while they sit in a pigpen and their filthy babies play with the pigs. In this 1868 cartoon artist Thomas Nast appears sympathetic with the freedman, but in later years his drawings would reveal disillusionment with African Americans and would both reflect and shape Northerners' increasing distaste for the reforms of Reconstruction.

May 7, 1874

For the first time in the nation's history, a colored man, Hon. Joseph H. Rainey of South Carolina, presided over the deliberations of the House of Representatives. The earth continues to revolve on its axis.

Black Landowners

Alongside family stability, education, and the right to vote, landownership figured prominently in freedmen's visions of what it would mean to be truly liberated. They knew that only by owning land would they be able to fully participate in the economy, support their families, and protect their political rights. After hundreds of years of working for nothing, many former slaves believed they had earned title to the lands that had belonged to their masters. Not only blacks, but also some Northern whites, understood landownership to be a fundamental necessity for freedpeople. In the following speech to Congress in March 1867, the radical Republican Thaddeus Stevens explains why land redistribution was necessary to procure equal rights for African Americans.

African-American men gathered in Nashville, Tennessee, for the Colored National Convention in 1876. The outcome of the 1876 election was of major concern to African Americans who watched increasingly clear signs that the gains of Reconstruction were eroding.

Four million persons have just been freed from a condition of dependence, wholly unacquainted with business transactions, kept systematically in ignorance of all their rights and of the common elements of education, without which none of any race are competent to earn an honest living, to guard against the frauds which will always be practiced on the ignorant, or to judge of the most judicious manner of applying their labor. But few of them are mechanics, and none of them skilled manufacturers. They must necessarily, therefore, be the servants and victims of others unless they are made in some measure independent of their wiser neighbors. The guardianship of the Freedmen's Bureau, that benevolent institution, cannot be expected long to protect them. It encounters the hostility of the old slaveholders, whether in official or private station, because it deprives these dethroned tyrants of the luxury of despotism. In its nature it is not calculated for a permanent institution. Withdraw that protection and leave them a prey to the legislation and treatment of their former masters, and the evidence already furnished shows that they will soon become extinct, or be driven to defend themselves by civil war. Withhold from them all their rights, and leave them destitute of the means of earning a livelihood, the victims of the hatred or cupidity of the rebels whom they helped to conquer, and it seems probable that the war of races might ensue which the President feared would arise from kind treatment and the restoration of their rights. I doubt not that hundreds of thousands would annually be deposited in secret, unknown graves. . . . Make them independent of their old masters, so that they may not be compelled to work for them upon unfair terms, which can only be done by giving them a small tract of land to cultivate for themselves, and you remove all this danger. You also elevate the character of the freedman. Nothing is so likely to make a man a good citizen as to make him a freeholder. Nothing will so multiply the productions of the South as to divide it into small farms. Nothing will make men so industrious and moral as to let them feel that they are above want and are the owners of the soil which they till. It will also be of service to the white inhabitants. They will have constantly among them industrious laborers, anxious to work for fair wages. How is it possible for them to cultivate their lands if these people were expelled? . . . Have they not a right to [land]? I do not speak of their fidelity and services in this bloody war. I put it on the mere score of lawful earnings. They and their ancestors have toiled, not for years, but for ages, without one farthing of recompense. They have earned for their masters this very land and much more. Will not he who denies them compensation now be accursed, for he is an unjust man?

Stevens advocated confiscating the land of Confederate citizens and giving it to freedpeople. William Tecumseh Sherman, the triumphant Union general who had led his soldiers on devastating marches across the South, instituted this very policy in January 1865 with his Special Order Number 15. In this announcement, Sherman took possession of lands on the Sea Islands and along the coast of South Carolina and Georgia that had been abandoned by Confederates fleeing his oncoming army. Answering the dreams of thousands of freedmen and women, he divided the land up and parceled it out to

Racism in the House

Even in the House of Representatives, black members often faced outright racist treatment. John T. Harris, a Democrat from Virginia, and Alonzo J. Ransier, a black congressman from South Carolina, verbally spar with each other in the following exchange.

Harris: There is not a gentleman on this floor who can honestly say he really believes that the colored man is created his equal.

Ransier: I can.

Harris: Of course you can, but I am speaking to the white men of the House and I do not wish to be interrupted again. . . . Admit it is prejudice, yet the fact exists and you, as members of Congress, are bound to respect that prejudice—that the colored man was inferior to the white.

Ransier: I deny that.

Harris: Sit down. I am talking to white men. I am talking to gentlemen.

Alonzo Ransier died in poverty in 1882, after spending his last years as a night watchman at the Charleston Custom House and as a city street sweeper.

individual families. A total of 400,000 acres, along 30 miles of coastline, became home to 40,000 ex-slaves who took up farming in the abandoned rice fields and plantations.

The islands from Charleston [South Carolina], south, the abandoned rice fields along the rivers for thirty miles back from the sea, and the country bordering the St. Johns River, Florida, are reserved and set apart for the settlement of the negroes now made free by acts of war and the proclamation of the President of the United States. . . .

[O]n the islands, and in the settlements hereafter to be established, no white person whatever, unless military officers and soldiers, detailed for duty, will be permitted to reside; and the sole and exclusive management of affairs will be left to the freedpersons themselves, subject only to United States military authority and acts of Congress. . . .

Whenever a negro has enlisted in the military service of the United States, he may locate his family at any one of the settlements at pleasure, and acquire a homestead, and all other rights and privileges of a settler, as though present in person.

In order to carry out this system of settlement, a general officer will be detailed as Inspector of Settlements and plantations, whose duty it shall be to visit the settlements, to regulate their police and general management, and who will furnish personally to each head of a family, subject to the approval of the President of the United States, a possessory title in writing, giving as near possible a description of the boundaries; and who shall adjust all claims or conflicts that may arise under the same, subject to like approval, treating such titles altogether as possessory.

Sherman's proclamation left vague the question of whether or not the new possessors of the land actually had title to it, thus owning it outright. Some freedpeople assumed that they did, while others realized there was no guarantee but hoped it would turn into a permanent situation.

This fervent dream was smashed on May 29, 1865, when Andrew Johnson announced his sweeping amnesty for Confederates. His pardon returned to them not only their political rights, but title to their abandoned and confiscated lands as well. The men and women who had so joyously taken up farming on the Sea Islands were angry and defiant. They were supported by black soldiers, who encouraged them not

Taken in 1862 by Timothy O'Sullivan, this is one of the first photographs of Southern black life ever exhibited. These ex-slaves were freed in 1861 when their owners fled upon the federal army's occupation of the Sea Islands coastal area near Beaufort, South Carolina. In what is called the Port Royal experiment, the army and a group of Northern missionaries tried to prove that local plantations could be run with paid black laborers, and that free African Americans could be responsible wage earners.

to give up their land, and agents of the Freedmen's Bureau, who were hesitant to return the land to the old owners.

In October 1865 President Johnson sent Freedmen's Bureau Commissioner Oliver O. Howard to South Carolina to explain that the freedpeople would have to leave their land. Howard spoke to 2,000 farmers at a local church on Edisto Island. He later wrote in his autobiography, "My address met with no apparent favor. They did not hiss, but eyes flashed unpleasantly and with one voice they cried, 'No, no!' One very black man, thick set and strong, cried out from the gallery: 'Why, General Howard, why do you take away our lands? You take them from us who are true, always true to the Government! You give them to our all-time enemies! That is not right!'"

Howard requested that the freedpeople set up a three-man committee to decide how to proceed with returning the land to the white planters. Instead, the men drafted the following response.

General, we want Homesteads, we were promised Homesteads by the government. If it does not carry out the promises its agents made to us, if the government haveing concluded to befriend its late enemies and to neglect to observe the principles of common faith between its self and us its allies in the war you said was over, now takes away from them all right to the soil they stand upon save such as they can get by again working for *your* late and their *all time* enemies . . . we are left in a more unpleasant condition than our former. . . . You will see this is not the condition of really freemen.

You ask us to forgive the land owners of our island. . . . The man who tied me to a tree and gave me 39 lashes and who stripped and flogged my mother and my sister and who will not let me stay in his empty hut except I will do his planting and be satisfied with his price and who combines with others to keep away land from me well knowing I would not have anything to do with him if I had land of my own—that man, I cannot well forgive. Does it look as if he had forgiven me, seeing how he tries to keep me in a condition of helplessness?

In the end, despite some serious resistance in South Carolina and Georgia, most of the freedpeople were forced to leave the land. Only 2,000 of the original 40,000 blacks actually received the acres they had been promised.

There is one great difficulty in the way of the country's hope and the freedmen's success: it is the idea which has been insidiously and sedulously instilled into the blacks that the government would give them lands and that each family should have its freehold possession—an idea which the military authorities have earnestly endeavored to remove, but which still pervades the mass and is cherished with a tenacity which nothing can overcome. To be an estated man is at present the height of the freedman's ambition—an ambition which Radical legislation seems disposed to gratify. If Congress persists in surrendering to them the Sea Islands and rice lands—the cream of the state—it will not only inflict irreparable injury upon individuals and the commonwealth to the full value of the estates involved, but it will by that one act give a galvanic shock to the entire labor system of the interior. It is yet an open question whether such a gift on the part of the government . . . would be a blessing to the recipients.

—Julius Fleming Sumter, column for the *Charleston Courier*, 1866

The Limits of Reconstruction

The loss of the land and the dream of 40 acres and a mule, a hope raised by Sherman's Special Order Number 15, was only one of many crushing disappointments that freed men and women faced in the years of Reconstruction. In the following excerpt of an interview conducted long after the war, ex-slave Mattie Curtis recalls her life in the early years of freedom. Her memory underlines both the possibilities that Reconstruction opened up to blacks, and the severe limits it placed on them.

I got married before de war to Joshua Curtis. I always had craved a home an' plenty to eat, but freedom ain't give us notin' but pickled hoss meat an' dirty crackers an' not half enough of dat. Josh ain't really care 'bout no home but through dis land corporation I buyed dese fifteen acres on time. I cut down de big trees dat was all over dese fields an' I hauled out de wood an sold hit, den I plowed up de fields an' planted dem. Josh did help to build de house an' he worked out some. All of dis time I had nineteen chilluns an' Josh died, but I kep' on.

I'll never fergit my first bale of cotton an' how I got hit sold. I was some proud of date bale of cotton, an' atter I had hit ginned I set out wid hit on my steercart for Raleigh. De white folks hated de nigger den, 'specially de nigger what was makin' something so I dasen't ax nobody whar de market was. I rid all day an' had to take my cotton home wid me dat night 'case I can't find no place to sell hit at. But dat night I think hit over an' de next day I axes a policeman 'bout de market.

I done a heap of work at night too, all of my sewin' and such an de piece of lan' near de house over dar ain't never got no work cept at night. I finally paid for the land.

While Mattie Curtis managed to buy her own land through years of arduous work, millions of other blacks were prevented from meeting that goal. Instead they became enmeshed in a system of work contracts and sharecropping that kept them endlessly indebted to white landowners, living a life that many said was little better than slavery.

Even after the Reconstruction Acts demolished the harsh Black Codes of the earlier period, there was a continuous struggle between whites and blacks to restructure the ways in

which they would deal with each other, especially regarding work. Col. Samuel Thomas, Assistant Commissioner of the Freedmen's Bureau for Mississippi and N. E. Louisiana, described the situation as he saw it on September 28, 1865.

Wherever I go—the street, the shop, the house, the hotel, or the steamboat—I hear the people talk in such a way as to indicate that they are yet unable to conceive of the negro as possessing any rights at all. Men who are honorable in their dealings with white neighbors will cheat a negro without feeling a single twinge of their honor. To kill a negro they do not deem murder; to debauch a negro woman they do not think fornication; to take the property away from a negro they do not consider robbery. The people boast that when they get freedmen affairs in their own hands, to use their own classic expression, "the niggers will catch hell."

The reason of all this is simple and manifest. The whites esteem the blacks their property by natural right, and however much they may admit that the individual relations of masters and slaves have been destroyed by the war and by the President's emancipation proclamation, they still have an ingrained feeling that the blacks at large belong to the whites at large, and whenever opportunity serves they treat the colored people just as their profit, caprice or passion may dictate.

In this context, one of the Freedmen's Bureau's most important functions was to adjudicate disagreements over work contracts. The writer John William DeForest, a Connecticut native who had fought in the Union army, served as an agent for the Freedmen's Bureau after the war. In several articles, DeForest described his experiences in the bureau. In the following, "A Bureau Major's Business and Pleasures," published in _Harper's Magazine_ in November 1868, he recounts some of the problems he encountered over contracts.

Most of the difficulties between whites and blacks resulted from the inevitable awkwardness of tyros in the mystery of free labor. Many of the planters seemed to be unable to understand that work could be other than a form of slavery, or that it could be accomplished without some prodigious binding and obligating of the hireling to the employer. Contracts which were brought to me for approval contained all sorts of ludicrous provisions. Negroes must be respectful and polite; if they were not respectful and polite they

Freedmen's Bureau agent Lt. S. Merrill interviews both former slaveholders and ex-slaves. Men, women, and children have come to get his help in settling various disputes, or in some cases simply to get financial aid.

must pay a fine for each offense; they must admit no one on their premises unless by consent of the landowner; they must have a quiet household and not keep too many dogs; they must not go off the plantation without leave. The idea seemed to be that if the laborer were not bound body and soul he would be of no use. . . .

One prevalent fallacy was the supposition that the farmer could, of his own authority, impose fines; in other words, that he could withhold all or part of the laborer's pay if he left the farm before the expiration of his contract. The statement, "You can not take your man's wages for July because he has refused to work for you during August," was quite incomprehensible from the old-fashioned, patriarchal point of view.

"But what am I to do with this fellow, who has left me right in the hoeing season?" demands a wrathful planter.

"You have no remedy except to sue him for damages resulting from a failure of contract."

"Sue him! He ha'nt got nothing to collect on."

"Then don't sue him."

Exit planter, in helpless astonishment over the mystery of the new system, and half inclined to believe that I have been making game of him. I could, of course, have sent for the delinquent and ordered him to return to his work; but had I once begun to attend personally to such cases I should have had business enough to kill off a regiment of Bureau officers; and, moreover, I never forgot that my main duty should consist in educating the entire population around me to settle their difficulties by the civil law; in other words, I considered myself an instrument of reconstruction.

Sharecropping

Since whites refused to sell land to African Americans, and the government did not give it to them as they had hoped, most African Americans had to work for whites. They strongly resisted the kind of work that the planters would have preferred them to do—laboring in gangs under a white overseer—because it smacked so strongly of slavery. Instead, they preferred to work in small family groups away from white supervisors. Because it offered them the chance for this kind of day-to-day independence, blacks began to accept a farming system known as sharecropping. In this type of arrangement, they received a parcel of land from the owner, which they farmed during the year, and agreed to hand over a portion of their crops at harvest time. They were not paid in cash, receiving nothing at all until after the harvest. In fact, during the year they had to buy all their supplies on credit from the farmer himself—often for exorbitant prices. In many cases they received such a small share of the crop, and paid out so much money for the goods they bought, that at the end of the year they ended up owing the farmer rather than making a profit. Forced to remain on the land in order to pay back what they owed, over time many sharecroppers sank deeper and deeper into debt and continued to work for nothing. In essence, the sharecropping system became no different from slavery.

In 1866, Martin R. Delaney, a well-known black abolitionist editor who was one of the highest ranking black officers in the Freedmen's Bureau, was put in charge of Hilton Head, a large area of the Sea Islands. He tried on many occasions to ensure that the blacks there were treated fairly and would have a chance at financial success. In 1867, he wrote this description of sharecropping in his region.

A prevailing custom, very disadvantageous to the progress of the freedmen is the taking advantage of his ignorance, making him pay double and treble what an article is worth. For instance, he is made to pay $10 and $11 dollars a barrel for grits which cost the trader only $5 or $6, and if he gets it on credit he is compelled to give his obligation for $14 or $15. And corn meal which cost the purchaser two cents a pound, the freedman is compelled to pay six and eight cents for. Indeed, whatever of bread stuffs the blacks buy, they are made to pay the most extravagant prices.

"We made crops on shares for three years after freedom, and then we commenced to rent. They didn't pay everything they promised. They taken a lot of it away from us. They said figures didn't lie. You know how that was. You dassent dispute a man's word then."
—Ex-slave Richard Crump

The disposal of their cotton is a subject of much importance. Totally ignorant of trade regulations, of prices and rates of exchange, they are incapable at present of disposing of their own staple without protection by the authorities. A deep laid scheme and system are at work to obtain the produce of these uneducated people for little or nothing. Cotton worth from $1 to $1.40 per pound prepared are got from the producers at from twelve cents to twenty cents per lb. in the seed. When I came to the Island they were disposing of it at prices ranging from six cents to ten cents a lb.

A Reign of Terror

At the beginning of Reconstruction, many Southern whites had reacted with a combination of bitterness and resignation. But as time went on they became more and more determined to crush the ex-slaves' newfound freedom and return them as much as possible to a state of dependence on and subservience to whites. Increasingly whites used violence to meet this goal.

In the following testimony taken at Congressional hearings on Reconstruction-era violence, H. S. Hall, a former lieutenant colonel of the 43rd U.S. Colored Troops who was Sub-Assistant Commissioner for Freedmen in the northeastern district of Texas, described the situation in his state around 1866.

Q. What would be the state of the country in which you have been, should the military force be withdrawn, and the officers of the Freedmen's Bureau be also withdrawn?—A. Judging from the state of the country in counties where there is no military force, I can say there would be neither safety of person nor of property for men who had been loyal during the war; and there would be no protection whatsoever for the Negro.

Q. What would be the condition of the Negro under the circumstances, as compared with his former condition as a slave?—A. He would be, in many instances, forced to labor without any compensation, under some system of compulsion, nearly the same as formerly. He would be liable to worse treatment than ever before—to assaults in many instances, and even murder. Frequent instances of murder have occurred in those counties where there has been no military force.

One freedman is being sold as a punishment for larceny and another is whipped, leading cartoonist Thomas Nast to question whether slavery is dead. The Slave Codes passed by state governments after the Civil War, which reinstated extremely restrictive laws and harsh punishments for African Americans, persuaded many Republicans that the South needed the strong arm of the federal government to protect freedmen's rights.

Q. Can you particularize some of those instances?—A. One case I can cite was that of a Negro woman named Lucy Grimes. She was taken into the woods in the month of December last, by two men, and there stripped and beaten until she died. These men—named Anderson and Simpson—were well known in the county. On the case being presented to the chief justice of the county, who was appointed by Governor Hamilton, he stated that he could not issue a warrant for the arrest on the evidence of a Negro, as there was no other evidence but that of the son of the murdered woman, and that he could do nothing whatever in the case. I made an effort to arrest the murderers, but they could not be found. They were secured and concealed by parties in the neighborhood.

Q. Do you state these matters from your own personal knowledge?—A. From my own personal knowledge. The case was brought before me. A complaint was made to me of the murder, in the first place.

Q. What were the circumstances attending or leading to the murder of this woman?—A. A child of this Negro woman had taken some money which was lying about some part of the house occupied by Mrs. Grimes, for whom she was working. The child had taken it out of the house and was playing with it. Mrs. Grimes accused the child of stealing the money, and required the mother to whip it; the mother declined in doing so. Then Mrs. Grimes went and had an interview with these two men—Anderson and Simpson. The next morning they came and took away the Negro woman, Lucy, saying that they designed taking her to Marshall to present the case to me; instead of which, they took her to a piece of woods two miles from the house, where they stripped her and beat her. She lived till next morning. The son found her and reported the case to me, and I immediately sent out a surgeon with some cavalry. The body was found, and the facts were reported to me by the surgeon. No trace of the murderers could be found.

Q. State the condition in which the body was; and all the circumstances, as you learned from the surgeon.—A. The body was found entirely naked, with the exception of a shirt. The back was very much beaten and bruised, apparently with some sort of whip or strap. Across the head and the face there were several severe bruises, evidently made with a club; and, finally, there was a break in the skull, which the surgeon stated undoubtedly caused the death of the woman, made by a club.

Q. Were there antecedents of the murderers?—A. They were discharged rebel soldiers. Anderson was the son of a gentleman who was considered quite respectable in Harrison County. Simpson was a desperado, not a resident of that part of the country, but of Georgia or Alabama.

Q. Was the mistress of this woman examined by you?—A. She was not.

Q. What part did she take in the matter, so far as you could learn?—A. I could not learn of her taking any part, except conferring with Simpson and Anderson, requesting them to have this Negro punished in some way, simply because she refused to whip the child.

Q. How old was the child?—A. Ten or Twelve years.

Q. Who came to see you about it?—A. A grown man; a Negro man twenty-one or twenty-two years of age; a son of the woman who was killed. He came to report the murder of his mother. . . .

Q. Do you know of any other instances in which outrages have been committed on colored people? If so, state them.—A. During the month of November a young man named Webster fired upon a Negro woman who was in his employment for some language which he considered impudent. The ball struck her in the back of the head, resulting in a serious wound, but not causing death. For that offence he was arrested by the military authorities and tried, and fined $100. That was before I arrived at that post. The post was then commanded by Brevet Brigadier General Sheetz, of the Eighth Illinois Regiment of infantry.

Q. Is that the usual penalty imposed by military officers down there for shooting colored people?—A. That was the usual punishment in that part of the state. It had been for the reason that there were no other means of punishment in the hands of the military authorities. That portion of Texas has never been considered as belonging to General Canby's department. I have never made any written communication to his headquarters, but I asked General A. J. Smith what I should do in case I succeeded in arresting men who committed murder, where there was no testimony but Negro testimony. His reply was that General Canby would not permit any citizen to be punished by military commission. That, of course, left the military authorities there perfectly powerless to punish adequately any offences upon Negros. Another case of outrage was reported to me as having occurred at Navarro County. There is a family of Ingrahams there, very wealthy and influential. An unknown Negro came along and asked for work. A son of Hugh Ingraham, and son-in-law, said they would give him work. They armed themselves with revolvers, took the Negro a short distance from the house, in a piece of woods, and there tied him and flogged him to death.

Q. How do you know these facts?—A. This case was reported to me by a citizen of that county. His name I am not able to give; but it is on the records of the office.

Q. Did you take such testimony in the case as satisfied you of the truth of the statement that you now make?—A. Yes, sir; I applied to the commander of the post for a force to send out to arrest those parties. For two or three weeks I was unable to obtain it; the force there not being adequate. The gentlemen who reported these facts further stated that he had designed to remove his family to Arkansas; that he had engaged a number of Negros in the neighborhood of Ingraham's, and started them for a plantation in Arkansas; that his family had been stopped and taken back to his house, the house surrounded by citizens of that part of the country, and threats made that if he ever made his appearance there again they would take his life. I was never able to get a force of troops to send there, and am not able to give the result. The place is ninety-five miles distant from where I am stationed.

Not only were individuals whipped, beaten, and killed, but in several instances, the entire black population of a city was the target of premeditated murder. In 1866 and 1867, riots rocked Memphis, Tennessee, and New Orleans, Louisiana, with white mobs attacking blacks with the help of policemen and political officials. Almost 100 men, women, and children were killed, and hundreds more were wounded.

On the morning of May 2, 1866, racist whites shot down African Americans at Memphis, Tennesee, on a citywide rampage that also included rape and burning down blacks' homes.

In order to understand what happened, Congress held hearings in which they gathered testimony from eyewitnesses, from which the following excerpts are taken.

In Memphis most of the victims were ex-slaves who had been freed early in the war and had joined the Union army or worked for the government. Jane Sneed was the wife of a black soldier.

On Wednesday, they came into my house and searched for arms and not finding any, went away. Before they came to my house they went to Adam Lock's, right alongside of mine. With Rachael, my daughter, I went out to help get the things out of his house. The house had been set on fire and was burning. There was a man in the house asleep and some of the people asked me to go in and wake him. When I went back, I walked upon the body of Rachael. She was dead and the blood running out of her mouth. Her clothes were all burned off from her.

Q—How old was your daughter?

A—About fourteen years old.

Frances Thompson, a washerwoman, was one of five women raped during the riot.

Tuesday night, seven men, two of whom were policemen, came to my house. They said they must have supper and asked me what I had, and said they must have some eggs and ham and biscuit. They all sat down and ate. A girl lives with me; her name is Lucy Smith; she is about 16 years old. When they had eaten supper they said they wanted some woman to sleep with. I said we were not that kind of women. They said "that didn't make a damned bit of difference." One of them hit me on the side of my face and, holding my throat, choked me. Lucy tried to get out of the window when one of them knocked her down. They drew their pistols and said they would shoot us and fire the house if we did not let them have their way with us. All seven of the men violated us. Four of them had to do with me, and the rest with Lucy.

Primus Lane was a brewery worker in Memphis.

On Wednesday, they came to my house about midnight. They said "Make a light—make a light damn quick." I lighted a match and they looked around and found a piece of a candle. Then they set the house afire. When we came out I was in my shirt-tail and [my wife] in her chemise. I ran in and got my old pantaloons and a dress for my wife. I lost all I had and I had a good deal for me to lose. I had a couple of hogs that weighed two hundred and they burned up. They burned about twenty chickens and little stuff that was in the cabin. I had right smart of garden stuff there too and all that was destroyed.

With the arrival of Radical Reconstruction, violence in the South became even more widespread and well-organized. Several clandestine societies sprang up, the most famous of which is the Ku Klux Klan (KKK). The KKK was in all practicality a military arm of the Democratic Party; its main goal was to restore the Democrats to power by terrorizing and murdering black and white Republican activists. KKK members also whipped and lynched African Americans who had managed to save money, or learned to read and write—in fact, any black person who seemed to be succeeding in life.

Abram Colby, a member of the Georgia legislature, testified at a congressional investigation into Klan violence.

On the 29th of October, 1869, they broke my door open, took me out of bed, took me to the woods and whipped me three hours or more and left me for dead. They said to me, "Do you think you will ever vote another damned radical ticket?" I said, "I will not tell you a lie." I supposed they would kill me anyhow. I said, "If there was an election tomorrow, I would vote the radical ticket." They set in and whipped me a thousand licks more, with sticks and straps that had buckles on the ends of them.

Q—What is the character of those men who were engaged in whipping you?

A—Some are first-class men in our town. One is a lawyer, one a doctor, and some are farmers. They had their pistols and they took me in my night-clothes and carried me from home. They hit me five thousand blows. I told President Grant the same that I tell you now. They told me to take off my shirt. I said, "I never do that for any man." My drawers fell down about my feet and they took hold of them and tripped me up. Then they pulled my shirt up over my head. They said I had voted for Grant and had carried the Negroes against them. About two days before they whipped me they offered me $5,000 to go with them and said they would pay me $2,500 in cash if I would let another man go

The caption to this KKK woodcut in a Southern newspaper read, "The above cut represents the fate in store for those great pests of Southern society——the carpet-bagger and scalawag——if found in Dixie's land after the break of day on the 4th of March next."

to the legislature in my place. I told them that I would not do it if they would give me all the county was worth.

The worst thing about the whole matter was this. My mother, wife and daughter were in the room when they came. My little daughter begged them not to carry me away. They drew a gun and actually frightened her to death. She never got over it until she died. That was the part that grieves me the most.

Q—How long before you recovered from the effects of this treatment?

A—I have never got over it yet. They broke something inside of me. I cannot do any work now, though I always made my living before in the barber shop, hauling wood, &c.

Q—You spoke about being elected to the next legislature?

A—Yes, sir, but they run me off during the election. They swore they would kill me if I staid. The Saturday night before the election I went to church. When I got home they just peppered the house with shot and bullets.

Q—Did you make a general canvas there last fall?

A—No, sir. I was not allowed to. No man can make a free speech in my county. I do not believe it can be done anywhere in Georgia.

Q—You say no man can do it?

A—I mean no Republican, either white or colored.

Despite the white hoods of Klansmen, their victims often recognized these racist criminals. "I knew him. Me and him were raised together," said an Alabama freedman of a KKK member who had brutally attacked his son with a knife.

In 1871 Congress passed the Ku Klux Act, which granted the federal government the power to use the army to crush the KKK by imprisoning anyone who disguised themselves and deprived other people of their equal protection under the law. Like other Radical Reconstruction acts, it greatly increased the power of the federal government over the states.

Sec. 2. That if two or more persons within any State or Territory of the United States . . . shall conspire together, or go in disguise upon the public highway or upon the premises of another for the purpose, either directly or indirectly, of depriving any person or any class of persons of the equal protection of the laws, or of equal privileges or immunities under the laws, or for the purpose of preventing or hindering the constituted authorities of any State from giving or securing to all persons within such State the equal protection of the laws, . . . or by force, intimidation, or threat to prevent any citizen of the United States lawfully entitled to vote from giving his support or advocacy in a lawful manner towards or in favor of the election of any lawfully qualified person as an elector of President or Vice-President of the United States, or as a member of the Congress of the United States, or to injure any such citizen in his person or property on account of such support or advocacy, each and every person so offending shall be deemed guilty of a high crime, and, upon conviction thereof in any district or supreme court of any Territory of the United States having jurisdiction of similar offenses shall be punished by a fine not less than five hundred nor more than five thousand dollars, or by imprisonment, with or without hard labor, as the court may determine, for a period of not less than six months nor more than six years, as the court may determine, or by both such fine and imprisonment as the court may determine. . . .

Sec. 3. That in all cases where insurrection, domestic violence, unlawful combinations, or conspiracies in any State shall so obstruct or hinder the execution of the laws thereof, and of the United States, as to deprive any portion or class of the people of such State of any of the rights, privileges, or immunities, or protection, named in the Constitution and secured by this act, and the constituted authorities of such State shall either be unable to protect, or shall from any cause fail in or refuse protection of the people in such rights, such facts will be deemed a denial by such State of the equal protection of the laws to which they are entitled under the Constitution of the United States; and in all such cases, . . . it shall be lawful for the President, and it shall be his duty to take such measures, by the employment of the militia or the land and naval forces of the United States, or of either, or by other means, as he may deem necessary for the suppression of such insurrection, domestic violence, or combinations. . . .

Sec. 4. That whenever in any State or part of a State the unlawful combinations named in the preceding section of this act shall be organized and armed, and so numerous and powerful as to be able, by violence, to either overthrow or set at defiance the constituted authorities of such State, and of the United States within such State, or when the constituted authorities are in complicity with, or shall connive at the unlawful purposes of, such powerful and armed combinations . . . it shall be lawful for the President of the United States, when in his judgment the public safety shall require it, to suspend the privileges of the writ of habeas corpus, to the end that such rebellion may be overthrown: Provided, . . . That the President shall first have made proclamation, as now provided by law, commanding such insurgents to disperse: And Provided also, That the provisions of this section shall not be in force after the end of the next regular session of Congress.

If a man sees proper to associate with negroes, to eat at the same table, ride on the same seat with them in cars, or sees proper to send his children to the same schools with them, and place himself upon the same level with them in any regard, I would not abridge his right to do so; but that is a very different thing from compulsory social equality and association with those whose company is distasteful to him.

—Kentucky Rep. Henry Davis McHenry, speech opposing passage of the second Civil Rights Bill banning segregation in public facilities and transportation, 1872

The Ku Klux Act worked. After a series of trials and the imprisonment of many KKK leaders, the society died out by 1872 (although it would be reborn later in the century and still exists in some areas of the country today). But the success was a double-edged sword. While it brought peace to the region for the first time since the end of the Civil War, it also made many Northerners feel that the task of Reconstruction was over. They began to grow weary of hearing about the South's troubles, and, influenced by writings such as Pike's *The Prostrate State*, many felt that blacks were not capable of managing the independence that freedom had given them. In 1873, a severe economic depression swept the North, turning people's attention to their own troubles and away from those down South.

Republican Reconstruction governments began to be supplanted by the election of Democratic legislatures. In order to speed up this process of "redemption," Democrats turned once again to violence as a political tool. No longer disguised or riding at night like the KKK, these men murdered black teachers, ministers, and Republican organizers in broad daylight. In 1875 in Mississippi, Democrats followed a pattern that was soon copied in other states, known as the Mississippi Plan. A congressional committee investigating it described it as follows:

(1.) The committee find that the young men of the State, especially those who reached manhood during the war, or who have arrived at that condition since the war, constitute the nucleus and the main force of the dangerous element.

As far as the testimony taken by the committee throws any light upon the subject, it tends, however, to establish the fact that the democratic organizations, both in the counties and in the State, encouraged the young men in their course, accepted the political advantages of their conduct, and are in a large degree responsible for the criminal results.

(2.) There was a general disposition on the part of white employers to compel the laborers to vote the democratic ticket. This disposition was made manifest by newspaper articles, by the resolutions of conventions, and by the declarations of landowners, planters, and farmers to the workmen whom they employed, and by the incorporation in contracts of a provision that they should be void in case the negroes voted the republican ticket.

In western Tennessee, two members of the White Man's League shot and killed Julia Hayden, a black graduate of Nashville's Central College. She had arrived in their town only three days earlier to take up a position as schoolteacher.

MISS JULIA HAYDEN, THE MURDERED SCHOOL-TEACHER.—[FROM A PHOTOGRAPH.]

(3.) Democratic clubs were organized in all parts of the State, and the able-bodied members were also organized generally into military companies and furnished with the best arms that could be procured in the country. The fact of their existence was no secret, although persons not in sympathy with the movement were excluded from membership. Indeed their object was more fully attained by public declarations of their organization in connection with the intention, everywhere expressed, that it was their purpose to carry the election at all hazards.

In many places these organizations possessed one or more pieces of artillery. These pieces of artillery were carried over the counties and discharged upon the roads in the neighborhood of republican meetings, and at meetings held by the democrats. For many weeks before the election members of this military organization traversed the various counties, menacing the voters and discharging their guns by night as well as by day. . . .

(4.) It appears from the testimony that, for some time previous to the election, it was impossible, in a large number of the counties, to hold republican meetings. In the republican counties of Warren, Hinds, Lowndes, Monroe, Copiah, and Holmes meetings of the republicans were disturbed or broken up, and all attempts to engage in public discussion were abandoned by the republicans many weeks before the election.

(5.) The riots at Vicksburgh on the 5th of July and at Clinton on the 4th of September, were the results of a special purpose on the part of the democrats to break up the meetings of the republicans, to destroy the leaders, and to inaugurate an era of terror, not only in those counties, but throughout the State, which would deter republicans, and particularly the negroes, from organizing or attending meetings, and especially deter them from the free exercise of the right to vote on the day of the election. The results sought for were in a large degree attained.

(6.) Following the riot at Clinton, the country for the next two days was scoured by detachments from these democratic military organizations over a circuit of many miles, and a large number of unoffending persons were killed. The number has never been ascertained correctly, but it may be estimated fairly as between thirty and fifty. . . .

(8.) The committee find that in several of the counties the republican leaders were so overawed and intimidated, both white and black, that they were compelled to withdraw from the canvass those who had been nominated, and to substitute others who were

September 5, 1875

Dear Blanche,
I had finished my letter to you yesterday and was looking for George to mail it when Capt. Fisher came to me out of breath and out of heart to tell me of a riot which had just taken place at Clinton (a village ten miles west of here) and from which he had just escaped, with his wife.... There were present at a Republican barbecue about fifteen hundred colored people, men, women, and children. Seeking the opportunity white men, fully prepared, fired into this crowd. Two women were reported killed, also two children.... This is but in keeping with the programme of the Democracy at this time.

—Mississippi Gov. Adelbert Ames, to his wife

named by the democratic leaders, and that finally they were compelled to vote for the ticket so nominated, under threats that their lives would be taken if they did not do it. . . .

(10.) . . . on the day of the election, at several voting places, armed men assembled, sometimes not organized and in other cases organized; that they controlled the elections, intimidated republican voters, and, in fine, deprived them of the opportunity to vote the republican ticket. . . .

(12) . . . where intimidation and force did not result in securing a democratic victory . . . fraud was resorted to.

Reconstruction Ends

Using tactics like the ones outlined in the Mississippi Plan, Redeemers had captured almost every state government in the South by 1875. In the Presidential election of 1876, Democrats nominated New Yorker Samuel J. Tilden, and the Republicans put forward Ohio governor Rutherford B. Hayes. In the South, Democrats continued their reign of terror to frighten black and white Republicans out of voting. In South Carolina, Louisiana, and Florida, the results were so contentious, with each side claiming fraud by the other, that neither could claim victory. No clear winner emerged from the national election in November.

Congress set up a commission to figure out what to do. Eventually, behind closed doors and without any official written record, the legislators reached a series of compromises. In effect, their ideal meant that Hayes was elected President, and in return, he promised to withdraw federal troops from Louisiana and South Carolina, the only states that still had Republican governments. As soon as the troops withdrew in 1877, the governments of these two states collapsed and thus every Southern state had been returned to Democratic control. Reconstruction came to an end.

In 1879, Albion Tourgee wrote a book about his experiences as a carpetbagger who had believed in the possibility of truly reconstructing the South and titled it *A Fool's Errand*. Looking back at Reconstruction today, most historians agree that it was, overall, a failure. After 1877 the Southern white elites regained political as well as financial and social power and, with continued violence, prevented African Americans from assuming their rights as U.S. citizens.

Reconstruction had planted some important seeds, how-ever. Families were reunited; public education took root in the South; and African Americans began to build churches, schools, and other institutions that nurtured their communi-ties. From these institutions, as well as from the Constitution-al amendments passed during Reconstruction, eventually the Civil Rights movement of the 1950s and 1960s would grow. Nevertheless, the outcome of Reconstruction must be under-stood as a tragedy for the nation.

Looking back on Emancipation and then the govern-ment's refusal to grant land to the newly freed slaves, Freder-ick Douglass put the case in a biblical and historical context:

You say that you have emancipated us. You have and I thank you for it. But what is your emancipation?

When the Israelites were emancipated they were told to go and borrow of their neighbors—borrow their coin, borrow their jewels, load themselves down with the means of subsistence; after they should go free in the land which the Lord God gave them. When the Russian serfs had their chains broken and were given their liberty, the government of Russia—aye the despotic govern-ment of Russia—gave to these poor emancipated serfs a few acres of land on which they could earn their bread.

But when you turned us loose, you gave us no acres. You turned us loose to the sky, to the storm, to the whirlwind, and worst of all, you turned us loose to the wrath of our infuriated masters.

In 1903, in his book *The Souls of Black Folk*, the prominent black intellectual W. E. B. Du Bois summed up the results of Reconstruction's failures.

[D]espite compromise, war, and struggle the Negro is not free. In the backwoods of the Gulf States, for miles and miles, he may not leave the plantation of his birth; in well-nigh the whole rural South the farmers are peons, bound by law and custom to an eco-nomic slavery, from which the only escape is death or the peni-tentiary. In the most cultured sections and cities of the South the Negroes are a segregated servile caste, with restricted rights and privileges. Before the courts, both in law and custom, they stand on a different and peculiar basis. Taxation without representation is the rule of their political life. And the result of all of this is, and in nature must have been, lawlessness and crime.

Federal Government Withdraws

Because Southern leaders swore as part of the Compro-mise of 1877 to support the equal rights of blacks once home rule was established, President Rutherford B. Hayes believed state governments would continue the work of Reconstruction. He states this opinion in his inaugural address, delivered in March 1877:

The evils which afflict the Southern States can only be removed or remedied by the united and harmonious efforts of both races, actuated by motives of mutual sympathy and regard; and while in duty bound and fully determined to protect the rights of all by every constitu-tional means at the disposal of my Admin-istration, I am sincerely anxious to use every legitimate influence in favor of honest and efficient local *self*-government as the true resource of those States for the promotion of the contentment and prosperity of their citi-zens. In the effort I shall make to accomplish this purpose I ask the cordial cooperation of all who cherish an interest in the welfare of the country, trusting that party ties and the prejudice of race will be freely surrendered in behalf of the great purpose to be accom-plished....

Let me assure my countrymen of the Southern States that it is my earnest desire to regard and promote their truest interests—the interests of the white and of the colored peo-ple both and equally—and to put forth my best efforts in behalf of a civil policy which will forever wipe out in our political affairs the color line and the distinction between North and South, to the end that we may have not merely a united North or a united South, but a united country.

Timeline

March 2, 1821
The Missouri Compromise passes Congress

Jan. 1, 1831
William Lloyd Garrison publishes the first issue of his abolitionist newspaper, the *Liberator*

Aug. 21, 1831
Nat Turner leads a rebellion of about 70 slaves

June 1845
Narrative of the Life of Frederick Douglass published

May 13, 1846
War declared with Mexico

Aug. 8, 1846
Congressman David Wilmot proposes a proviso excluding slavery from land acquired by the Mexican War

Aug. 9, 1848
Free-Soil Party formed

Feb. 2, 1848
The United States signs Treaty of Guadalupe Hidalgo, ending war with Mexico

Sept. 9–12, 1850
Congress passes Compromise of 1850, temporarily settling the question of slavery in territories won in the Mexican War

Feb. 28, 1854
Republican Party launched in Ripon, Wisconsin

May 26, 1854
Kansas-Nebraska Act passes Senate, allowing settlers in the new territories to determine the status of slavery for themselves

May 22, 1856
Sen. Charles Sumner caned in Senate by Rep. Preston Brooks in retaliation for Sumner's derogatory comments about Sen. Andrew Butler, Brooks's cousin

March 6, 1857
Supreme Court decides *Dred Scott v. Sanford*, a proslavery ruling that angers Northern abolitionists and deepens the rift in the Democratic Party

Aug.–Oct. 1858
Abraham Lincoln debates U.S. Senator Stephen A. Douglas seven times in the campaign for the Illinois seat, making the conflict between slavery and freedom his main theme and establishing a national reputation

Oct. 16, 1859
Abolitionist John Brown and 21 followers raid Harpers Ferry, Virginia

Nov. 6, 1860
Abraham Lincoln elected President

Dec. 20, 1860
South Carolina secedes

Feb. 4, 1861
Confederacy formed

April 12, 1861
The Civil War begins at Fort Sumter, South Carolina

May 23, 1861
Union General Benjamin F. Butler names fugitive slaves "contraband of war"

July 21, 1861
First Battle of Bull Run in Virginia, the first major battle of the war

July 22–25, 1861
Crittenden-Johnson Resolutions pass, stipulating that the North's objective is only "to defend and maintain the supremacy of the Constitution, and to preserve the Union"

April 6–7, 1862
Battle of Shiloh, in Tennessee, ends in unprecedented number of deaths with 20,000 casualties

Aug. 30, 1862
Confederate Gen. Robert E. Lee eliminates immediate Union threat to northern Virginia by outmaneuvering Union generals John Pope and George B. McClellan with nearly half as many troops at Second Battle of Bull Run

Sept. 17, 1862
Battle of Antietam, with 25,000 casualties, the most in one day during the war

Dec. 13, 1862
Battle of Fredricksburg, site of Union defeat that demoralizes Northerners

Jan. 1, 1863
Emancipation Proclamation takes effect

April 2, 1863
Richmond bread riots

May 2–4, 1863
Lee again defeats Union army with half as many troops, this time at Battle of Chancellorsville, Virginia

July 1–3, 1863
Lee's army retreats back to Virginia after the Battle of Gettysburg, Pennsylvania, biggest battle ever fought on North American soil

July 4, 1863
Confederate Army surrenders to Gen. Ulysses S. Grant at Vicksburg

July 13–16, 1863
New York City draft riots

July 18, 1863
Black soldiers of the 54th Massachusetts Regiment fight at Fort Wagner

Dec. 8, 1863
Lincoln announces his 10 Percent Plan for Reconstruction, promising Presidential recognition of former Confederate states in which 10 percent of voters in 1860 take an oath of loyalty and organize state governments loyal to the Union

June 3, 1864
Grant orders an all-out charge against the Confederate position at the Battle of Cold Harbor; 8,000 Union troops die in 10 minutes

July 2, 1864
Congress passes the Wade-Davis Bill, stating that Reconstruction may not start in a rebel state until military resistance to the U.S. government is completely crushed in that state and a majority of its voters in 1860 take a loyalty oath

Nov. 8, 1864
President Lincoln re-elected

Nov. 15, 1864
Gen. William T. Sherman's march from Atlanta to the sea begins

Jan. 16, 1865
Sherman issues Special Order Number 15, granting abandoned Confederate lands on the Sea Islands and in coastal South Carolina and Georgia to ex-slaves

March 3, 1865
Freedmen's Bureau created to oversee ex-slaves' transition to freedom

April 3, 1865
Richmond falls to the Union

April 9, 1865
Confederate Gen. Robert E. Lee surrenders at Appomattox

April 14, 1865
Lincoln assassinated by John Wilkes Booth

May 29, 1865
President Andrew Johnson offers amnesty to former Confederates

Jan. 31, 1865
13th Amendment passes Congress, abolishing slavery

April 9, 1866
Civil Rights Bill of 1866 passes, defining all persons born in the United States, black or white, as citizens

May 1–4, 1866
Anti-black riot takes place in Memphis, Tennessee

June 13, 1866
14th Amendment passes Congress, making equality before the law a basic right for all

March 2, 1867
Congress passes First Reconstruction Act

Feb. 26, 1869
15th Amendment passes Congress, granting citizens the right to vote regardless of race, color, or former enslavement

April 20, 1871
Ku Klux Act passed, allowing federal government to use the army to crush the KKK

1872
Freedmen's Bureau dismantled

1873
Financial panic of 1873 cripples North

Feb. 1877
Rutherford B. Hayes wins Presidency after secret negotiations

April 1877
Troops leave New Orleans, effectively ending Reconstruction

Further Reading

General Works

Basler, Roy P., ed. *The Collected Works of Abraham Lincoln.* New Brunswick, N.J.: Rutgers University Press, 1953.

Commager, Henry Steele and Milton Cantor, eds. *Documents of American History.* 10th ed. Englewood Cliffs, N.J.: Prentice Hall, 1988.

Foner, Eric. *Free Soil, Free Labor, Free Men: The Ideology of the Republican Party Before the Civil War.* New York: Oxford University Press, 1970.

Friedheim, William, ed. *Freedom's Unfinished Revolution: An Inquiry into the Civil War and Reconstruction.* New York: New Press, 1996.

Harris, Neil et al., eds., *American History, 1600 to the Present, Source Readings.* New York: Holt, Rinehart & Winston, 1969.

Holt, Michael F. *The Political Crisis of the 1850s.* New York: W.W. Norton & Co., 1978.

Jimerson, Randall C. *The Private Civil War: Popular Thought during the Sectional Conflict.* Baton Rouge: Louisiana State University Press, 1988.

Linden, Glenn M. and Thomas J. Pressly, eds. *Voices from the House Divided: The United States Civil War as Personal Experience.* New York: McGraw-Hill, 1995.

McPherson, James M. *Battle Cry of Freedom: The Civil War Era.* New York: Ballantine Books, 1988.

McPherson, James M. *Ordeal by Fire: The Civil War and Reconstruction.* 2nd ed. New York: McGraw-Hill, Inc., 1992.

Paludan, Philip Shaw. *A People's Contest: The Union and Civil War 1861–1865.* 2nd ed. Lawrence: University Press of Kansas, 1996.

Perman, Michael, ed. *Major Problems in the Civil War and Reconstruction.* Lexington: D.C. Heath & Co., 1991.

Smith, George Winston and Charles Judah. *Chronicles of the Gringos: The U.S. Army in the Mexican War, 1846–1848.* Albuquerque: University of New Mexico Press, 1968.

———. *Life in the North During the Civil War: A Source History.* Albuquerque: University of New Mexico Press, 1966.

Southern Pamphlets on Seccession. Chapel Hill: University of North Carolina Press, 1996.

Soldiers

Linderman, Gerald F. *Embattled Courage: The Experience of Combat in the American Civil War.* New York: Free Press, 1987.

McPherson, James M. *For Cause and Comrades: Why Men Fought in the Civil War.* Oxford University Press, 1997.

Mitchell, Reid. *Civil War Soldiers: Their Expectations and Their Experiences.* NewYork: Simon & Schuster, 1988.

Silber, Nina and Mary Beth Sievens, eds. *Yankee Correspondence, Civil War Letters Between New England Soldiers and the Home Front.* Charlottesville: University Press of Virginia, 1996.

Wiley, Bell I. *The Life of Billy Yank: The Common Soldier of the Union.* Baton Rouge: Louisiana State University, 1983.

———. *The Life of Johnny Reb: The Common Soldier of the Confederacy.* New York: Bobbs-Merrill Co., 1943.

Women

Attie, Jeannie. *Patriotic Toil: Northern Women and the American Civil War.* Ithaca: Cornell University Press, 1998.

Bunkers, Suzanne L., ed. *The Diary of Caroline Seabury, 1854–1863.* Madison: University of Wisconsin Press, 1991.

Burr, Virginia Ingraham, ed. *The Secret Eye: The Journal of Ella Gertrude Clanton Thomas, 1848–1889.* Chapel Hill: University of North Carolina Press, 1990.

Clinton, Catherine and Nina Silber, eds. *Divided Houses: Gender and the Civil War.* New York: Oxford University Press, 1992.

Faust, Drew Gilpin. *Mothers of Invention: Women of the Slaveholding South in the American Civil War.* Chapel Hill: University of North Carolina Press, 1996.

Leonard, Elizabeth. *Yankee Women: Gender Battles in the Civil War.* New York: Norton, 1994.

Rable, George. *Civil Wars: Women and the Crisis of Southern Nationalism.* Urbana: University of Illinois Press, 1989.

Whites, LeeAnn. *The Civil War as a Crisis in Gender: Augusta, Georgia: 1860–1890.* Athens: University of Georgia Press, 1995.

African Americans and Native Americans

Berlin, Ira, et al., eds. *Freedom: A Documentary History of Emancipation, 1861–1867.* New York: Cambridge University Press, 1985.

Douglass, Frederick. *Life and Times of Frederick Douglass, Written by Himself.* Hartford, Conn.: Park Publishing Co., 1882.

Litwack, Leon F. *Been in the Storm So Long: The Aftermath of Slavery.* New York: Vintage Books, 1980.

Ripley, Peter C., ed. *Witness for Freedom: African American Voices on Race, Slavery, and Emancipation.* Chapel Hill: University of North Carolina Press, 1993.

Sterling, Dorothy, ed. *The Trouble They Seen: The Story of Reconstruction in the Words of African Americans.* New York: Da Capo Press, 1994.

Vogel, Virgil J. *This Country Was Ours: A Documentary History of the American Indian.* New York: Harper & Row, 1972.

Reconstruction

Foner, Eric. *Reconstruction: America's Unfinished Revolution, 1863–1877.* New York: Harper & Row, 1988.

Foner, Eric and Olivia Mahoney, eds. *America's Reconstruction: People and Politics after the Civil War.* New York: HarperPerennial, 1995.

Silber, Nina. *The Romance of Reunion: Northerners and the South, 1865–1900.* Chapel Hill: University of North Carolina Press, 1993.

Stalcup, Brenda, ed. *Reconstruction: Opposing Viewpoints.* San Diego: Greenhaven Press, 1995.

Text Credits

Main Text

15: Michael Perman, ed. *Major Problems in the Civil War and Reconstruction*, 1st ed. (Lexington, Mass.: D.C. Heath, 1991), 43–44.

15–16: Perman, ed. *Major Problems in the Civil War and Reconstruction*, 38.

16: Frederick Law Olmsted, *New York Times*, January 12, 1854. Reprinted in Michael Perman, ed. *Major Problems in the Civil War and Reconstruction*, 1st ed. (Lexington, Mass.: D.C. Heath, 1991), 35–36.

17: Abraham Lincoln, September 30, 1859, speech to Wisconsin State Agricultural Society, Milwaukee, Wisc. Reprinted in Roy P. Basler, ed., *The Collected Works of Abraham Lincoln*, vol. 3 (New Brunswick, N.J.: Rutgers University Press, 1953), 478–79.

18: *Subterranean*, September 13, 1845. Reprinted in Sean Wilentz, *Chants Democratic: New York City and the Rise of the American Working Class, 1788–1850* (New York: Oxford University Press, 1984), 332.

19: *David Walker's Appeal*, September 28, 1829. Reprinted in Eric Foner and Olivia Mahoney, eds., *America's Reconstruction: People and Politics after the Civil War* (New York: HarperPerennial, 1995), 31.

20: *Liberator*, January 1, 1831. Reprinted in Henry Steele Commager and Milton Cantor, eds., *Documents of American History*, vol.1, 10th ed. (Englewood Cliffs, N.J.: Prentice Hall, 1988), 277.

21: Channing Seabury and Family Papers, diary of Caroline Seabury, Minnesota Historical Society, St. Paul, Minn. Reprinted in Suzanne L. Bunkers, ed., *The Diary of Caroline Seabury, 1854–1863* (Madison: University of Wisconsin Press, 1991), 40.

23–24: James D.B. DeBow, "The Non-Slaveholders of the South." Reprinted in Michael Perman, ed. *Major Problems in the Civil War and Reconstruction*, 1st ed. (Lexington, Mass.: D.C. Heath, 1991), 39–41.

24–25: *The Diary of Bennet H. Barrow*. Reprinted in Neil Harris et al., eds., *American History 1600, Present Source Readings* (New York: Holt, Rinehart & Winston, 1969), 228–31.

26–27: Virginia Ingraham Burr, ed., *The Secret Eye: The Journal of Ella Gertrude Clanton Thomas, 1848–1889* (Chapel Hill: University of North Carolina Press, 1990), 132–33, 157–58. Copyright (1990 by Virginia Ingraham Burr and Gertrude T. Despeaux. Used by permission of the publisher.

27–28: Benjamin Drew, ed., *A Northside View of Slavery: The Refugee, or the Narratives of Fugitive Slaves in Canada, Related by Themselves* (Boston: John P. Jowett, 1856), 41–44. Reprinted in Nancy F. Cott et al., eds., *Root of Bitterness: Documents in the Social History of American Women*, 2nd ed. (Boston: Northeastern University Press, 1996), 252–53.

28–29: Frederick Douglass, *Life and Times of Frederick Douglass, Written by Himself with an Introduction by Mr. George L. Ruffin* (Hartford: Park Publishing, 1882), 62–63, 72–73.

32–33: Howard Zinn, *A People's History*, (New York: Harper Perennial, 1990), 129–30.

33: Col. Ethan Allen Hitchcock, quoted in Zinn, *A People's History*, 149.

34: Henry Steele Commager and Milton Cantor, eds., *Documents of American History*, vol.1, 10th ed. (Englewood Cliffs, N.J.: Prentice Hall, 1988).

35: Bernardo Garza, Antonio Treneria, O.F. Janes, "Camp Peyton near Burrita," to Col. Balie Peyton, June 26, 1846, Letters Received, Army of Occupation, Record Group 94, Adjutant General's Office, National Archives, Washington, D.C. Reprinted in George Winston Smith and Charles Judah, eds., *Chronicles of the Gringos: The U.S. Army in the Mexican War, 1846–1848* (Albuquerque: University of New Mexico Press, 1968), 286.

36–38: *Pennsylvania Freeman*, October 31, 1850. Reprinted in C. Peter Ripley, ed., *Witness for Freedom: African-American Voices on Race, Slavery, and Emancipation* (Chapel Hill: University of North Carolina Press, 1993), 180–81.

40: *Frederick Douglass' Newspaper*, June 2, 1854. Reprinted in Ripley, ed., *Witness for Freedom*, 182–83.

41: Stephen A. Douglas, Text of a Letter to the St. Joseph Convention of January 9, 1854, dated Washington, December 17, 1853, and published in *St. Joseph Gazette*, March 15, 1854. Reprinted in Virgil J. Vogel, *This Country Was Ours: A Documentary History of the American Indian* (New York: Harper & Row, 1972), 142–44.

41–42: Edward E. Hale, *Kanzas and Nebraska: The History, Geographical and Physical Characteristics, and Political Position of those Territories; An Account of the Emigrant Aid Companies, and Directions to Emigrants* (Boston: Phillips, Sampson, 1854), 242.

42: Hale, *Kanzas and Nebraska*, 227.

43: Miriam Davis Colt, *Went to Kansas* (Watertown: L. Ingalls & Co., 1862). Reprinted in March of America Facsimile Series, no. 91 (Ann Arbor, Mich.: University Microfilms, 1966), 43–46.

45: Charles Sumner, *The Works of Charles Sumner* (Boston: Lee & Shepard, 1871). Reprinted in Neil Harris et al., eds., *American History, 1600 to the Present, Source Readings* (New York: Holt, Rinehart & Winston, 1969), 261–65.

45: P.S. Brooks, May 28, 1856. Reprinted in Harris et al., eds., *American History, 1600 to the Present, Source Readings*, 265–66.

46–47: *Dred Scott v. Sanford*, 19 Howard, 393, 1857. Reprinted in Henry Steele Commager and Milton Cantor, eds., *Documents of American History*, vol.1, 10th ed. (Englewood Cliffs, N.J.: Prentice Hall, 1988), 339–45.

47: Robert Purvis, speech at American Anti-Slavery Society's 1857 annual meeting in New York City. Reprinted in C. Peter Ripley, ed., *Witness for Freedom: African-American Voices on Race, Slavery, and Emancipation* (Chapel Hill: University of North Carolina Press, 1993), 177.

51–53: Lincoln-Douglas Debate #7, Alton, Ill., October 15, 1858. Reprinted in Henry Steele Commager and Milton Cantor, eds., *Documents of American History*, vol.1, 10th ed. (Englewood Cliffs, N.J.: Prentice Hall, 1988), 353–54.

54–55: John Brown's last speech, November 2, 1859. From John Davison Lawson, ed. *American State Trials*, vol. 6 (St. Louis: Thomas Law Book Co., 1914–), 800 ff. Reprinted in Commager and Cantor, eds., *Documents of American History*, 361.

56–57: Harold Holzer, ed., *Dear Mr. Lincoln: Letters to the President* (Reading, Mass.: Addison-Wesley Publishing Co., 1993), 46–47.

58–59: *Charleston Mercury*, January 4, 1861. Reprinted in Philip Van Doren Stern, *Prologue to Sumter: The Beginnings of the Civil War from the John Brown Raid to the Surrender of Fort Sumter* (Greenwich, Conn.: Fawcett Publications, 1961), 196.

59: Van Doren Stern, *Prologue to Sumter*, 155.

60–61: Henry Steele Commager and Milton Cantor, eds., *Documents of American History*, vol.1, 10th ed. (Englewood Cliffs, N.J.: Prentice Hall, 1988), 369–71.

62–65: James D. Richardson, ed. *A Compilation of the Messages and Papers of the Presidents, 1789–1897*, vol. 6 (Washington, D.C.: Goverment Printing Office, 1896–99. Published by authority of Congress), 5 ff. Reprinted in Commager and Cantor, eds., *Documents of American History*, 385.

65–67: C. Vann Woodward, ed., *Mary Chestnut's Civil War* (New Haven: Yale University Press, 1981), 42–46.

71: *Daily Richmond Examiner*, April 15, 1861. Reprinted in William Joseph Kimball, *Richmond in Time of War* (Boston: Houghton Mifflin, 1960), 4.

72–73: Letters of Fred Spooner and Henry Joshua Spooner, Henry J. Spooner Papers, MSS 732, Manuscript Collection, Rhode Island Historical Society Library, Providence. Reprinted in Nina Silber and Mary Beth Sievens, eds., *Yankee Correspondence, Civil War Letters Between New England Soldiers and the Home Front* (Charlottesville: University Press of Virginia, 1996), 55–57.

74: Eric Foner and Olivia Mahoney, eds., *America's Reconstruction: People and Politics after the Civil War* (New York: HarperPerennial, 1995), 67.

75–77: Letters of George H. Sargent, 1976-3 (m), New Hampshire Historical Society, Concord. Reprinted in Nina Silber and Mary Beth Sievens, eds., *Yankee Correspondence, Civil War Letters Between New England Soldiers and the Home Front* (Charlottesville: University Press of Virginia, 1996), 25–26.

78–80: Allan Nevins and Milton Halsey Thomas, eds., *The Diary of George Templeton Strong*, abridged by Thomas J. Pressly (Seattle: University of Washington Press, 1988), 236–41. Reprinted in Glenn M. Linden and Thomas J. Pressly, eds. *Voices from the House Divided: The United States Civil War as Personal Experience* (New York: McGraw-Hill, 1995), 114–18.

80–81: Letters of Thomas D. Freeman, Brown Family Papers, courtesy American Antiquarian Society, Worcester, Mass. Reprinted in Nina Silber and Mary Beth Sievens, eds., *Yankee Correspondence, Civil War Letters Between New England Soldiers and the Home Front* (Charlottesville: University Press of Virginia, 1996), 47–48.

81–82: *Documents of the United States Sanitary Commission*, vol. 1, pamphlet no. 24, "General Instructions to Sanitary Inspectors" (New York, 1866).

83: *Charleston Daily Courier*, August 30, 1862. Reprinted in J. Cutler Andrews, ed., *The South Reports the Civil War* (Pittsburgh: University of Pittsburgh Press, 1985), 198–99.

83–84: Letter from James T. Miller to Wiliam J. Miller, June 8, 1863, James T. Miller Papers, James S. Schoff Civil War Collection, William L. Clements Library, University of Michigan, Ann Arbor. Reprinted in Gerald F. Linderman, *Embattled Courage: The Experience of Combat in the American Civil War* (New York: Free Press, 1987), 24.

84: Frank Wilkeson, *Recollections of a Private Soldier in the Army of the Potomac* (New York: G.P. Putnam's Sons, 1886), 113–14. Reprinted in Linderman, *Embattled Courage*, 241–2.

84–85: Letter from Charles Harvey Brewster to his mother, July 12, 1862. Reprinted in Michael Perman, ed. *Major Problems in the Civil War and Reconstruction*, 2nd ed. (New York: Houghton Mifflin, 1998), 128–29.

85–86: Michael Perman, ed. *Major Problems in the Civil War and Reconstruction*, 1st ed. (Lexington, Mass.: D.C. Heath, 1991), 210.

86–87: Holmes, James Edward. Letter to Abbie Holmes, 21 May 1863. Holmes Family Papers, Massachusetts Historical Society, Boston. Reprinted in Nina Silber and Mary Beth Sievens, eds., *Yankee Correspondence, Civil War Letters Between New England Soldiers and the Home Front* (Charlottesville: University Press of Virginia, 1996), 44–45.

88: Gerald F. Linderman, *Embattled Courage: The Experience of Combat in the American Civil War* (New York: Free Press, 1987), 244.

88–89: Frank Wilkeson, *Recollections of a Private Soldier in the Army of the Potomac* (New York: G.P. Putnam's Sons, 1886), 166–68. Reprinted in Linderman, *Embattled Courage*, 241–42.

92: Henry Steele Commager and Milton Cantor, eds., *Documents of American History*, vol.1, 10th ed. (Englewood Cliffs, N.J.: Prentice Hall, 1988), 395–96.

93–95: 111–13: Michael Perman, ed. *Major Problems in the Civil War and Reconstruction*, 2nd ed. (New York: Houghton Mifflin, 1998), 279–80.

95: Ira Berlin et al., eds., *Free At Last: A Documentary History of Slavery, Freedom, and the Civil War* (New York: New Press, 1992), 34.

96: *Douglas Monthly*, September 1862.

98–99: Francis B. Carpenter, *Six Months at the White House with Abraham Lincoln* (New York: Hurd & Houghton, 1867), 20–24.

100: Gerald F. Linderman, *Embattled Courage: The Experience of Combat in the American Civil War* (New York: Free Press, 1987), 73–74.

101: T.J. Stiles, ed. *Civil War Commanders* (New York: Berkeley Publishing Group, 1995), 61.

101–2: Russell Duncan, ed., *Blue-Eyed Child of Fortune: The Civil War Letters of Robert Gould Shaw* (Athens: University of Georgia Press, 1992), 245–47.

103: Ira Berlin et al., eds., *Freedom: A Documentary History of Emancipation, 1861–1867*, vol. 1 (New York: Cambridge University Press, 1985), 231.

103: Ira Berlin et al., eds., *Freedom: A Documentary History of Emancipation, 1861–1867*, vol. 1 (New York: Cambridge University Press, 1985), 235.

104–5: Henry Steele Commager and Milton Cantor, eds., *Documents of American History*, vol.1, 10th ed. (Englewood Cliffs, N.J.: Prentice Hall, 1988), 420–21.

106–7: Ira Berlin et al., eds., *Free at Last: A Documentary History of Slavery, Freedom, and the Civil War* (New York: New Press, 1992), 439–41.

108–11: T.J. Stiles, ed. *Civil War Commanders* (New York: Berkeley, 1995), 152, 165–74.

111–13: Michael Perman, ed. *Major Problems in the Civil War and Reconstruction*, 2nd ed. (New York: Houghton Mifflin, 1998), 101–2.

113: Christine Jacobson Carter, ed. *Diary of Dolly Lunt Burge, 1848–1879*, (Athens: University of Georgia Press, 1997), 158–63.

115: Glenn M. Linden and Thomas J. Pressly, eds. *Voices from the House Divided: The United States Civil War as Personal Experience* (New York: McGraw-Hill, 1995), 243–44.

116: Linden and Pressly, eds. *Voices from the House Divided*, 249–50.

120–23: L. Merrit Anderson Letters, Orbison Collection, Pennsylvania State Archives, Harrisburg, Penn.

123: Letters of Thomas O. Nickerson, Misc. CS Letters, vol. 5, Providence Public Library Manuscript Collection, Providence, R.I. Reprinted in Nina Silber and Mary Beth Sievens, eds., *Yankee Correspondence, Civil War Letters Between New England Soldiers and the Home Front* (Charlottesville: University Press of Virginia, 1996), 28–29.

125–26: Letter from Hattie L. Carr to Abraham Lincoln, January 29, 1864, Record Group 94, Adjutant General's Office, Enlisted Branch Papers, letters received, 1864. National Archives, Washington, D.C.

126: John Higgins, Lt. Colonel, 116th Reg. NY Volunteers, report written on Hattie Carr to Abraham Lincoln, January 29, 1864, Enlisted Branch, 1864.

127: *Fincher's Trades Review*, April 2, 1864.

127: Letter from Mary A. Cooper to her brother William, December 1, 1861, William Cooper Papers, U.S. Army Military History Institute, Carlisle Barracks, Carlisle, Penn.

128: Samuel Alexander to Agnes Alexander, November 14, 1861, Alexander Letters, Civil War Miscellaneous Collection, U.S. Army Military History Institute, Carlisle, Penn.

128: Letter from Albert Rake to his wife Lucy, Rake Family Papers, U.S. Army Military History Institute, Carlisle Barracks, Carlisle, Penn.

129: Papers of the Philadelphia Ladies' Aid Society, and the papers of its Secretary, Ellen Matilda Orbison Harrison, Orbison Family Papers, Manuscript Group 98, 111, A & B. Pennsylvania State Archives, Harrisburg, Penn.

131: Sarah Morgan Dawson, *A Confederate Girl's Diary* (Boston: Houghton Mifflin, 1913), 36–7. Reprint, *The Civil War Diary of Sarah Morgan*, ed. Charles East (Athens: University of Georgia Press, 1991), 78.

132–33: Sara Agnes Rice Pryor, *Reminiscences of Peace and War* (New York: Macmillan, 1904), 237–9. Reprinted in William Joseph Kimball *Richmond in Time of War* (Boston: Houghton Mifflin, 1960), 76–77.

134–35: Letter from Captain W.D. Bradford to Brig. Gen. J.J. Pettigrew, December 13, 1862, B-2932 1862, Letters Received, ser. 12, Adjt. & Insp. Gen., Record Group 109 [F-258], National Archives, Washington, D.C. Reprinted in Ira Berlin et al., eds., *Freedom: A Documentary History of Emancipation, 1861–1867*, vol. 1 (New York: Cambridge University Press, 1985), 771.

135–37: Reprinted by permission of Louisiana State University Press from *Brokenburn: The Journal of Kate Stone*, by John Q. Anderson (Baton Rouge: Louisiana State University Press, 1972), 108–10. Copyright (1995 Louisiana State University Press.

138–41: Nancy Johnson's testimony to the Southern Claims Commission, claim of Boson Johnson, Liberty Co., Georgia case files, Approved Claims, ser. 732, Southern Claims Commission, 3d. Auditor, Record Group 217 [I-5], National Archives, Washington, D.C. Reprinted in Ira Berlin et al., eds., *The Destruction of Slavery*, series 1, vol. 1, *Freedom: A Documentary History of Emancipation, 1861–1867* (New York: Cambridge University Press, 1985), 150–54.

142: Marinda Branson Moore, *The Dixie Speller* (Raleigh, N.C.: Branson & Farrar, 1864), 23. Reprinted in Drew Gilpin Faust, *Mothers of Invention: Women of the Slaveholding South in the American Civil War* (Chapel Hill: University of North Carolina Press, 1996), 239.

143: Allan Nevins and Milton Halsey Thomas, eds., *The Diary of George Templeton Strong*, abridged by Thomas J. Pressly (Seattle: University of Washington Press, 1988), 294–5. Reprinted in Glenn M. Linden and Thomas J. Pressly, eds. *Voices from the House Divided: The United States Civil War as Personal Experience* (New York: McGraw-Hill, 1995), 253.

156–57: *The Writings of Abraham Lincoln*, Federal ed., vol. 7 (New York: G.P. Putnam's Sons, 1905–6), 20. Reprinted in Henry Steele Commager and Milton Cantor, eds., *Documents of American History*, vol.1, 10th ed. (Englewood Cliffs, N.J.: Prentice Hall, 1988), 428–29.

157–60: James D. Richardson, ed. *A Compilation of the Messages and Papers of the Presidents, 1789–1897*, vol. 6 (Washington, D.C.: Goverment Printing Office, 1896–99. Published by authority of Congress). Reprinted in Brenda Stalcup, ed., *Reconstruction: Opposing Viewpoints* (San Diego: Greenhaven Press, 1995), 28–31.

160–61:From Henry Winter Davis, "The Wade-Davis Manifesto," *New York Daily Tribune*, August 5, 1864. Reprinted in Stalcup, ed., *Reconstruction*, 32–37.

162: U.S. Constitution, amend. 13, secs. 1 and 2.

163–65: Henry Steele Commager and Milton Cantor, eds., *Documents of American History*, vol.1, 10th ed. (Englewood Cliffs, N.J.: Prentice Hall, 1988), 452–55.

166–67: U.S. Constitution, amend. 14.

167–68: *Colored Tennessean*, August 12 to October 14, 1865. Reprinted in Leon F. Litwack, *Been in the Storm So Long: The Aftermath of Slavery* (New York: Vintage Books, 1980), 232.

168: Sydney Andrews, quoted in the *Joint Report on Reconstruction*, 39th Congress, 1st session, 1866. Reprinted in William Friedheim, ed., *Freedom's Unfinished Revolution: An Inquiry into the Civil War and Reconstruction* (New York: New Press, 1996), 178.

169–70: Frederick Douglass, "What the Black Man Wants," *Liberator*, February 1865. Reprinted in John W. Blassingame and John R. McKivigan, eds., *The Frederick Douglass Papers*, series 1, vol. 4, *Speeches, Debates, and Interviews* (New Haven, Conn.: Yale University Press, 1991), 59–69.

171: U.S. Constitution, amend. 15.

173–74: James S. Pike, *The Prostrate State* (New York: D. Appleton, 1874), chapter 1. Reprinted in Brenda Stalcup, ed. *Reconstruction: Opposing Viewpoints* (San Diego: Greenhaven Press, 1995), 170–77.

174–76: Dorothy Sterling, ed., *The Trouble They Seen: The Story of Reconstruction in the Words of African Americans* (New York: Da Capo Press, 1994), 172–74.

176–77: Thaddeus Stevens, a speech to Congress, March 19, 1867, in Beverly Wilson Palmer, ed., *The Selected Papers of Thaddeus Stevens*, vol. 2 (Pittsburgh: University of Pittsburgh Press, 1998), 283–84.

178: William J. Friedheim, ed., *Freedom's Unfinished Revolution: An Inquiry into the Civil War and Reconstruction* (New York: New Press, 1996), 128–29.

179: O.O. Howard, *Autobiography* (New York: Baker & Taylor Co., 1907). Quoted in Eric Foner, *Short History of Reconstruction, 1863–1877* (New York: Harper & Row, 1990), 73.

180: Michael Perman, ed. *Major Problems in the Civil War and Reconstruction*, 2nd ed. (New York: Houghton Mifflin, 1998), 345.

181: Col. Samuel Thomas, Assistant Commissioner, Bureau of Refugees, Freedmen, and Abandoned Lands for Mississippi and N.E. Louisiana, to Gen. Carl Schurz, September 28, 1865, 39th Congress, 1st session, Senate Exec. Doc. 2, "Report of Carl Schurz on the States of South Carolina, Georgia, Alabama, Mississippi, and Louisiana." Reprinted in

Leon F. Litwack, *Been in the Storm So Long: The Aftermath of Slavery* (New York: Vintage Books, 1980), 364.

181–82: John William DeForest, "A Bureau Major's Business and Pleasures," *Harper's Magazine*, 37 (November 1868): 767–71. Reprinted in Robert W. Johannsen, *Reconstruction: 1865–1877: Sources in American History* (New York: Free Press, 1970), 119–20.

183–84: Dorothy Sterling, ed., *The Trouble They Seen: The Story of Reconstruction in the Words of African Americans* (New York: Da Capo Press, 1994), 86.

184–87: Testimony taken from the Hearings of the Joint Committee on Reconstruction, the Select Committee on the Memphis Riots and Massacres, and the Select Committee on the New Orleans Riots-1866 and 1867. Reprinted in Hans L. Trefousse, ed., *Background for Radical Reconstruction* (Boston: Little, Brown, 1970), 146–51.

188: *House Report No. 101*, 39th Congress, 1st session. Reprinted in Dorothy Sterling, ed., *The Trouble They Seen: The Story of Reconstruction in the Words of African Americans* (New York: Da Capo Press, 1994), 92–94.

189: U.S. Congress, *Testimony Taken by the Joint Select Committee to Inquire into the Condition of Affairs in the Late Insurrectionary States* (Washington: Government Printing Office, 1872). Reprinted in Dorothy Sterling, ed., *The Trouble They Seen: The Story of Reconstruction in the Words of African Americans* (New York: Da Capo Press, 1994), 374–75.

190–91: Henry Steele Commager and Milton Cantor, eds., *Documents of American History*, vol.1, 10th ed. (Englewood Cliffs, N.J.: Prentice Hall, 1988), 502–4.

192–94: United States. Congress. Senate. Select committee to inquire into the Mississippi election of 1875. *Mississippi in 1875. Report of the Select committee to inquire into the Mississippi election of 1875, with the testimony and documentary evidence ...* Senate Reports, no. 527 (44th Congress, 1st session), III, ix–xxxix. Reprinted in Robert W. Johannsen, ed. *Reconstruction, 1865–1877* (New York: Free Press, 1970), 173–82.

195: William J. Friedheim ed., *Freedom's Unfinished Revolution: An Inquiry into the Civil War and Reconstruction* (New York: New Press, 1996), 257.

195: W.E.B. DuBois, *The Souls of Black Folk* (Chicago: A.C. McClurg & Co., 1903), 41. Reprinted in John David Smith, ed. *Black Voices from Reconstruction* (Brookfield, Conn.: Millbrook Press, 1996), 150.

Sidebars

20: Elizabeth Cady Stanton, Susan B. Anthony, Matilda Joslyn Gade, eds. *History of Woman Suffrage* (Salem, N.H.: Ayer Co., 1985). Reprint.

29: Frederick Douglass, "What to the Slave Is the Fourth of July?," speech given to the Rochester (New York) Ladies' Anti-Slavery Society, July 5, 1852. Reprinted in John W. Blassingame, ed., *The Frederick Douglass Papers* 2 (New Haven: Yale University Press, 1982), 359–88.

32: Lewis Cass, quoted in Howard Zinn *A People's History*, (New York: Harper Perennial, 1990), 130.

38: Jane H. Pease and William H. Pease, eds., *The Fugitive Slave Law and Anthony Burns* (Philadelphia: Lippincott, 1975), 43.

40: *Frederick Douglass' Paper*, June 9, 1854.

42: Miriam Davis Colt, *Went to Kansas* (Ann Arbor, Mich.: University Microfilms, 1966), 32–33.

44: *Richmond Enquirer*, June 9, 1856.

47: Eric Foner, *Free Soil, Free Labor, Free Men: The Ideology of the Republican Party Before the Civil War* (New York: Oxford University Press, 1970), 87.

53: *The Writings of Abraham Lincoln*, Federal ed., vol. 7 (New York: G.P. Putnam's Sons, 1905–6). Reprinted in Henry Steele Commager and Milton Cantor, eds., *Documents of American History*, vol.1, 10th ed. (Englewood Cliffs, N.J.: Prentice Hall, 1988), 345.

54: Letter from John Copeland to Father and Mother, November 26, 1859, Oswald G. Villard–John Brown Manuscripts, Rare Book and Manuscript Library, Columbia University. Reprinted in C. Peter Ripley, ed., *Witness for Freedom: African-American Voices on Race, Slavery, and Emancipation* (Chapel Hill: University of North Carolina Press, 1993), 204.

55: Oswald Garrison Villard, *John Brown, 1800–1859: A Biography Fifty Years After* (New York: Houghton Mifflin Co., 1910). Reprinted in James M. McPherson, *Ordeal by Fire: The Civil War and Reconstruction*, 2nd ed. (New York: McGraw-Hill, 1992), 498–99, 554.

57–58: Speech delivered by Jabez L. M. Curry at the Talladega Methodist Church in Alabama, November 26, 1860. Reprinted in John L. Wakelyn, ed. *Southern Pamphlets on Secession* (Chapel Hill: University of North Carolina Press, 1996), 35.

62: David Herbert Donald, *Charles Sumner and the Coming of the Civil War* (New York: Fawcett Columbine, 1960), 368.

67: *Augusta Daily Constitutionalist*, March 30, 1861. Reprinted in James M. McPherson, *Ordeal by Fire: The Civil War and Reconstruction*, 2nd ed. (New York: McGraw-Hill, 1992), 131.

73: *Richmond Daily Whig*, May 22, 1861. Reprinted in William Joseph Kimball *Richmond in Time of War* (Boston: Houghton Mifflin, 1960), 8.

77: James M. McPherson, *Ordeal by Fire: The Civil War and Reconstruction*, 2nd ed. (New York: McGraw-Hill, 1992), 207.

79: Eric Foner, *Reconstruction: America's Unfinished Revolution, 1863–1877* (New York: Harper & Row, 1988), 96.

81: Letter from Rachel Ann Wickford to "President Andrew," September 12, 1864, Colored Troops Records, Letters Received, Box 109, National Archives, Washington, D.C.

82: Alexander Hunter, *Johnny Reb and Billy Yank* (New York: Neale Publishing Co., 1905). Reprinted in Gerald F. Linderman, *Embattled Courage: The Experience of Combat in the American Civil War* (New York: Free Press, 1987), 230–1.

92: Michael Perman, ed. *Major Problems in the Civil War and Reconstruction*, 2nd ed. (New York: Houghton Mifflin, 1998), 158.

99: Mark Diedrich, ed., *Dakota Oratory: Great Moments in the Recorded Speech of the Eastern Sioux, 1695–1874* (Rochester, Minn.: Coyote Books, 1989), 66–67.

108: From *The War and Its Heroes*, (Richmond: Ayres & Wade, 1864). Reprinted in Richard B. Harwell, ed. *The Confederate Reader: How the South Saw the War* (New York: Dover Publications, 1989), 117.

111: William J. Friedheim, ed., *Freedom's Unfinished Revolution: An Inquiry into the Civil War and Reconstruction* (New York: New Press, 1996), 112.

114: James M. McPherson, *Ordeal by Fire: The Civil War and Reconstruction*, 2nd ed. (New York: McGraw-Hill, 1992), 463.

117: Richard B. Harwell, ed. *The Confederate Reader: How the South Saw the War* (New York: Dover Publications, 1989), 189.

132: Varina Howell Davis, *Jefferson Davis, Ex-president of the Confederate States of America; A Memoir by His Wife* (New York: Belford, 1890).

134: *Official Records of the Union and Confederate Armies*, series I, vol. XVIII. Reprinted in William Joseph Kimball *Richmond in Time of War* (Boston: Houghton Mifflin, 1960), 80.

137: John B. Jones, *A Rebel War Clerk's Diary* (Philadelphia: Lippincott, 1866). Reprinted in James M. McPherson, *Ordeal by Fire: The Civil War and Reconstruction*, 2nd ed. (New York: McGraw-Hill, 1992), 377.

143: Glenn M. Linden and Thomas J. Pressly, eds. *Voices from the House Divided* (New York: McGraw-Hill, 1995), 267–68.

157: Brenda Stalcup, ed., *Reconstruction: Opposing Viewpoints* (San Diego: Greenhaven Press, 1995), 29.

159: James M. McPherson, *Ordeal by Fire: The Civil War and Reconstruction*, 2nd ed. (New York: McGraw Hill, 1992), 393.

162: Eric Foner, *Reconstruction: America's Unfinished Revolution 1863–1877* (New York: Harper & Row, 1988), 67.

167: William J. Friedheim, ed. *Freedom's Unfinished Revolution: An Inquiry into the Civil War and Reconstruction* (New York: New Press, 1996), 207–8.

173: Brenda Stalcup, ed., *Reconstruction: Opposing Viewpoints* (San Diego: Greenhaven Press, 1995), 166.

177: *Congressional Record*, 43rd Congress, 1st Session. Reprinted in Dorothy Sterling, ed., *The Trouble They Seen: The Story of Reconstruction in the Words of African Americans* (New York: Da Capo Press, 1994), 183.

179: Brenda Stalcup, *Reconstruction: Opposing Viewpoints* (San Diego: Greenhaven Press, 1995), 158.

183: Leon Litwack, *Been in the Storm So Long: The Aftermath of Slavery* (New York: Vintage Books, 1980), 448.

191: Henry Davis McHenry, *Congresional Globe*, 42nd Congress, 2nd session, April 13, 1872. Reprinted in Brenda Stalcup, ed., *Reconstruction: Opposing Viewpoints* (San Diego: Greenhaven Press, 1995), 179.

193: *Chronicles from the Nineteenth Century: Family Letters of Blanche Butler and Adelbert Ames*, vol. 2 (Clinton, Mass.: 1957), 163–4. Michael Perman, ed. *Major Problems in the Civil War and Reconstruction*, 2nd ed. (New York: Houghton Mifflin, 1998), 386–7.

194: Brenda Stalcup, ed., *Reconstruction: Opposing Viewpoints* (San Diego: Greenhaven Press, 1995), 204.

Picture Credits

Index

Acknowledgments

I want to thank my students at Carleton College for their enthusiasm about these documents and their myriad meanings. Nancy Toff and Karen Fein of Oxford University Press have consistently provided enthusiasm and skill for which I am very grateful. Special thanks to my parents, Linda and Irving Seidman, and to Peter Filene, Erica Rothman, and Jeanette Falk, who have each in their own way made major contributions to my work and my sanity. No one else has shared so completely the satisfactions and the hard work of this project as Benjamin Filene. Without his steady presence and generous love I never would have made it through. Eliza and Hazel Filene are completely and wonderfully responsible for making it so hard to finish this book, and I thank them from the bottom of my heart.

About the Author

Rachel Filene Seidman teaches in the history department of Carleton College. Her work on Northern women during the Civil War is forthcoming in two collections, *Making and Remaking Pennsylvania's Civil War* and *The North's Civil War: The Yankee Homefront and the Union War Effort*. She lives in Saint Paul, Minnesota, with her husband and two daughters.